MW00804719

Imperfect Victims

GENDER AND JUSTICE

Edited by Claire M. Renzetti

This University of California Press series explores how the experiences of offending, victimization, and justice are profoundly influenced by the intersections of gender with other markers of social location. Cross-cultural and comparative, series volumes publish the best new scholarship that seeks to challenge assumptions, highlight inequalities, and transform practice and policy.

1. *The Trouble with Marriage: Feminists Confront Law and Violence in India,* by Srimati Basu

2. *Caught Up: Girls, Surveillance, and Wraparound Incarceration,* by Jerry Flores

3. *In Search of Safety: Confronting Inequality in Women's Imprisonment,* by Barbara Owen, James Wells, and Joycelyn Pollock

4. *Abusive Endings: Separation and Divorce Violence against Women,* by Walter S. DeKeseredy, Molly Dragiewicz, and Martin D. Schwartz

5. *Journeys: Resiliency and Growth for Survivors of Intimate Partner Abuse,* by Susan L. Miller

6. *The Chosen Ones: Black Men and the Politics of Redemption,* by Nikki Jones

7. *Decriminalizing Domestic Violence: A Balanced Policy Approach to Intimate Partner Violence,* by Leigh Goodmark

8. *Imperfect Victims: Criminalized Survivors and the Promise of Abolition Feminism,* by Leigh Goodmark

Imperfect Victims

CRIMINALIZED SURVIVORS AND THE
PROMISE OF ABOLITION FEMINISM

Leigh Goodmark

UNIVERSITY OF CALIFORNIA PRESS

University of California Press
Oakland, California

© 2023 by Leigh Goodmark

Cataloging-in-Publication Data is on file at the Library of Congress.

ISBN 978-0-520-39110-9 (cloth : alk. paper)
ISBN 978-0-520-39112-3 (pbk. : alk. paper)
ISBN 978-0-520-39113-0 (ebook)

Manufactured in the United States of America

31 30 29 28 27 26 25 24 23 22
10 9 8 7 6 5 4 3 2 1

For Rudeara, Tressie, Jody, Renee, Keri, Desalashia, Dixie, Ashley, Tanisha, Eraina, and all of you who, for your own safety, I can't name here. You trusted me with your stories. I hope I did them justice.

There are no criminals here at Riker's Island Correctional Institution for Women (New York), only victims. Most of the women (over 95%) are black and Puerto Rican. Many were abused children. Most have been abused by men and all have been abused by "the system."

—Assata Shakur, "Women in Prison: How It Is with Us"

Contents

Preface

In 2018, I co-facilitated a support group for women serving life sentences at the Maryland Correctional Institution for Women. My students and I represented several of the women in the group who were eligible for parole and had been working with them to write their life stories for their parole packets. Looking for a new group project, we coalesced around writing a book—the women would write their stories, and I would frame their narratives using law and social science research. Although some at the prison were open to the idea, the Maryland Department of Public Safety and Correctional Services vetoed the project. The women then asked me to tell their stories myself. This book is the result of that request.

I have been telling the stories of victims of gender-based violence in various forms for more than twenty-five years: as a lawyer, in legislative advocacy, and as a scholar. But until 2013 my work with criminalized survivors was largely academic. The exception: in 2006, I read about Dixie Shanahan, a woman subjected to unspeakable abuse who killed her husband, Scott, after he threatened to murder her and their unborn child. I learned about Dixie through news articles, obtained the transcripts of her trial, and tried to figure out how anyone could believe that incarcerating Dixie after the nineteen years of abuse she had already endured could constitute justice. I wrote a law review article about her case and, after the article's publication, became involved with the effort to seek commutation of Dixie's sentence and began trading letters with Dixie.

I was very clear about the injustice of Dixie's incarceration, but I wasn't doing anything to help women closer to home. That changed in 2013, when I began teaching at the University of Maryland Carey School of Law. I started a new clinic, the Gender Violence Clinic, whose mission was to handle any case where gender and violence intersected. Looking for new types of cases to work on with students, I connected with Mary Joel Davis. Mary Joel is a legend in Maryland. At fifty, Mary Joel founded Alternative Directions, an organization providing services to incarcerated and formerly incarcerated people. After her retirement, at seventy-five, Mary Joel founded Second Chance for Women, which assists incarcerated people preparing for parole. Now well into her eighties, Mary Joel continues to go into prisons regularly, trailing her oxygen tank and getting into the best kind of trouble on behalf of incarcerated people. She referred me my first criminalized survivor client seeking parole and gave me the basics I needed to represent my client properly.

Since then, my students and I have represented numerous criminalized survivors seeking parole, commutations, and pardons in both the state and federal systems. We have spent hours upon hours in prisons, delivering news both good and devastating. We have seen how police, prosecutors, judges, parole commissioners, and governors disbelieve, disdain, and dismiss our clients' claims of victimization. And how our clients sit in prison year after year, doing their best to grow and find meaning in their incarceration, enduring trauma and losing hope.

I came late in my career to representing criminalized survivors. I came even later to abolition feminism. At twenty-five, when I began representing victims of violence, I firmly believed that everyone who perpetrated violence was a monster and that swift and harsh intervention by the criminal legal system was essential to stop that violence. My clients quickly taught me to look at intimate partner violence in more nuanced ways. The more I represented people in the legal system, the more I doubted how effective those interventions were.

In 2018, by the time I published my second book, *Decriminalizing Domestic Violence*, I had been a critic of the legal system's response to intimate partner violence for many years. In that book I argued that the criminal legal system was not deterring or decreasing intimate partner violence and that criminalization had serious negative consequences for the people it was meant to benefit. Nonetheless, I ended that book by saying that although "one could make a credible, even strong, case for decriminalizing intimate partner violence," decriminalizing domestic violence was "unlikely, and probably unwise." I was not yet ready to embrace abolition. Instead, I offered reforms to the carceral system that I suggested could make it more just and less likely to spur the trauma that contributes to the perpetration of intimate partner violence—the kind of reforms that I criticize in this book.

I've talked about *Decriminalizing Domestic Violence* hundreds of times. But the context for that conversation is very different now than it was when I finished writing the book in 2016. Continuous police killings of Black people brought police and prison abolition to the consciousness of those of us not previously steeped in it. I learned from feminist abolitionists like Angela Y. Davis, Mariame Kaba, Andrea Ritchie, and Beth Richie that abolition was not only consistent with efforts to end gender-based violence but essential to those efforts.

And I was going into prisons regularly to represent my own clients. The people the criminal legal system had labeled "murderers" I experienced as kind, caring, funny, warm, thoughtful, empathetic human beings. I came to understand that the violence of incarceration can never solve the problem of gender-based violence and that caging people can never be just. By the time I began writing *Imperfect Victims*, it was clear to me that abolition is the only solution to the revictimization of survivors by the criminal legal system. I hope in reading this book it becomes clear to you as well.

Acknowledgments

I have been extraordinarily lucky throughout my career as a lawyer to find fulfilling work. But representing incarcerated survivors of violence is the most meaningful work I have ever done. And my clients are the reason that I love this work so much. Working with and learning from them has been the greatest privilege of my career. Maintaining relationships with clients who have been released is a gift. I struggle to find the words to describe just how much their trust, friendship, and love mean to me. I hope they know. I think they do.

I co-facilitated the lifers group described in this book's preface with Mary Joel Davis. In 2013, Mary Joel gave me my first parole case, and I could not be more grateful to her. Lila Meadows was among the first Gender Violence Clinic students to work on a parole case. She took on as many cases as I would give her, often urging me to take cases even though our docket was full, just because she could not stand to see someone go unrepresented. Lila's knowledge of the parole system quickly eclipsed mine, and over time she went from being a student to the Gender Violence Clinic's staff attorney to the director of her own clinic and a trusted friend. There is no one who understands the parole system in Maryland better than Lila and no fiercer advocate for her clients. I am thankful for her commitment, her energy, her friendship, and the dark humor we share on those days (and they are the majority) when the criminal legal system proves yet again that the cruelty is the point.

In 2017, I learned about the work of Survived and Punished, a coalition of people and projects working to support and free criminalized survivors of gender-based violence. I have been in awe of their work ever since. For letting me learn from and struggle with them, I thank Alisa Bierria, Mariame Kaba, Colby Lenz, Andrea Ritchie, Emily Thuma, Survived and Punished New York, Survived and Punished California, the California Coalition for Women Prisoners, MUAVI, and Love and Protect.

There are people (lawyers and nonlawyers) throughout the United States advocating for criminalized survivors at various stages in the legal system. We share stories, strategies, and commiserations, and I appreciate them tremendously. I am grateful to Sandra Babcock, Margaret Byrne, Courtney Cross, Carrie Hempel, Carol Jacobsen, and Anne Rather for taking the time to talk with me about these ideas and their work. And to my friend and co-conspirator, Kate Mogulescu, thank you for your immense knowledge and even greater wisdom and for always dragging me into your projects.

This book relies heavily on the stories of criminalized survivors documented by journalists throughout the United States. Without these journalists, so much of what happens to criminalized survivors in courts and prisons would be shielded from public view. I am particularly grateful for the work of Victoria Law, Justine van der Leun, Natalie Schreyer, Jessica Pishko, Melissa Gira Grant, and Melissa Jeltsen. Read their stuff! Additional appreciation to Victoria Law, who published *Tenacious* (cited frequently in this book), a zine written and illustrated by formerly and currently incarcerated people, for almost twenty years (and who is likely burning her lunch as I write this).

The University of Maryland Carey School of Law is one of the best places in the country to be a clinical law professor. I am deeply grateful to the School of Law for supporting my scholarship and the Gender Violence Clinic's work with incarcerated survivors. I am particularly indebted to Professor Michael Pinard and Bay Golfin-Byrd, the Gender Violence Clinic's staff attorney—both are unbelievably supportive colleagues who took on significant extra work to free me up to write *Imperfect Victims*.

Five classes of law students have helped me amass the research for this book and offered their insights about how to shape it. My thanks to Chelsea van Orden, Monica Gasey, Sydney Goetz, Joanna Woodson, Isabel Restall, and Hayley Wolf for doing all of the things I hate to do and for quickly answering random "Can you get this for me?" emails at all hours of the day and night with good humor (even when I could have Googled it myself).

Special thanks to Alisa Bierria, Alesha Durfee, Jill McCorkle, Kate Mogulescu, and Michael Pinard for their detailed feedback on the draft of this book, which improved the final version immeasurably (all mistakes are mine, of course).

This is my second book with the University of California Press, and I never considered publishing it anywhere else. Maura Roessner is the best editor a person could ask for—the perfect balance of critical probing and encouragement and excitement. And I am proud to again be part of Claire Renzetti's Gender and Justice series for UC Press, proving that I was right when I said in the acknowledgments to *Decriminalizing Domestic Violence* that Claire would keep me fully employed for the next several years.

The ideas in *Imperfect Victims* were workshopped at the University of Nevada Las Vegas Boyd School of Law, the LEX Research Network, and the Washington State Coalition Against Domestic Violence. Parts of the book were adapted from articles published in the *Kansas Law Review*, the *Yale Journal of Law and Feminism*, the *Penn State Dickinson Law Review*, and the *International Journal for Crime, Justice, and Social Democracy*.

This book was written in the middle of a pandemic. At various times, two, three, and four of my family members were simultaneously in the house, all working on our own projects and managing not to drive each other crazy. I am unbelievably lucky to have the love and support of those three other people. To my children, Juliet and Carter: you make me laugh, you make me think, and you make me proud every single day. This book took a lot of my time (as does the work it describes), but there is nothing more important to me than being your mom. Doug, I could not do any of this without you. I am so grateful for that disastrous blind date and for all the years that have followed. I love you and I promise to keep going to the office four days per week (during the semester, of course).

1 The Criminalization of Survival

Some of their names may be familiar.

Marissa Alexander fired a gun into the ceiling of her home after her ex-husband, Rico Gray, threatened her. No one was injured during the incident. Gray had a long history of abusing women. He admitted to attacking Alexander at least four or five times. During one incident, Gray pushed Alexander backward, causing her to hit her head on a bathtub, resulting in an injury requiring medical attention. Gray admitted that, as Alexander had said, he chased her around her house and was refusing to leave when Alexander fired her gun into the air. Alexander was charged with three counts of aggravated assault—one for each of the people in the house at the time she fired the gun. After twelve minutes of deliberation by the jury, Alexander was convicted and sentenced to twenty years of incarceration.

Bresha Meadows was eight years old when her father began sexually abusing her. He first raped Meadows when she was twelve. She does not remember a time when her father did not physically abuse her mother. Meadows's mother sought a protective order, detailing how her husband "cut me, broke my ribs, fingers, the blood vessels in my hand, my mouth, blackened my eyes. . . . If he finds us, I am 100 percent sure he will kill me and the children." Ultimately Meadows's mother returned home with the children. Meadows's father continued to rape her until July 28, 2016, when Meadows killed him with his gun while he was passed out, drunk, on the couch. Just before she shot, Meadows remembers, "I sat there thinking and pictures kept flashing in my head, like my mom's funeral casket, and then my sister and brother are old enough to move out, and it is just me and [her father] left in the house."[1] Meadows did not believe that she would be arrested. She thought it was clear that she had acted in self-defense. But she was arrested the night of the shooting and charged with aggravated murder. Fifteen-year-old Bresha Meadows pled to involuntary manslaughter and was sentenced to a year and a day in juvenile detention, plus six months in a mental health facility.[2] Had she been tried and convicted as an adult, Meadows could have been sentenced to life in prison.

Others appear primarily in headlines ("Domestic violence victim charged with murdering husband") or as hashtags (#FreeLiyah; #Bring MsPrettyHome). Whether named or not, these people share two things. They are victims of gender-based violence.[3] And they were punished by the criminal legal system as a direct result of that violence.[4] They are imperfect victims.

For the past forty years, the criminal legal system has been the primary societal response to gender-based violence (which includes intimate partner violence, rape and sexual assault, and human trafficking) in the United States.[5] Antiviolence advocates tout legislative victories, increased enforcement of laws criminalizing gender-based violence by police and prosecutors, and longer penalties as proof of society's dedication to ensuring that those who do violence are held accountable. Criminalization was meant to increase awareness of gender-based violence and decrease that violence by changing community norms about its acceptability. But those efforts have also led to increased rates of arrest, prosecution, conviction, and incarceration of those who the changes were meant to protect: victims of violence. So many victims of violence have been caught up in the criminal legal system that an entire movement—known by the hashtag #SurvivedandPunished—has emerged to protest their revictimization by the criminal legal system.

Punitive intervention by the criminal legal system as a response to survivors' efforts to defend themselves or otherwise address gender-based violence is not a new phenomenon, however. On June 23, 1855, an enslaved woman named Celia fought off her master, Robert Newsom, with a stick, killing him. Newsom had repeatedly raped Celia over the five years since purchasing her when she was fourteen. Celia told Newsom that she would fight if he tried to rape her again and asked his daughters to stop him. But Newsom persisted. After killing Newsom, Celia put his body into the fire and removed his bones the following day. Missouri law permitted women to argue self-defense when resisting rape, but the judge in Celia's case refused to give the jury that instruction. By law, Celia was property, not a person, and therefore could not be raped. Instead, the judge told the jury that if Newsom had been used to "having intercourse" with Celia, went to her cabin to do so, and she struck and killed him, she would be guilty of first-degree murder. On November 1, 1855, Celia was found guilty of first-degree murder. She was hanged on December 21, 1855.[6]

Lena Baker was hired to nurse Ernest Knight back to health after he broke his leg. Knight's adult son abused Baker, while Knight essentially held Baker captive (and may have been raping her). In August 1944, Knight locked Baker in his mill; when he returned, Baker shot Knight after a struggle. Tried by an all-white jury, Baker was convicted of murder and sentenced to death. During her trial she testified: "What I done, I did in self-defense, or I would have been killed myself. Where I was I could not overcome it." Baker became the first and only woman killed in Georgia's electric chair. She was pardoned in 2005, sixty years after the state of Georgia killed her.[7] Many of the women tried and convicted for attempting to protect themselves in that era were, like Celia and Lena Baker, Black women.[8]

Rose and Joe Lucas had been married for twenty-three years by 1956. Around 1951, Joe, a highway patrolman, began abusing his wife. On December 5, 1956, Rose called police when her husband threatened to kill her. After a five-minute investigation, the officers left. They told Rose to make a complaint through the District Attorney's office (something Rose had tried to do two years earlier, with no success). Joe resumed his threats. In response, Rose loaded his revolver and said, "Joe, I can't go on like this, we can't go on like this any longer. I have to talk to you ... I don't want you to kill me."[9] Joe lunged toward his wife. She shot him four times. Prosecutors contended that "to acquit this defendant ... is to give every married person in San Francisco the license to kill."[10] Rose Lucas was convicted of manslaughter.[11]

Historically, law professor Carolyn Ramsey has argued, judges and juries were not uniformly unsympathetic to women's self-defense arguments. By the 1970s, however, women were much more likely to plead guilty in such cases than to be acquitted.[12] At about the same time, the anti-rape movement began to encourage women to use force in response to sexual violence. In the July 1970 edition of *It Ain't Me Babe*, a newsletter founded by members of Berkeley Women's Liberation, a member named Erin argued that if they wanted to protect themselves from rape, "we women must take action and do it ourselves. We must be willing to fight to protect ourselves."[13] Claiming the right to defend oneself from rape challenged the idea that only the state, via the criminal legal system, had the right to respond to rape.

The anti-rape and battered women's movements actively organized in support of women who were prosecuted for using violence in self-defense. In 1974 feminists rallied around Joan Little, a twenty-year-old Black woman charged with killing Clarence Alligood, a sixty-two-year-old white correctional officer at the Beaufort County, North Carolina, jail. Alligood was found dead on the bunk in Little's cell with semen on his thigh. He had been stabbed eleven times. Little claimed that Alligood came to her cell carrying an ice pick, which he used to force her to perform oral sex. Alligood grabbed Little's neck and shoved her to the ground. While Little was complying, Alligood loosened his grip on the ice pick. Little grabbed the ice pick and stabbed Alligood with it.[14] Little escaped from jail but turned herself in after several days. Her attorney, Karen Galloway, explained Little's predicament: "Joan knew that nobody was going to believe her. Alligood had already told her that .... And she knew that was true. No one was going to believe her. She's in Jail. She's a black woman. He's white. He's a male. He believes he can do anything he wants to a black woman. He's been taught that his whole life."[15] And Alligood wasn't just any white man—he was a white law enforcement officer.

Little's case highlighted what anti-rape activists saw as the two primary problems with the operation of the criminal legal system in cases like Little's: first, that women rather than their rapists were criminalized, and second, that women were denied the right to defend themselves at all.

Anti-rape activists picketed the courthouse carrying signs proclaiming, "Why Have a Trial—the Criminal is Dead." The slogan of the Free Joan Little Movement was "Power to the Ice Pick."[16] After a little over an hour, a jury consisting of both Black and white members acquitted Little—who then returned to prison to finish serving her original sentence.[17] Anti-rape activists hoped that Little's acquittal would encourage other women to fight back. As Celine Chenier, a founder of the Joan Little Defense Fund explained, "Joan Little has inspired me and countless others to deal with any rapist."[18]

But not all women who defended themselves faced a sympathetic jury. Also in 1974, Luis Castillo and Miguel Jimenez raped Inez Garcia. From a few blocks away, they then called to taunt her. Garcia loaded her rifle and went to look for the men. When she found them, Jimenez threatened Garcia with a knife. She shot and killed him.[19] At trial, Garcia was unrepentant, saying, "I'm not sorry I did it. . . . I'm only sorry I missed Luis."[20] She left the courtroom during the prosecutor's cross-examination. The judge refused to allow the jury to consider self-defense, saying that Castillo and Jimenez's rape of Garcia earlier that night was not relevant and prohibiting Garcia from testifying about it.[21] Garcia was convicted of second-degree murder and sentenced to five years to life. She served fifteen months in prison before being granted bail after the California Court of Appeal overturned her conviction. At a second trial Garcia was permitted to argue self-defense. She testified about the rape and told a different story about the shooting, explaining that she left her house because she believed Castillo and Jimenez would come back and kill her. Garcia's lawyers argued that she did not tell police about the rape when she was initially arrested because she was ashamed to talk about it. Castillo invoked his privilege against self-incrimination rather than testifying. Garcia was acquitted.[22]

Judy Ann Laws was fifteen and pregnant when she married John (J. T.) Norman. Starting about five years into their marriage, J. T. Norman abused his wife regularly and brutally, beating her with his fists, a baseball bat, bottles, glasses, an ashtray, a shoe. He forced Judy to eat from a dog dish and sleep on the floor. He took his wife to truck stops and forced her to sell sex, beating her if she did not bring home enough money. The day before J. T.'s death in June 1985, Judy called police, who told her they could do nothing if she did not seek a warrant for her husband's arrest (which was not required by North Carolina law). Despite the bruises on her face, police left without making an arrest. That night, Judy was briefly hospitalized after overdosing on sleeping pills. After her release later that night and throughout the next day, J. T.'s abuse, which included putting his cigarette out on Judy's collarbone, continued. When J. T. finally fell asleep, Judy went to look for headache medicine in her mother's purse. She also found a gun. Judy Norman shot J. T. Norman three times while he slept.[23]

Judy Norman was charged with first-degree murder. At trial the defense introduced extensive evidence of J.T. Norman's history of abusing his wife. Judge John Gardner refused, however, to give the jury an instruction on self-defense.[24] The jury found Judy Norman guilty of manslaughter. Prosecutor Alan Leonard said, "I was concerned from day one about the example that would be set in this case.... If Mrs. Norman didn't get some active sentence, that would in effect give the court's approval to an intentional homicide."[25] The media shared Leonard's concern, with outlets like CBS's *60 Minutes* reporting that women were "getting away with murder."[26] Judy Norman was sentenced to six years of incarceration.[27] Her case was not unusual for the time. As gender and sexuality studies professor Emily Thuma has noted, "most abuse survivors who killed in self-defense in the 1970s and early 1980s were convicted rather than acquitted, and incarcerated rather than sentenced to probation."[28] Acquitted women were newsworthy because "they were the exception and not the rule."[29]

The stories of Little, Garcia, and Norman are fairly well known (or were at the time). But for every one of these stories, there are countless others we know little about. They appear as headlines for a day—"Police: Woman Shoots Husband after Reports of Domestic Violence Earlier This Year"—then largely vanish from public view. After conviction, most all but disappear altogether. As Cyntoia Brown-Long has observed in her autobiography, *Free Cyntoia: My Search for Redemption in the American Prison System*, "America's prisons are full of women who were arrested [for killing abusive partners]. They're forgotten, left to waste away in prison, with no one interested in showing them mercy."[30]

Some people escape criminal punishment. Occasionally the media reports the story of someone like Letoya Ramseure, who killed her boyfriend after he threatened to kill her, pushed his way into her home in violation of a protective order, and assaulted both Ramseure and her mother. Ramseure was originally charged with third-degree murder but ultimately tried for manslaughter. Although the prosecutor argued that Ramseure's motive was jealousy, not fear, and that she lacked visible injuries after the incident, a jury found Ramseure not guilty.[31] Edna Louise Pipkins killed her boyfriend after two years of abuse and twenty-three calls to police. When the charges against her were ultimately dropped, the Women Free Women in Prison Project commented, "In legal terms it is said that Edna Louis Pipkin [*sic*] won her case. It would be more accurate to say that she escaped the usual punishment of imprisonment faced by most poor women of color who fight back against their batterers."[32] But that freedom comes at a cost—time spent in jail or prison, money paid toward bail, separation from children and loved ones, the trauma of the criminal legal process.

Several factors may be responsible for the prosecution of people for crimes related to their own victimization. In the context of intimate partner violence, for example, Ramsey has suggested that women's increasing economic power and the liberalization of divorce laws have created expectations that women would simply end violent relationships. When women failed to take advantage of this ostensible newfound freedom to leave their violent partners, their self-defense claims were seen as not credible, prompting prosecutors to pursue them.[33]

But law reform itself has also had a substantial impact on law enforcement's determination to press these cases. Feminist antiviolence advocates championed law reform, believing that state intervention via the criminal legal system was essential if gender-based violence was to be taken seriously. In the late 1970s and 1980s, antiviolence advocates lobbied for substantial changes to rape and domestic violence law. These changes were intended to make prosecution more frequent and more successful and to signal the state's condemnation of gender-based violence. States removed barriers to prosecuting rape cases, including requirements that victims vigorously resist their rapists, have witnesses corroborate their claims, and report their rapes immediately. Given the liberalization of rape law, rape victims were expected to bring their claims to court—not take matters into their own hands by defending themselves. In the context of intimate partner violence, states enacted mandatory arrest laws (requiring police to make arrests in all cases where they had probable cause to do so) and no-drop prosecution policies (committing prosecutors to pursuing any case of intimate partner violence where sufficient evidence existed).

The Violence Against Women Act (VAWA), enacted as part of 1994's Violent Crime Control and Law Enforcement Act, incentivized the adoption of such policies and funded increased criminalization through grants to police, prosecutors, and courts that now total in the billions of dollars. The antiviolence advocates behind these reforms—who had "a vision of social justice as criminal justice, and of punitive systems of control as the best motivational deterrents for men's bad behavior"—were dubbed "carceral feminists" by the sociologist Elizabeth Bernstein.[34] As the social work professor Mimi Kim has explained, although antiviolence advocates initially thought they could control how law enforcement intervened in gender-based violence cases, law enforcement's goals and strategies soon eclipsed the policy aims of advocates—a dance Kim describes as "the carceral creep."[35] The push for criminal anti-trafficking laws has largely followed the intimate partner violence playbook, establishing the centrality of criminal prosecution in governmental anti-trafficking strategies and using the law to punish behavior ranging from giving someone a place to stay to holding money for them to selling people for sex.

The criminalization of gender-based violence championed by carceral feminists has been ineffective in decreasing that violence.[36] Rape is still underreported and rarely prosecuted. Rates of intimate partner violence have decreased since the inception of legal reforms, but those rates decreased in tandem with the overall crime rate between 1994 and 2016 and have fluctuated in the past few years. Criminalization has also had significant consequences for the victims of that violence, something that some antiviolence feminists, particularly feminists of color, foresaw from the beginning of the reform movement.[37] While many white feminists believed the criminal legal system would protect victims of gender-based violence, people of color were primarily focused on preventing that system from doing harm.[38] Black feminists noted that support for the criminal legal system strengthened institutions that not only targeted those who used violence but also passed judgment on those who defended themselves from violence.[39]

To benefit from legal system reforms, survivors of violence had to perform their victimization in very specific ways: they had to be perfect victims. The gendered rhetoric of criminalization created unrealistic stereotypes of people subjected to abuse. Blameless victims (usually meek, passive women) were pitted against monstrous perpetrators (usually men).[40] Blamelessness guaranteed that victims would be treated sympathetically; "the 'true' or 'worthy' victim loses some of her halo if her presentation falters."[41] Victimization is a constructed identity—that is, claims of victimization are believed only to the extent that others accept those claims as true.[42]

But victims of violence don't always—or even often—conform to these stereotypes. Australian scholar Heather Nancarrow has described a discussion about intimate partner violence with Indigenous women, during which one Aboriginal woman noted that women in her community used violence. Nancarrow writes, "We all nodded politely but said nothing and moved on: we simply did not know how to respond."[43] The legal system is similarly confounded by victims who fail to fit stereotypes—who use force to defend themselves or who are angry, for example. Such victims face a hostile legal system skeptical of their claims. A woman who was being stalked by an ex-boyfriend against whom she had a protective order repeatedly called police, to no avail. She finally fought back against her stalker, who was later tried for violating the protective order. A judge noted her requests for help but said, "At the same time, she seems to put up a fairly tough exterior here." The woman's "tough exterior" coupled with her willingness to confront her stalker likely led to his acquittal—despite his admission that he had violated the order on numerous occasions.[44]

Some victimization claims are deemed more credible than others. "Women who are abrasive and argumentative, who are aggressive towards their abusers for any reason (including self-defense), or who otherwise fail to conform to traditional female gender roles" are imperfect victims.[45] Sex workers are imperfect victims, as are lesbians and trans people.[46] So are women of color, particularly Black women.[47] As anti-trafficking activist Holly Joshi has argued, Black women have never been seen as survivors or "good" victims, but rather tools that the criminal legal system can use to punish Black men.[48] Imperfect victims are more likely to be arrested.[49]

Once victimized women become criminal defendants, the opportunity to be seen as a perfect victim all but vanishes. As the sociologist Elizabeth Comack has written, "crime categories are premised on a binary opposition or dualism between 'the criminal' and 'the law abiding.' Those who are processed through the system and end up in prison are relegated to the criminal side of the equation. The net effect is to cast criminal women as Other—and the underlying message is clear: they are not like the rest of us."[50] A system so reliant on this kind of binary leaves little room for the complicated stories of criminalized survivors—for imperfect victims. The portrayal of the victim-defendant in a criminal trial is hotly contested ground. Prosecutors and defense attorneys in Joan Little's trial, for example, offered competing visions of Little. While prosecutors characterized her as a "violent and scheming seductress," the defense realized that she needed to be seen as "sympathetic and respectable" to be acquitted.[51] Violence is gendered male. Women who use force deviate from gender norms and may be punished severely for doing so.[52]

Criminalization undoubtedly increased enforcement of laws prohibiting gender-based violence, particularly in the context of intimate partner violence (and later, trafficking). Mandatory arrest and no-drop prosecution policies in intimate partner violence cases ensured that police made arrests whenever they had probable cause and that prosecutors pursued cases whenever they had sufficient evidence. Police and prosecutors often enforced those policies without looking beyond isolated incidents or asking whether the defendant was actually the victim of violence.[53] When women used force or were accused of using force, they were subject to criminalization. "In the name of equal justice," criminologist Meda Chesney-Lind has explained, the criminal legal system enforced laws against women just as it did against men, a phenomenon Chesney-Lind calls "vengeful equity."[54] Or as Oklahoma prosecutor Steve Kunzweiler has argued: "If women are equal, then they are equal in all ways, including the idea that there are women to whom you have to say, 'Goodbye!' "[55]

Arrest rates of women after the adoption of mandatory arrest policies tell the vengeful equity story. Jurisdictions across the United States logged significant increases in the numbers of women arrested, both in dual arrests (both parties were arrested) and in arrests of women only, after such laws were adopted.[56] After the passage of mandatory arrest laws in California, for example, men's arrests rose by 60 percent; women's arrests increased by 400 percent. In Kenosha, Wisconsin, arrests of women increased twelve times following the enactment of mandatory arrest laws.[57]

These increases would be warranted if the research suggested that women were eluding arrest prior to the passage of mandatory arrest laws or had grown more violent after such laws were enacted. Indeed, some claim that women are as violent as men.[58] But other research shows that women are more likely to use emotional abuse (which is not generally criminalized) than physical violence. When they do use violence, they do so in self-defense.[59] Women are not usually the primary perpetrators of intimate partner violence.[60] And women did not become more violent after the passage of mandatory arrest laws. Instead, as sociology professor Alesha Durfee has explained, the jump in arrest rates is at least in part "directly attributable to the implementation of mandatory arrest policies and not simply an increased use of violence by women in intimate relationships."[61]

The criminalization of gender-based violence—and the consequences of criminalization for victims of violence—must be situated in the larger context of mass incarceration in the United States. As of 2020, almost 2.3 million people were incarcerated in the United States.[62] Around 10 percent of those incarcerated were women and girls, making the United States "one of the top incarcerators of women in the world."[63] Incarceration of women in state prisons increased by 834 percent between 1978 and 2015—twice the rate of the increase in men's incarceration.[64] As Chesney-Lind has noted, "For most of the 20th century, we imprisoned about 5,000 to 10,000 women. At the turn of the new century, we now have more than 100,000 women doing time in U.S. prisons."[65] By the 2000s, the rate of incarceration of women in the United States equaled the total incarceration rate for western Europe.[66]

The growth in women's incarceration is attributable not to increases in women's criminality but to how the criminal legal system treats women.[67] Black women make up a substantial portion of the increased prison population. Black women are incarcerated at twice and Latinas 1.3 times the rate of white women.[68] Native women are also incarcerated at disproportionate rates.[69] Rates of incarceration are inflated for lesbian, gay, bisexual (LGB) and transgender and gender-nonconforming (TGNC) people as well. LGB and TGNC people are three times as likely to be incarcerated as the general population.[70] Black trans women are ten times as likely to be incarcerated.[71] And 42 percent of women in prison and 35 percent of women in jails (but only about 1 percent of the population of the United States) are lesbians.[72]

WHO ARE CRIMINALIZED SURVIVORS?

Most women in prison have one thing in common: they have experienced gender-based violence. In that sense most incarcerated women are criminalized survivors. Studies consistently show that anywhere from 50 percent to 95 percent of incarcerated women have been raped, sexually assaulted, or subjected to abuse by intimate partners.[73] Criminologist Beth Richie has noted that she has never met an incarcerated Black woman who has not experienced some form of gender-based violence.[74] Kwaneta Harris, incarcerated in Texas, says the same.[75] Similar rates of victimization are found among adjudicated girls. One researcher found that 74 percent of the girls held in an Ohio facility for "delinquent" girls were abused by family members—65 percent by people unrelated to them. And 52 percent had been sexually abused by nonfamily members, 22 percent by family members.[76]

Incarcerated women are much more likely to be victims of violence than men—seven times more likely to have been sexually abused and four times more likely to have been physically abused.[77] Many women experience more than one type of victimization, often being abused by multiple people.[78] Enduring gender-based violence is a "defining experience" for incarcerated women.[79] Although there is little data on prior victimization among incarcerated TGNC people, surveys of TGNC people reveal that physical, psychological, sexual, and identity-based victimization is common.[80] A substantial number of incarcerated TGNC people have likely experienced some form of gender-based violence.

The definition of "criminalized survivor" used in this book is a bit narrower. Criminalized survivors are women, trans people, and gender-nonconforming people whose punitive encounters with the criminal legal system are directly linked to their own gender-based victimization (rape/

sexual assault, intimate partner violence, or trafficking—or some combination thereof, given the co-occurrence of these forms of violence).[81] As Survived & Punished New York (a collective dedicated to ending the criminalization of survival) has explained: "We focus on women, trans folks, and gender non-conforming folks because they—we—are the main targets of gender violence, and of criminalization of survival actions."[82]

In a survey of women incarcerated in Oregon's Coffee Creek Correctional Facility, 44 percent of the women reported that the relationships they were in at the time of their arrests contributed to their convictions; 69 percent linked trauma to their incarceration.[83] A 2020 survey of people incarcerated in women's prisons for murder or manslaughter found that 41 percent of those who experienced intimate partner violence prior to their incarceration were in prison for killing a partner; 30 percent of all respondents said they were incarcerated for attempting to prevent physical or sexual violence against them or a loved one.[84] A 2011 study reported that more than 90 percent of women convicted of killing intimate partners in New York State had previously been abused by a partner.[85] Because women and girls are the focus of the vast majority of research on criminalized survivors, the data and stories in this book primarily describe their experiences. The experiences of TGNC people are documented whenever possible.

CONFRONTING THE CRIMINAL SYSTEM

Survivors encounter the criminal legal system in a variety of ways. Some come to the criminal legal system seeking assistance. For example, Tiawanda Moore called the police for help after her boyfriend assaulted her. Chicago police officer Jason Wilson came into Moore's room to interview her and during that interaction he groped her breast. Moore reported the assault to police and met with internal affairs officers, who attempted to discourage her from reporting. Feeling pressured to drop her complaint, Moore recorded the meeting on her phone. After police became aware that Moore was recording the meeting, they notified her that it was illegal to record a conversation without the consent of all parties and arrested her for felony eavesdropping. Moore spent the next two weeks in jail. More than a year later, a jury found her not guilty. Wilson was never disciplined or charged with a crime.[86]

Others seek assistance through the civil system but find themselves punished. In 2017, for instance, Kassandra Jackson sought a civil order protecting her from her partner. When the order was denied, Jackson hit a sign on the wall. Hamilton County, Ohio, magistrate Michael Bachman ordered her incarcerated for five days for contempt of court because of her "belligerence." In 2018, Jackson returned to court to seek another order. When told she was too late, she pleaded with a man in the hallway. Bachman left his courtroom, chased Jackson down, grabbed her, and directed her to his courtroom, where he found her in contempt and sentenced her to ten days imprisonment—again, because she was "belligerent."[87] Still others are punished by police, prosecutors, and judges for failing to act "like victims": refusing to cooperate with police investigating an incident, declining prosecutors' requests to testify, or failing to appear for court after being subpoenaed.

Criminalized survivors also come to the attention of the criminal legal system as defendants. Researchers studying women's criminality have identified several pathways women take to crime. Pathways explain "how the abuse and oppression of women and girls narrows their options and may place them on a trajectory where crime may be the most logical response."[88] In her original articulation of pathways theory, sociologist Kathleen Daly described how "harmed-and-harming" women, who were abused and neglected as children, and "battered" women, who were in or had been in relationships with violent men, arrived in felony court.[89] Subsequent studies have identified dysfunctional intimate relationships, violence, victimization, and relationships with men engaged in criminal behavior as pathways to crime.[90]

While the pathways approach can illuminate the circumstances that lead women to crime, women's and gender studies professors Jodie Lawston and Erica Meiners have argued that it is "limited, in that it does not fully account for the ways in which gender, race, and sexuality coalesce so that *certain* women and girls are *targeted* by the criminal justice system for incarceration."[91] Richie, for example, explains that criminalized Black survivors are often "compelled to crime."[92] Richie argues that "gender entrapment"—that is, "the socially constructed process whereby African

American women who are vulnerable to men's violence in their intimate relationship are penalized for behaviors they engage in even when the behaviors are logical extensions of their racialized gender identities, their culturally expected gender roles, and the violence in their intimate relationships"—explains "how some women who participate in illegal activities do so in response to violence, the threat of violence, or coercion by their male partners."[93]

The paradigmatic image of the criminalized survivor is the woman who uses force against her partner. While often characterized as either "mad" (mentally unstable or mentally ill) or "bad," women use force against their partners for a variety of reasons. In a study of 208 women arrested and sent to intervention programs for using force, women identified asserting their dignity, defending themselves from violence, aggression, and fending off an anticipated attack as motivations for their violence.[94] Retaliation for past violence, expressing emotion, relieving tension, getting attention, asserting power, and establishing a tough identity have also been offered as justifications for women's actions.[95] Self-defense, however, is the most frequent explanation for criminalized survivors' use of force. For people who believe that the legal system will not protect them, particularly Black people, violence may seem to be (and may in fact be) the only way to protect themselves.[96] As a result, Black women may be more likely to fight back against their partners.[97]

Sometimes violence has the desired effect. As one woman explained: "He, uh, never hits me now. 'Cause, uh, I fought back. I figured, 'Why let this person treat me the way he does or, when I tried and treat him nice, you know? So I started fighting back. And then he quit. Because I guess he knew, uh, I wasn't going to take no shit from him."[98] Other women find that not only does the violence continue, but they are punished for defending themselves: "In the last seven years, Eileen has started to fight back. I asked her what happens when she does and she replied, 'I *always* end up in court.' Eileen has been charged four times in the past seven years. In one incident, where her husband hit and kicked her and she then hit him in return, he got 30 days and she got 8 months."[99]

People also become enmeshed in the criminal legal system when they commit crimes at the direction of, and out of fear of, their partners. For example, women and girls convicted of prostitution are frequently sold for sex by abusive partners.[100] Women are much more likely to be involved in serious crimes if they have at least one male co-offender. Often those women are coerced into crimes.[101] A 2020 survey found that 33 percent of people incarcerated in women's prisons for murder or manslaughter had been convicted of a crime involving a male partner; 13 percent were convicted of committing crimes with the people who abused them.[102] A survey of incarcerated women in Oklahoma found that over 80 percent of women whose husbands were involved in their crimes and more than 75 percent of those whose boyfriends were involved had been abused by their partners.[103]

Ramona Brant was a first-time offender when she received a mandatory minimum life sentence for conspiracy to distribute drugs. Brant's codefendant husband, who ran the drug business, regularly abused her and refused to take a plea deal that would spare her from prosecution, saying that if he couldn't have her, no one would.[104] Brant's sentence was commuted after she served twenty-one years in federal prison. She died two years after being released.[105] Eraina Pretty was convicted of first-degree murder at age eighteen after her boyfriend, Ronald Brown, ordered her to accompany him to rob her employer's Baltimore store. Brown told Pretty to tie up her employer and another man who was in the store. Brown assured Pretty he would not harm the men. Pretty did as she was told, then fled the store as soon as she could. As she ran, she heard gunshots. Pretty was sentenced to life imprisonment for the murder of the store owner and released in 2020, after forty-two years of incarceration. The fear of what an abusive partner will do if a person fails to participate in his crime is hard to overstate. As a criminalized survivor named Letisha explained to Richie: "I know it's hard for people to believe, but I really thought he would kill me if I refused to go along with his scheme.... The risk of being arrested was much less scary for me than being killed by my husband."[106]

In her study of Black women "compelled to crime," Richie also found women who, having been abused by partners in the past, used force to protect themselves from people other than their partners. "When some women were the constant victims of abuse, enduring years of denial, rationalization and failed efforts to change the abuser," Richie wrote, "they responded almost instinctively to protect themselves from other men."[107] Selma, for example, shot a man who tried to steal her jacket. Her lawyer said that Selma's history of being abused had no bearing on the crime.

Selma disagreed. "For me, it explains why I shot that man," she explained. "I would have *never* done anything like that if I wasn't well trained by my family to take care of myself and if I hadn't learned from my husband that men will do anything to get me and I'd better to try to protect myself when a man was coming to hurt me."[108] Survivors are also criminalized for the mechanisms they use to cope with violence, through prosecution for illegal substance use, fraud, and theft.[109]

Victims of violence are held accountable for crimes committed by others. Mothers subjected to abuse are frequently charged with failing to protect their children from their partners' abuse. Sebina described how her husband abused both her and her son for four years, increasing his abuse when she tried to fight back. Her husband beat the child to death, then raped Sebina. The police saw that Sebina was beaten badly and had witness statements about the husband's violence. Nonetheless, Sebina was charged with second-degree murder for failing to protect her son.[110]

The creation and increased enforcement of criminal laws against trafficking have had similar consequences for victims of trafficking. Ashley Barnett befriended a young woman while living in Florida. Heavily addicted, Barnett sometimes spent time with two men who supplied her with drugs and to whom she introduced her friend. Concerned for her friend's well-being, Barnett gave her a code word—pineapple—to use if the young woman felt unsafe. After a few nights of partying together, during which the young woman opted to stay with the men after Barnett chose to leave, Barnett did not see her friend again—until Barnett's trial. Barnett later learned that the men were selling young women, including the friend Barnett had introduced to them, for sex. Having been raped, physically abused, and commercially sexually exploited herself, Barnett was devastated that she inadvertently brought the young woman into that world. Despite her own history of victimization and her unwitting involvement in the younger woman's trafficking, Barnett was prosecuted for sex trafficking a minor.

THE FOUNDATION FOR *IMPERFECT VICTIMS*

Imperfect Victims tells the stories of criminalized survivors who interact with the criminal legal system—the system that promises to protect them but that so often fails to make good on that promise. The book owes a debt to and relies heavily on decades of writing, organizing, and advocacy on behalf of criminalized survivors, much of it done by Black women and other women of color. Scholar/activists such as Angela Y. Davis, Beth Richie, Andrea Ritchie, Mariame Kaba, Emily Thuma, and Alisa Bierria—all of whom are cited throughout this book—have interrogated the history, mechanics, and consequences of the criminal legal system's punishment of survivors of gender-based violence. Three books have been especially important to the development of *Imperfect Victims*. In 1996, Richie published *Compelled to Crime: The Gender Entrapment of Black Battered Women*, which examined how Black survivors of violence were drawn into the criminal legal system and how they were treated within that system. Richie's theory of gender entrapment provides an essential foundation for understanding the criminalization of survival. In 2005's *Victims as Offenders: The Paradox of Women's Violence in Relationships*, criminologist Susan Miller explored how the criminal legal system responded to women's use of force in intimate relationships, illuminating the reasons for women's use of force and arguing that criminal system interventions designed to protect women were responsible for their criminalization. And in 2021's *We Do This 'Til We Free Us*, Kaba, who came to abolition through her work in the antiviolence movement, brings together almost a decade's worth of writing and interviews on the criminalization of survival and abolition as theory, politics, and practice.

The work of generations of organizers, grassroots activists, and lawyers also informs this book. The National Clearinghouse for the Defense of Battered Women has supported and advocated for criminalized survivors for more than thirty years, while lawyers and advocates such as Andrea Bible and Carol Jacobsen provided representation to criminalized survivors in parole and clemency. Incarcerated people in several states, through groups like Looking Inward for Excellence in Ohio and Convicted Women Against Abuse in California, organized clemency campaigns for criminalized survivors in the 1990s. In 2001 members of the prison abolitionist group Critical Resistance and INCITE! Women of Color Against Violence disseminated their "Statement on Gender Violence & the Prison Industrial Complex," which highlighted the role that the antiviolence movement played in increasing the reach of the criminal legal system into the lives of

survivors, documented the failures of the criminal legal system in addressing violence, and acknowledged the failure of the antiprison movement
to attend to the needs of survivors of violence, both interpersonal and
state.[111]

More recently, defense campaigns such as the Free Marissa Now Mobi-
lization Campaign and #FreeBresha have brought public attention to
criminalized survivors who might otherwise have disappeared into the
criminal legal system. These and similar campaigns are the reason that
Marissa Alexander's and Bresha Meadows's names entered the public
discourse. Journalists like Victoria Law have written hundreds of stories
about the experiences of criminalized survivors. Organizations including Survived & Punished, the California Coalition for Women Prisoners,
Moms United Against Violence and Incarceration, New York's Coalition
for Women Prisoners, Free Battered Women, and Love and Protect build
public awareness of how the legal system criminalizes individual survivors
and demand their release, working with rather than on behalf of criminalized survivors. Bierria has found that the term "criminalized survivor"
was not widely used until Survived & Punished popularized it; previously
such people were usually known as "victim defendants." That rhetorical
shift situates the organizing and advocacy of these groups in a broader
critique of the criminal legal system and the destruction wrought by
criminalization.[112]

Imperfect Victims would not exist without this foundation. The book's
contribution to this body of work is to explain not just *what* happens to
criminalized survivors, but *why*—how police, prosecutors, judges, immigration officials, governors, and even the US president use (or fail to use)
the legal system and, as a result, do grave harm to survivors. The book
tells that story using court documents, legal and social science scholarship, media accounts, and in some cases (and with their permission) the
narratives of my own clients, who were the impetus for this book. The
book pays special attention to the experiences of those who are disproportionately represented in the criminal legal system—people of color, particularly Black people. Professor of Africana Studies Jasmine Syedullah
has described sharing the narratives of criminalized survivors as a form
of "political self-defense" that undermines the systemic silencing of those
who are otherwise seen as having "no selves to defend."[113]

The stories of criminalized survivors can be hard to read. The violence they have experienced, both at the hands of individuals and the state, is extreme. Narratives about and from those who are directly affected convey that violence in a visceral way and bring to light what many criminalized survivors have struggled with and continue to endure. These stories are offered not because they are sensational but because they are ordinary—they capture the violence inflicted on criminalized survivors every day.

The criminal legal system's treatment of survivors of gender-based violence raises broader questions about the intersection of the criminal legal system and the antiviolence movement. The antiviolence movement was built through grassroots organizing. Survivor defense, as in the case of Joan Little, was very much a part of that grassroots effort. But the antiviolence movement was also an early adopter of criminal system reforms, advocating for mandatory arrest and strict prosecution policies as early as the 1970s. Some in the antiviolence movement championed VAWA not despite, but rather because of, its support for criminal responses to gender-based violence (and funding to implement those policies). Others swallowed concerns they may have had about forging close alliances with the criminal legal system to ensure VAWA's passage. Advocates then championed VAWA reauthorizations that required the antiviolence movement to formalize its relationships with the criminal legal system to be eligible for funding.

Over time, antiviolence organizations and law enforcement have become increasingly enmeshed, so much so, Bierria has observed, that it is "rare for folks who are in direct service organizations to have the capacity to imagine a response outside of the usual paradigm of either direct services or pro-criminalization."[114] Even as antiviolence organizations recognized the harms done to victims of gender-based violence because of criminalization, most continued to advocate for and benefit from VAWA and related criminal laws and institutions. Bierria and organizer Hyejin Shim have noted that mainstream domestic violence organizations were reluctant to join survivor defense campaigns for criminalized survivors Marissa Alexander and Nan-Hui Jo. In Alexander's case, prosecutor Angela Corey actively pressured antiviolence organizations to withhold their support. Although Shim was not certain that similar pressure was exerted in Jo's case, she did "wonder if the reliance of domestic violence orgs on the DA to prosecute batterers and thus legitimize domestic violence work is a barrier" to publicly supporting criminalized survivors.[115]

Survived & Punished New York has raised similar concerns about how dependence on funding available to antiviolence organizations through the Manhattan District Attorney's office "chains these organizations to prosecutors" and precludes them from publicly condemning police abuses.[116] That the work of calling attention to and supporting criminalized survivors and holding the criminal system accountable for their mistreatment has largely been done by organizers outside of large mainstream antiviolence organizations reflects the divided (at best) loyalties of many of these organizations.

The treatment of criminalized survivors also implicates broader questions about the legitimacy of law enforcement and the criminal legal system. For example, the need to be protected from rape and intimate partner violence is regularly raised in response to demands to defund the police. But police pose a serious threat to victims of gender-based violence: when police abuse their own partners and the people they encounter while on duty, when victims are arrested as perpetrators, and when people come forward as victims or witnesses. Similarly, reliance on law enforcement assumes that prosecution benefits victims of gender-based violence. But prosecutors can do great damage to victims, given the disproportionate power prosecutors hold in the criminal legal system. That use and misuse of prosecutorial power is clear in the stories of criminalized survivors. These larger themes are woven throughout this book.

This story starts at the point where many criminalized survivors have their first encounter with the legal system—as children. Children come into the system as victims of, witnesses to, and "perpetrators" of illegal acts. Chapter 2 documents the increase in the numbers of girls and TGNC youth brought into the criminal legal system (often, but not always, the juvenile system) and connects that increase to their experiences of gender-based violence. Chapter 2 looks at how specific laws meant to address gender-based violence, like mandatory arrest and anti-trafficking laws, have led to growing numbers of young people entering the system. The chapter documents the harm done to children when they enter the legal system, particularly when they are detained, and argues that the criminal legal system's failure to see these young people as children or as victims of violence contributes to their arrest, prosecution, and detention and exacerbates the trauma they have already experienced.

Decisions about arrest and prosecution have profound implications for victims of violence. Chapter 3 examines arrest, charging, bail, and prosecutorial decisions to question what police, prosecutors, and judges hope to accomplish by criminalizing survivors. The chapter begins with arrest, asking what factors influence the arrests of survivors of violence and how the criminalization of gender-based violence has changed arrest decisions. The chapter next turns to prosecution, beginning with the criminalization of victims of violence as witnesses and focusing on the use of material witness warrants to compel testimony from victims of violence. The chapter explores how prosecutors use their discretion in bail, charging, and plea bargaining and considers the effectiveness of self-defense law and duress and coercion defenses. The chapter highlights how the incident-based focus of criminal law prevents police and prosecutors from understanding the broader history of violence and trauma that creates a context for survivors' actions. That narrow view makes it easier to justify criminalization.

Chapter 4 focuses on punishment. The chapter first questions whether the theories underlying criminal punishment justify the punishment of survivors of violence. The chapter next focuses on sentencing and incarceration. Prosecutors sometimes argue that criminalizing survivors can be beneficial, allowing survivors to access services for which they would not otherwise be eligible and taking them out of abusive environments. Indeed, some survivors have made the same assertion. The chapter looks at the experience of incarceration for criminalized survivors, asking whether incarceration can ever be "good" for people subjected to abuse and concluding that incarceration is cruel for everyone, especially so for victims of trauma. The chapter examines immigration detention as a form of punishment and details the harms that accrue when victims of gender-based violence are held in detention. Some criminalized survivors find themselves saddled with punishments specific to their convictions that seem inappropriate at best and unduly harsh at worst, given their experiences with violence. The chapter considers these specialized forms of punishment, including the requirement that criminalized survivors of sex trafficking register as sex offenders and that those convicted of intimate partner violence attend batterer intervention counseling. The chapter argues that these punishments are problematic for many people and wholly inappropriate for victims of gender-based violence.

Once a criminalized survivor is convicted, the ability to make claims about victimization and to use victimization to provide a context for one's actions becomes considerably more constrained. Conviction negates victimization, either through a factual finding that the abuse did not occur or because victimization has been dismissed as irrelevant to the crime. Attempts to re-raise victimization claims after conviction are often met with attitudes ranging from skepticism to outright hostility. Criminalized survivors are forced to negotiate this tricky terrain when seeking resentencing and clemency. Chapter 5 describes and analyzes the effectiveness of both the general and the gender-violence specific resentencing laws enacted in recent years, including New York's Domestic Violence Survivors' Justice Act. The chapter ends with clemency—parole and commutation. Over the past thirty years, high-profile clemency campaigns involving criminalized survivors—from the Framingham (Massachusetts) Eight to Cyntoia Brown—have captured public attention. The chapter notes the systemic obstacles to clemency for criminalized survivors and the barriers that exist when they are released.

Decreasing mass incarceration in the United States requires confronting how the criminal system responds to violence. But even some progressives exempt gender-based violence from conversations about decarceration. Responding to gender-based violence brings two core progressive ideas into tension: the need to decrease reliance on the criminal system and the importance of taking gender-based violence seriously. Chapter 6 argues that these priorities are mutually exclusive: as long as the criminal system intervenes in cases of gender-based violence, there will always be criminalized survivors. To protect survivors from revictimization by the criminal legal system, antiviolence advocates should embrace abolition feminism. Abolition feminism opposes the use of the carceral system to respond to all kinds of harms, including gender-based violence, and focuses on building structures and institutions that prevent violence, ensure people's well-being, and use constructive, community-based responses to facilitate active accountability.[117] Chapter 6 offers "nonreformist reforms" designed to decrease reliance on the criminal legal system while working toward a society free of carceral violence.

There are several parallel stories that this book is not telling: for example, about the criminalization of drug-dependent people, the criminalization of pregnancy, and the criminalization of parenthood via the child welfare system.[118] All of these stories highlight the United States' attempts to resolve social issues by using the criminal legal system or proxies for that system—what law professor Jonathan Simon has called "governing through crime."[119] And although other parts of the world are seeing similar increases in the criminalization of women and of gender-based violence—in part because of the United States' exportation of its punitive policies, laws, and ideas on responding to gender-based violence—this book focuses on the United States.

"Criminalization," historian Robin D. G. Kelley has written, "is to be subjected to regulation, containment, surveillance, and punishment, but deemed unworthy of protection."[120] Criminalized survivors experience criminalization in all of those ways. Criminalization harms victims of gender-based violence by using laws against them which were intended to benefit them; empowering police, prosecutors, and other government agents to harm them in the enforcement of those laws; creating an expectation that victims will turn to the criminal legal system, justifying harsher penalties for those who choose not to or cannot do so; and reinforcing stereotypes about victims and punishing them when they fail to conform to those stereotypes. Fixes that attempt to mitigate those harms have not worked well, if at all, because the criminal legal system is working in exactly the way that it was meant to function: policing and punishing the behavior of "nonconforming" people, particularly people of color, then "disappearing" those people.[121]

"Once the relevant connections are drawn between women's abuse histories and their troubles with the law," Comack has asked, "then it would seem relevant to query whether their incarceration serves any *benefit*—to the women themselves, to their families, to their communities or to the larger society."[122] By the end of this book, it should be clear that the answer is no—the criminal legal system is not benefitting any of these entities, and in fact it does serious harm to all of them. As long as criminalization is the primary response to gender-based violence, survivors will always be in danger of punishment. The only sure way to protect survivors from criminalization is abolition.

2 Youth

The criminalization of survival begins with girls and TGNC (transgender and gender-nonconforming) youth. Young people who do not present as perfect victims, challenge gendered expectations, and fail to behave "obediently, modestly, and cautiously" become trapped in a legal system that refuses to see them either as children or victims of gender-based violence.[1]

The criminalization of girls has increased significantly over the past several decades. Between 1989 and 1998 the arrest rate for girls rose 50 percent; arrests for serious violent offenses climbed 64 percent and for other assaults, 125 percent.[2] By 2005 the arrest rate for girls was about double what it had been in 1980.[3] Although arrest rates for girls declined after 2006, by 2012 girls made up 29 percent of children arrested nationally: 37 percent of arrests for simple assault, 38 percent of arrests for domestic violence, and 76 percent of those arrested for prostitution.[4] The number of girls referred to juvenile courts for disposition also increased substantially in the late 1980s and early 1990s, peaking around 2005 and dropping more recently. The proportion of juvenile court cases involving girls increased 9 percent between 1985 and 2009 and remained steady through 2015.[5] Since 1997, girls have consistently made up 13 percent to 15 percent of those detained in juvenile facilities after adjudication.[6] Lesbian, bisexual, and TGNC young people are disproportionately represented in the juvenile system. While 4 percent to 6 percent of young people identify as LGB (lesbian, gay, bisexual) and TGNC, LGB and TGNC youth account for 20 percent of those in the juvenile system.[7]

The growing number of girls arrested and adjudicated delinquent spawned a cottage industry in newspaper and magazine articles decrying girls' increasing criminality.[8] National publications ran stories with headlines like "Bad Girls Go Wild" and "Where Sugar and Spice Meet Bricks and Bats."[9] But researchers suggest that the data told a different story. Girls weren't becoming more violent, they argued. Instead, the legal system was reacting more aggressively to girls' behavior, "relabeling" behaviors like running away as criminal and punishing "marginally criminal" acts that had previously been handled outside of the juvenile system—a move described as "upcriming."[10] Decreased tolerance for girls "acting out" coupled with tough-on-crime policies on intimate partner violence and other forms of assault were responsible for the illusion that girls had suddenly become "bad." Gender bias also played a role, with girls being punished more harshly than boys for similar acts.[11]

The behavior prompting intervention by the juvenile system was often a reaction to girls' own experiences of gender-based violence.[12] Girls who had been sexually or physically abused and fought back against or ran away from their abusers were now being charged with violent crimes and status offenses. Victimization has been called the "first step" into the juvenile system.[13] Most girls involved in the juvenile system have a history of trauma.[14] Between 75 percent and 93 percent of girls have experienced some form of physical, sexual, or emotional abuse before coming into the juvenile system.[15] Many girls report multiple experiences of abuse and trauma.[16] A Maryland study found that 45 percent of justice-involved girls had had five or more adverse childhood experiences (ACES), including physical and sexual abuse.[17]

Girls also witness significant violence at home.[18] As many as 67 percent of girls in the juvenile system have been diagnosed with post-traumatic stress disorder, though reported rates in studies vary significantly.[19] System professionals' experiences echo the data. A juvenile probation officer observed, "I hardly ever get a girl who hasn't been raped, sexually abused, or physically abused."[20] Given the number of ACES reported by TGNC youth, including emotional, physical, and sexual abuse and neglect, as well as exposure to domestic violence in the home, TGNC youth entering the system likely have significant histories of trauma as well.[21] The overwhelming prevalence of abuse among system-involved young people, and the links between the trauma they have experienced and the incidents that bring them into the system, has led researchers to argue that children are experiencing the "criminalization of trauma."[22]

HOW YOUNG PEOPLE COME INTO THE SYSTEM

Young people come into the juvenile system as witnesses to and victims of crimes. Detention, for example, is sometimes used to compel a child to participate in prosecution. Fourteen-year-old Miranda "spent a month in juvenile detention, even though she wasn't charged with a crime. No, this time Miranda's locked up because she agreed to testify against her pimp, and juvenile is where she must wait for the trial to start."[23] Afraid that young people will run away rather than testify or return to their traffickers if released, prosecutors ask courts to issue material witness warrants (known in some jurisdictions as body attachments or courtesy holds) to detain them until they testify.[24] Material witness warrants empower courts to detain young people indefinitely. Those being held on material witness warrants are generally not entitled to post bail to secure their release.[25] In Miranda's case, that meant being held for thirty-eight days in a secure facility. Miranda was released only because her trafficker pled guilty. Her testimony was no longer needed.[26]

Legal system professionals recognize the damage caused by detaining young people as witnesses. But their determination to prosecute traffickers outweighs their concerns about placing young people in detention. As Judge William Voy said, "We need an alternative to the detention center...[but] we have responsibilities to keep the girls here to testify against pimps."[27] Some public defenders concur: "We want to hang onto them, to keep them from running, and sometimes the only way to do that is in a secure environment."[28]

Young people who come into the system as witnesses say they feel like little more than "a piece of evidence" against their traffickers.[29] Che, for example, was subpoenaed to testify against her trafficker, "who had been the closest thing to family she had ever known."[30] To ensure that she appeared in court, Che was placed in a juvenile facility. She was later released to her mother in handcuffs and forced to testify, none of which gave her a "sense of justice."[31] Even when young people are willing to testify, the experience can be negative. At sixteen, Keiana Aldrich willingly testified against her twenty-six-year-old trafficker, believing that she had been promised counseling and safe housing in exchange for her testimony. But those services never materialized, her mother said: "She was treated like she did something wrong.... They didn't offer her no counseling, no nothing. Here, come testify and that's it, that's the last I ever heard of from those people."[32]

Young people also come into the system after reporting crimes. Danielle Hicks-Best was eleven years old when she was raped by two young men in her Washington, DC, neighborhood. After learning that police were looking for her, the young men released Hicks-Best and she made her way home. Hicks-Best's mother and a police officer were there when Hicks-Best arrived. They found blood in her underwear. A medical examination later found vaginal tears, cuts, and scrapes on the child. Hicks-Best's parents repeatedly called police but never received a reply. Almost a month later, Hicks-Best was kidnapped by one of the same men and again raped by both young men from the first incident.

Hicks-Best does not remember talking to the police after the second rape. "What I remember," she said, "was being confused, and I was exhausted, and I was still wearing the same clothes and I felt horrible." The medical report stated that when Hicks-Best was examined, she was "barely comprehendable." But police said that Hicks-Best purposely told inconsistent stories, concluding: "It became apparent that the Complainant was determined to get any story across that she could, regardless of how incredible it sounds." Officers closed the sexual assault case and instead requested a warrant for Hicks-Best's arrest, charging her with filing a false police report. In internal emails, police characterized the sex as consensual and blamed Hicks-Best's "promiscuous behavior" for her victimization. Because her parents were worried about the toll that a trial would take, Hicks-Best entered an Alford plea, maintaining her innocence while acknowledging that the state had sufficient evidence to convict, and was declared a ward of the court. Hicks-Best's father recalled, "She would say, 'Daddy, I got raped and I got locked up.' "[33]

Thirteen-year-old Maricella Chairez was a patient in an adolescent psychiatric unit in Racine, Wisconsin, when she was raped by a fifteen-year-old boy she knew. Chairez told the forensic nurse who examined her that the boy pinned her using his body weight and she told him no. The nurse noted vaginal tearing and bleeding. Chairez told the same story to police, who warned her to be honest. Police also interviewed the boy, who said he did not recall whether he had sex with Chairez. Despite the physical evidence and Chairez's account of the rape, police decided the sex had been consensual—and arrested both teenagers for second-degree assault, since neither had reached the age of consent. Chairez was never prosecuted, but she cycled in and out of hospitals and detention facilities until she died by suicide in a juvenile detention center at age sixteen.[34]

Status Offenses

Young people are detained for committing status offenses—truancy, running away, violating curfew, incorrigibility, and, in some states, morals offenses like "engaging in sexualized behavior" or associating with "dissolute" people.[35] Although the conduct is not criminal, state laws allow young people to be arrested and detained for status offenses. Girls are disproportionately impacted by these laws. Girls make up 15 percent of all incarcerated youth but 36 percent of those held for status offenses. The disparities are greater for status offenses based on running away; girls make up more than half of those detained.[36]

Status offenses punish "behaviors that violate idealized notions of femininity," including "fighting back against abuse, sleeping 'all day,' not doing chores, challenging parents' authority, overtly expressing sexuality, deviating from heteronormativity, or running away from home," the sociologist Jerry Flores has argued.[37] Frequently, those behaviors are linked to abuse. Young people often run away after being physically and sexually abused in their homes. As fifteen-year-old Julie Wood explained, "I was so pissed off after my mom's boyfriend raped me that I ran away from home."[38] Aracely told police that she did not want to return home because of her father's abuse. After police talked with her father, "they came back into the room and they told me to get up and put my hands behind my back and that's when I got arrested."[39] Law professor Kim Taylor-Thompson has noted the irony here: the same response expected of adult women subjected to abuse—that they leave home to escape the violence—results in girls being labeled status offenders.[40]

Young people cannot legally be incarcerated solely for committing status offenses. Detention requires that the young person also violate a court order (for example, an order prohibiting the young person from running away from home). Several states have exempted classes of status offenders from being held. A few states have prohibited detaining status offenders altogether.[41] Young people continue to be held for gender-nonconforming behavior, notwithstanding such prohibitions. That behavior has been relabeled criminal, particularly when young people fight back against their parents, and is contributing to increased arrest and detention rates for girls.[42] Charging girls with crimes of violence stemming from family dysfunction is creating a "new status offender."[43]

Domestic/Dating Violence

For years, increasing numbers of girls have come into the juvenile system as "perpetrators" of domestic violence. The adoption of mandatory arrest laws contributed to that increase. "Well-intentioned rules" like mandatory arrest laws "can punish and harm girls...by requiring arrest and detention when family fights result in calls to the police."[44] Few mandatory arrest laws exempt young people. As of 2015, only five states excluded domestic violence committed by minors.[45] Girls are more likely to be arrested for assaults against parents in jurisdictions with mandatory and preferred arrest laws.[46]

Girls, especially Black and Native girls, are disproportionately arrested and detained for domestic violence against family members, particularly mothers.[47] Many of these arrests arise from "nonserious, mutual combat situations with parents."[48] Parents are rarely injured in these fights.[49] Erica, for example, ran away after being raped repeatedly by her mother's ex-boyfriend. Confronted with her mother's anger, "Erica grabbed a bottle [of] rubbing alcohol and began to drink it; her mother attempted to stop her. The two began to push and shove each other. Her mother called the police. . . . The police took Erica to the hospital—and then filed assault and battery charges against her."[50]

Girls are frequently arrested for trying to protect themselves from or fighting back against abusive parents. When police confronted Diana after a fight with her mother, Diana said, "I was like: 'What the fuck, like look at my face she beat me up.' They are like: 'She called the cops on you, so you are at fault 'cause if she beat you up why didn't you call the cops on her?' Dude I don't want to get my mom in trouble plus anyways it's my word against her and although I am the one looking all torn up."[51] Girls are also arrested because it is easier to remove one child from the home than to arrest a parent and find shelter for the children. As a probation officer explained,

> Say the police respond to a case of domestic violence. You have a 3-year-old girl, a 16-year-old girl, and the mother fighting. Say the mother grabbed that girl and started pounding her face into cement. They're not going to take Mom to jail when there is a 3-year-old daughter there. But they need to separate the two of them. So a lot of times it really is the parent's fault but the kid gets hauled away.[52]

Although few of these cases ultimately result in detention (often because the violence is minor), law professor Francine Sherman has noted that girls are "traumatized by arrest, handcuffing, and in some case shackling, routine strip searches upon entry into detention, and the perception that she is being blamed for what is a family problem."[53]

Dating violence also brings young people into the juvenile system. About 16 percent of girls and 8 percent of boys experience physical or sexual dating violence; 22 percent of LGB young adults report dating violence.[54] Being subjected to intimate partner violence makes young people more vulnerable to juvenile system involvement. Girls are more likely to commit nonviolent delinquent acts (like running away) when experiencing intimate partner violence.[55]

Young people also become involved with the system because of their own violence. Girls use violence with partners to express anger and jealousy at a partner's infidelity, protest a partner's "emotional detachment," or get a partner's attention.[56] While some studies suggest that young men and women use violence in relationships at similar rates, those studies fail to account for the type, amount, impact, and reason for the violence. Girls' violence is generally less serious and causes less injury. Girls reportedly slap and pinch their partners most often, while boys are more likely to punch or sexually assault partners. Moreover, studies of heterosexual couples find that boys do not experience girls' violence as frightening or controlling. Half of boys report laughing at their female partners when they use violence. One-third ignored their partners when they were violent. Girls are also more likely to use violence defensively, fighting back against their partners.[57] Mandatory and preferred arrest laws that cover dating relationships have been linked to increased arrests of girls for dating violence, with Black girls most likely to be arrested.[58]

Commercial Sex Work and Trafficking

Significant numbers of young people enter the juvenile system after being involved in commercial sex work. In 2019 at least 290 children were arrested for prostitution-related offenses.[59] Most of the young people arrested for prostitution are girls.[60] LGB and TGNC youth are disproportionately involved in commercial sex, often as a means of survival. LGB young people in New York are seven times as likely as other unhoused young people to have traded sex for shelter. TGNC young people are eight times as likely.[61] In one survey of trafficking survivors, 42 percent reported being minors when first arrested.[62] Traffickers frequently seek out children of color, particularly Black children, and LGB and TGNC youth.[63]

The involvement of young people in commercial sexual activity creates a particular problem for the law. Criminalizing young people for commercial sexual activity means punishing them despite laws that establish a minimum legal age for consensually engaging in sexual activity. Statutory rape laws in several states set an age of consent (in most states, sixteen) to sexual activity. Sex involving people under the age of consent is per se illegal. Trafficking law similarly recognizes that underage people cannot consent to engage in sex. The federal Trafficking Victims Protection Act and many state statutes presume that children "lack the maturity and agency necessary to consent to a sexual act," and that therefore commercial sexual activity involving people below a certain age is inherently coercive.[64] As law professor Cynthia Godsoe has written, these conflicting provisions have created a "paradox of girlhood sex": "victim or offender?"[65]

In cases involving commercial sexual activity, criminal prosecution is used to punish what law enforcement sees as children's intentional criminal conduct. Law enforcement distinguishes "true" victims from those who "prostitute through their own volition," believing that some minors arrested for prostitution are "legitimate offenders" despite their age.[66] Police frequently fail to acknowledge that the young people they arrest for prostitution and related crimes are children. Fourteen-year-old Justice was trafficked and raped. When a police officer confronted her, "some of the first words of out his mouth were 'Stop fucking crying. You're pretending. You're acting like you're a victim and you're out here prostituting.'" Only when Justice told the officer that she was fourteen did he soften his tactics: "'He switched it up. He switched his whole personality up.'"[67] As criminologist Jennifer Musto has observed, "Even if law enforcement acknowledge youth ... victimization in name, they still have the power and the leverage of the criminal justice system to 'switch it up' and treat them like offenders."[68] Although prosecutors may acknowledge that they are dealing with children, they justify seeking punishment when a young person "lacked remorse" or needed to "face up" to her past.[69] Judges ascribe adult characteristics to children charged with prostitution. One judge described a thirteen-year-old girl who was paid for sex by a sixty-seven-year-old man as "an aggressor, particularly since she's the one who had to travel to" the man.[70]

Prostitution isn't the only activity that brings commercially sexually exploited youth to the attention of law enforcement. Survivors of trafficking are punished for other crimes directly related to their victimization. For example, Cyntoia Brown-Long was sixteen years old when she arranged to have sex for money with forty-three-year-old Johnny Allen. Brown-Long agreed to the arrangement because her abusive older boyfriend, Garion McGlothen (also known as Kut Throat), ordered her to make some money—and because she was in love. In her autobiography Brown-Long describes their relationship: "In my crazy, teenaged head, we were building a future together. He wasn't a pimp selling my body to fund his lifestyle. Our arrangement was only temporary, just until we could run away to Vegas and start our life."[71] When Brown-Long shot and killed Allen, she believed that law enforcement would understand that it was self-defense. Brown-Long testified that Allen had shown her multiple guns in the house, and she shot him because she believed he was reaching under the bed for a gun.[72] Brown-Long now recognizes that her experience in commercial sex affected the way she saw Allen: "Always feeling like I had to defend myself. Expecting, you know, for men to be violent towards me. And, you know, there's times I wonder, like, was I really, like, in real life in danger? Or was that just in my head?"[73]

Brown-Long quickly learned that no one in the legal system was interested in her self-defense claim. She describes how, after telling detectives that she was nineteen years old (to keep McGlothen from being accused of statutory rape), they became enraged when she admitted that she was only sixteen. "Lying was clearly an unforgivable sin in [the detective's] eyes. 'Now you're going to do life,' he hissed."

> [At trial the] D.A. never questioned the fact that a forty-three-year-old man was picking up a teenager for sex, and my attorneys didn't want to make the victim look bad. They never brought up Kut's age or described our relationship as statutory rape. . . . I was described as a teenaged prostitute, not a trafficking victim. . . . In the eyes of the prosecution, I was a murderous whore, an evil, out-of-control teen whom they were dead set on locking up.[74]

Brown-Long was tried as an adult and, in 2006, convicted of first-degree murder and aggravated robbery (for stealing $172 and Allen's truck—she was afraid to go back to McGlothen empty-handed) and sentenced to life in prison.

Young people are held responsible for crimes committed by their traffickers. Keiana Aldrich was seventeen and living on the streets of Sacramento when she sought refuge with a woman who trafficked her. The woman offered to sell Aldrich to two men making pornography. Instead, Aldrich and her trafficker robbed the men at gunpoint and put one of the men in the trunk of the car, took him to a store, and forced him to buy items and turn over money. Aldrich was charged as an adult, pled guilty, and was sentenced to almost ten years imprisonment.[75] Mia was sixteen when her trafficker took her to rob some men that they knew. Mia's role was to have sex with one of the men to distract him. The men were killed in the robbery, and Mia was charged with aggravated robbery and capital murder. Although the judge acknowledged that she had been trafficked, he nonetheless sentenced Mia to twenty years in prison, saying, "I believe that you went more or less willing [sic] along with the opportunity that the traffickers provided for you."[76] Punishing young people for their involuntary participation in the crimes of others highlights how unwilling the legal system is to acknowledge their victimization.

Fighting Back

Fighting back against sexual violence brings other young people into the legal system. A Girls for Gender Equity study found that one-third of the girls surveyed had been sexually harassed in schools.[77] That sexual harassment ranges from verbal insults to physical assaults, and teachers and other administrators often do not intervene.[78] Given their inaction, girls confront a problematic Catch-22, criminologist Jody Miller has explained: "On the one hand, failing to 'stand up for yourself' came with the likelihood of victim-blaming labeling and sometimes led to escalating abuse. On the other hand, young women's attempts to stand up to young men—verbally or physically—also placed them in a precarious position."[79] Girls who fight back are deemed "aggressive" or "assertive;" girls and TGNC youth, particularly youth of color, are blamed for their own victimization.[80] Carrying weapons to protect themselves from sexual harassment makes young survivors vulnerable to system involvement.[81] Zero-tolerance policies and the presence of police in schools make it more likely that when they fight back, young people will be arrested and charged.[82]

DETENTION

Intervention by the juvenile system can lead to incarceration—called "secure detention" in the juvenile system. "Every day, girls are securely detained for offenses that would not result in detention for a boy," Sherman has argued.[83] While some young people are detained because of the gravity of their offenses, others are held in a misguided attempt to help them. Young people are placed in secure detention to protect them from conflict in the home, danger on the streets, potentially abusive boyfriends, their own impulses, being commercially sexually exploited, and returning to their traffickers.[84] Prosecutors ask for young people to be held, and judges detain them because they see detention as the only way to provide young people with (or force them to accept) services.[85]

Young people are detained to ensure that they appear in court—either in their own cases or to testify against those who have harmed them—with the assumption that the legal process will somehow benefit the child.[86] Young people who come into the system as victims of commercial sexual exploitation are often detained by judges who believe that holding them will prevent them from being revictimized, sometimes without evidence that they are actually at risk.[87] In a Baltimore court, for example, an attorney explained that her client had been labeled as trafficked based on unsubstantiated information from a school resource officer; the girl did not understand why she was being described as a prostitute in court.[88] In their zeal to prevent trafficking, law enforcement officers and judges fail to recognize that involvement in the juvenile system makes young people more vulnerable to commercial sexual exploitation.[89] Musto calls this use of detention "carceral protectionism": "enforcement with a protective bent or carcerality inflicted with care."[90] Detention in a carceral protectionist world is not always meant as punishment, but instead is seen as a necessary evil intended to benefit young people.

Good intentions, however, don't make the experience of being incarcerated any easier for young people placed in secure detention. Judge Irene Sullivan has described the conditions she witnessed during her first visit to the Umatilla Academy for Girls, a secure facility for "high-risk" girls in Florida:

> He began the tour in a grimy, smelly cafeteria and continued down a corridor of girls' single rooms. They were tiny and windowless, as expected, and contained only a cot, mattress, and blanket, and a box for clothing. No photographs, cards, or personal items. We passed a bathroom, which I assumed was under construction, as the toilet lacked a door and the shower had no curtain. It turned out that there were never any doors or curtains.

On a later visit, Sullivan saw cosmetic changes, but serious problems remained:

Gangs of girls roamed the halls. Some were punched by staff. A guard was arrested for dragging a client by her ankles down the hallway, causing severe rug burns. A girl who'd swallowed nails wasn't taken to a hospital. Teens on suicide watch were left unsupervised.... Toilets and showers remained open, so that the girls could be seen at all times.[91]

Girls at Philadelphia's Youth Study Center described similar conditions: mice, lack of heat, overcrowding, girls sleeping on the floor, abuse by staff.[92] Video taken at a Nebraska "rehabilitation and treatment center" showed a girl having seizures "while lights flashed from fire alarms and water poured from a broken sprinkler head," other girls tried to help, and staff ignored her.[93] Lesbian and bisexual girls and TGNC youth face additional harms in detention: denial of gender-affirming clothing and health care, harassment and abuse by other young people and staff, conversion therapy, and "sexual-identity confusion counseling." TGNC youth are typically housed in facilities consistent with the sex assigned to them at birth and are often segregated. Young people are punished for acting in ways that are seen as sexually "deviant" or that fail to conform to gender norms, leading to longer stays in detention.[94]

Such conditions would be devastating for any young adult. They are particularly traumatic for those who have experienced gender-based violence. The complete control of their lives that young people experience in detention echoes the conditions that young people subjected to domestic violence endured in their homes. In one Texas facility, for example, girls' lives were constrained by a red line: "a large box painted on the dorm floors in front of the metal beds arranged on the edges of the room. Residents had to ask permission to cross this line to go to the bathroom or to sit at the metal tables and benches bolted to the floor in the center of the room, but they were also expected to sit or stand on the red line silently on a daily basis."[95] This kind of total control makes young people feel trapped and powerless. Bresha Meadows compared it to living in her father's abusive home. "It kind of triggered me, being in there... I'm like, y'all don't understand. I've been through this."[96] Highly restrictive programs for girls who have been trafficked run the same risk: "By telling them what to do, when to breathe, you're doing exactly what the traffickers did to them."[97]

Secure detention is particularly triggering for young people who have experienced physical and sexual abuse. Young people in secure detention are placed in handcuffs and restraints. They are strip-searched. They are touched, pushed, and hit by correctional staff.[98] For young people whose abusers were male, the presence of male correctional staff can be problematic. Having male staff conduct strip searches, supervise bathroom visits, or restrain them can be deeply traumatic. Having been trafficked, for example, Maricella Chairez reacted strongly when touched against her will, leading her to black out when restrained.[99] Juvenile facilities also use solitary confinement to control young people. About a third of all detained children spend time in solitary confinement, despite widespread condemnation of the practice as a form of torture. Although most states have banned the use of solitary confinement of juveniles as a form of punishment, most states allow isolation when other justifications, like safety, are given.[100] Solitary confinement can be deeply destructive. Young people describe feeling "crazy," "flipping out," and "losing it" while in solitary. One researcher saw girls punching walls, banging their heads, and attempting suicide while in isolation.[101]

The harm done by secure detention is particularly ironic given the reasons offered for that detention: keeping youth safe and providing them with needed services. Instead, detention often causes greater harm: depression, suicidal ideation, cutting.[102] As Genesis, who was detained in a Texas facility, explained,

> Some people have panic attacks. Some people think of the past. Some people get bored and start cutting themselves. Some people even start harming themselves by banging their head against the floor and putting bruises on their head. I've seen it before. I've seen all kinds of stuff. Some people even get so bored they start flooding their cell out, trying to hang themselves, 'cause "Dang, I'm locked up, I ain't got nothing to live for." It was just like, "Dang, why bother put us up in here if you're just making it worse?"[103]

These harms are associated with juvenile detention. But many girls and TGNC youth are transferred to the adult system for prosecution. Trying children as adults has become significantly easier over the past thirty years. By 1999 almost every state had enacted laws that increased the number of children tried as adults, leading to a substantial uptick in the number of girls, like Cyntoia Brown-Long, tried in the adult system.[104] The dangers to young people who are incarcerated as adults are substantial, including heightened risks of suicide and sexual assault.[105] And as chapter 4 details, being convicted as adults leads to collateral consequences that haunt criminalized survivors long after their cases are closed.

NOT CHILDREN, NOT VICTIMS

The link between gender-based violence and the criminalization of girls and TGNC youth is apparent in the reasons that they come into the criminal legal system. Regardless of the type of gender-based violence they have experienced, however, the legal system frequently refuses to see them as either children or victims, because criminalized youth fail to conform to stereotypes attached to both children (particularly girls) and victims. Girls who are not "ladylike"—who are perceived as angry or confrontational, run away, act in self-defense, use illegal substances, express sexuality, or engage in sexual behavior (voluntarily or involuntarily)—lose the protection that girlhood could confer and are sometimes punished more harshly as a result.[106] As Taylor-Thompson wrote,

> Police, prosecutors, judges and parents may be inclined to grant boys—particularly affluent white boys—some latitude in their misbehavior, subscribing to the notion that "boys will be boys."...[But] parents and juvenile authorities too often react to girls' delinquent conduct as though they have glimpsed the contours of a deeper pathology.[107]

Similarly, victims who fight back, who are angry, or who are arrested as perpetrators are no longer entitled to the protections that status as a victim confers—even when those victims are children.

The failure to see criminalized children as children or victims has profound consequences in criminal cases. For instance, Maryanne Atkins was sixteen when she was arrested for the murder of Emmanuel Gondo. Atkins already had a long history of sexual exploitation, including having been sexually assaulted as a child. Atkins contended that Gondo drugged and raped her and that she shot him in self-defense. When interviewed by Seattle police, Atkins acted in ways familiar to many parents—she cried, asked for her mother, and, after not receiving a response to her request to go to the bathroom, she threatened to urinate on the floor.[108]

After the state asked that Atkins be tried as an adult, her case was transferred to adult court. Prior to trial, Atkins's defense attorneys argued that because "jurors are to put themselves in the place of a 16 year-old girl, get the point of view which she had at the time of the tragedy, and view the conduct of . . . Mr. Gondo with all its pertinent sidelights as Maryanne was warranted in viewing it," testimony from experts on post-traumatic stress disorder and adolescent brain development was essential.[109] Experts would have testified to Atkins's long history of sexual exploitation and how that trauma could have caused her to experience flashbacks to previous abuse when she woke to find Gondo raping her. But the judge did not allow the defense to call the experts, leaving Atkins vulnerable to a life sentence if jurors failed to believe her self-defense claim at trial.[110] Atkins pled guilty to killing Gondo and was sentenced to more than nineteen years in prison.

The unwillingness to see criminalized children as either children or victims is a particular problem for young adults who have been commercially sexually exploited. Law enforcement officers have trouble distinguishing commercial sexual exploitation from sex work and believe that because girls "choose" to engage in prostitution, they should be held criminally accountable.[111] Alexis Martin, for example, was raped for the first of many times at age ten. At fourteen she was kidnapped and forced to become an exotic dancer. At fifteen Angelo Kerney began selling Martin for sex. Kerney made Martin quit school, regularly beat and raped her, and locked her in a basement without food and water. On November 7, 2013, Kerney was robbed and killed while Martin had sex (sex to which she was too young to consent) with Kerney's brother in another room.

Summit County, Ohio, prosecutors argued that, rather than being a victim of trafficking, Martin was the "manipulator" responsible for the crime. Prosecutors opposed defense motions to apply the safe harbor law specifically meant to protect trafficking survivors (discussed in chapter 6) in Martin's case. A judge found that Martin was "working" for Kerney's "escort service." Martin was convicted and sentenced to twenty-one years to life in prison. At her parole hearing in 2019, prosecutors dismissed Martin's claim that she had been commercially sexually exploited, calling the story a "'new narrative' she didn't disclose 'until she saw that she could get a benefit from it.'" But Martin had told the detectives investigating

Kerney's murder that Kerney was selling her for sex about five minutes into their interrogation.[112]

Failing to contextualize the actions of criminalized survivor children skews how the legal system interacts with these children. In her autobiography Cyntoia Brown-Long describes taking a class in prison with a professor who was also the prosecutor who opposed her appeal. The professor/prosecutor was stunned that the young woman whose participation he so valued was the same defendant he saw in his case file: "I just don't know how to reconcile the person I know from those court records with the person I know you to be." Brown-Long responded: "That's because I'm not that girl." Brown-Long told him how she had become involved in the murder for which she was incarcerated. "None of this was in the trial transcript," her professor said. Brown-Long replied: "Nope. It wouldn't have been. No one was too interested in finding out why I did what I did."[113]

The denial of childhood and victimization to criminalized children is particularly pernicious for girls of color and LGB and TGNC youth. The paradigmatic victim of gender-based violence looks much the same for children as for adults: white, heterosexual, cisgender, weak, meek, and passive. Perfect victim stereotypes predominate for victims of color as well: a "good" Latina girl, for example, is passive, quiet, and does not challenge authority.[114] Deviation from those stereotypes undermines the credibility of the victimization claims of survivors. Political science professor Joy James has described how when a fourteen-year-old Black girl named Tikki reported being raped by a white police officer, even her mother did not believe her.[115]

Most of the available data on the disproportionate impact of system intervention on girls of color compares the experiences of white and Black girls. Black girls are about six times more likely than white girls to experience police use of force.[116] Although white and Black girls commit status offenses and crimes at about the same rates, Black girls are overrepresented in the juvenile system.[117] Black girls make up 15 percent of the youth population but account for 35 percent of all delinquency cases and 52 percent of "person offenses" (e.g., assault, robbery, and sex offenses).[118] A national study in 2013 found that Black girls were three times more likely than white girls to be referred to juvenile court.[119] A more recent Baltimore study found that Black girls were five times more likely than white girls to be referred to the juvenile system. For reference, 33 percent of girls in Maryland are Black, but 60 percent of the girls in the system are Black.[120] Black girls are more likely than white boys and girls or Black boys to be arrested in jurisdictions with mandatory arrest policies, and Black girls are disproportionately arrested for prostitution.[121] Black girls are more likely to be referred to law enforcement for incidents that occur in schools, more likely to be charged with status offenses, and less likely to be diverted away from prosecution.[122]

Black girls consistently experience harsher treatment once they enter the juvenile system. White girls are much more likely to benefit from informal case dispositions or to have their cases dismissed than Black girls.[123] Black girls receive harsher sentences and are more likely to be detained. In Baltimore, for instance, 65 percent of girls placed in detention are Black.[124] In Florida, Black girls make up 23 percent of the population and 51 percent of the girls held in secure detention.[125] Black people are 6 percent of the population in San Francisco, but Black girls account for 58 percent of those detained in the juvenile system.[126] Nationally, 34 percent of girls in secure placements are Black. Black girls are more likely to be detained than white girls even when they are identified as victims of commercial sexual exploitation.[127]

Other girls of color and LGB and TGNC youth are also disproportionately represented in the juvenile system. A 2013 study found that American Indian/Alaska Native girls were 1.4 times as likely as white girls to become court-involved.[128] LGB and TGNC girls are more likely to be adjudicated delinquent and detained.[129] Girls of color spend more time in detention than white girls. In San Francisco, for example, white girls and TGNC youth averaged 21 days in juvenile hall, while Asian/Pacific Islanders averaged 178 days, Black girls and TGNC youth averaged 179 days, and Latinx girls and TGNC youth spent 276 days in detention.[130]

The disproportionately punitive focus on girls of color and LGB and TGNC youth, particularly Black girls and youth, is likely a function of the intersection of racist stereotypes and discretion. Widely held stereotypes about victims of gender-based violence prevent legal system professionals from recognizing the disproportionate impact of victimization on girls of color, particularly Black girls, and TGNC youth. Black women and girls are seen as angry, loud, aggressive, pushy, independent, street smart, mature, hypersexual, threatening, and invulnerable to abuse.[131] Black girls are perceived as needing less nurturing, protection, support, and comfort than white girls.[132] The "adultification" of Black girls makes it easier to characterize them as mature adults and their actions as intentionally criminal, depriving them of the protections extended to children and/or victims.[133] Stereotypes about Black girls influence legal system professionals' perceptions of the causes of their behavior as well: white girls act out because of stresses at home, Black girls are seen as innately criminal.[134] Police, prosecutors, and judges justify arrests and punitive sentences using racist and sexist stereotypes of Black girls. The broad discretion afforded to police officers, prosecutors, and judges allows them to shield these racist and sexist justifications for their actions from view.

Young victims of gender-based violence are retraumatized by the intervention of the juvenile and criminal legal systems, systems that fail to recognize either their age or their victimization and criminalize them for witnessing and experiencing violence. Attempts to prevent minors from entering the system or insulate minors from the worst abuses of the system are often ineffective. Whenever discretion is built into a system, those administering the system—police, prosecutors, judges, probation officers—will find ways to circumvent protective measures, often with the misguided belief that by doing so, they are saving young people from harm. Because stereotypes and racism are endemic in these systems, the harms will disproportionately fall on those who do not conform to those stereotypes, particularly Black girls and TGNC youth. Those harms extend well beyond childhood. Being ensnared in the juvenile system often leads to victimized girls and TGNC youth being "caught up" in the adult criminal system.[135]

3 Arrest and Prosecution

Simone Phoenix went to the Providence, Rhode Island, police station on January 23, 2017, to get an application for emergency housing funds. Phoenix had been assaulted by her husband the week before and wanted to move herself and her son out of the home they shared with her husband and closer to her new employer. Phoenix met with two "law enforcement advocates" employed by local antiviolence organizations, who, after asking her a number of questions, suggested that she needed a "mental health vacation."

Phoenix responded that she could not afford to take such a vacation, given her parenting responsibilities and new job. She realized that she needed to leave the meeting because her son would soon be home. Phoenix asked the advocates if she was free to leave. They confirmed that she was. Phoenix walked down the hall and tried to enter the elevator, but two police officers told her that she was not, in fact, free to leave. As the officers surrounded Phoenix, she told them she suffered from PTSD and they should not touch her. The officers grabbed her nonetheless. Phoenix, panicked, swung her arm to protect herself. The officers threw Phoenix to the ground, kicked her repeatedly, and handcuffed her so tightly that the fire department later had to remove the jammed cuffs. Officers dragged

Phoenix down the hallway by her hair, placed her in a holding cell, and left her there for three hours. Officers then transported Phoenix to the hospital and told hospital staff that Phoenix was suicidal. Police charged Phoenix with simple assault and malicious damage to property. After seven court appearances (and the loss of her job), all charges against Phoenix were dismissed.[1]

In July 2020, Rollinsford, Delaware, police arrested Sarah Letendre after her husband, R. J. Letendre, alleged she had assaulted him. R. J. told police that after he raised the issue of divorce, Sarah threatened to destroy his property, tried to rip his phone out of his hands when he attempted to call police, and bit him. But in a court filing, Sarah said that when she reached for her husband's phone (hers was in the car), he grabbed her and threw her to the ground. As she struggled to get free, he knelt on her sternum while she scratched at his chest, ripping his shirt. R. J. (once a mixed martial arts fighter) jammed his elbow into Sarah's ribcage. Police at the scene saw scratches on R. J.'s chest and no visible injuries to Sarah, although they noted that she complained of pain in her ribs. Police also learned that R. J. Letendre was an off-duty police officer.

Sarah Letendre was arrested and charged with simple assault, obstructing report of a crime, and resisting arrest. Sarah sought medical attention after the July incident. Her diagnosis: fractured ribs. In a later pleading, Sarah detailed several previous incidents of violence, including being held by her neck and thrown against a display case and being grabbed so hard that R. J. left fingerprint bruises. R. J. also allegedly placed a tracking device on Sarah's car and repeatedly called police to have her removed from their home. The charges against Sarah Letendre were later dropped.[2]

Melissa Ramlakhan was a fifteen-year-old virgin when she met Matthew Thompkins. Thompkins preyed on Ramlakhan's vulnerability. He raped her, telling her that if she loved him, she would have sex in any way that he wanted. He used those rapes to "teach" her what men might want from her. Then he sold her for sex—on the streets, stripping in brothels and strip clubs, and in peep shows. Thompkins told Ramlakhan that allowing him to sell her for sex would bring them closer together. Ramlakhan thought that Thompkins was the man she would marry and have children with. She did what he wanted. Ramlakhan was not the only woman Thompkins sold for sex. Thompkins brainwashed the women, convincing them that if the women allowed him to use them, they would have access to a life of wealth and prestige. But the money that Ramlakhan collected went directly to Thompkins; she and the other women were allowed to keep twenty dollars per day. Thompkins beat the other women he sold for sex. Ramlakhan feared that he would beat her as well. She did not see a way to escape.

Ramlakhan eventually had two children with Thompkins and, at his insistence, began to run various parts of his businesses, both illegal and legal. Thompkins continued to control all of Ramlakhan's actions and decisions. He used her name to apply for loans, open bank accounts, and make purchases to hide his illegal income. Desperate to give her children a father, unable to recognize the damage Thompkins was doing to her, and without resources, Ramlakhan complied with Thompkins's demands. Fourteen years after first being raped by Thompkins, Ramlakhan was convicted of conspiracy to engage in prostitution and conspiracy to commit money laundering.

All of these women were victims of violence. All of them were revictimized by being arrested and/or prosecuted.

ARREST

The criminalization of adult survivors begins with arrest. Although arrests are not findings of guilt, they are "fused" with guilt, law professor Anna Roberts has argued. Arrests can have consequences that suggest or presuppose guilt, including the creation of a permanent arrest record, bans on the receipt of public benefits, ineligibility for public housing, negative implications for child custody, and difficulty finding or keeping employment. Arrests are often publicized, while the dismissal of charges is not. The burden of arrest is unequally distributed. Lesbians and bisexual women are four times more likely than straight women to be arrested.[3] Low-income people and people of color are also more likely to be arrested.[4]

Arrest is a serious threat for victims of gender-based violence. In a 2015 survey of victims of intimate partner violence conducted by the National Domestic Violence Hotline, 24 percent of victims who called police said they were arrested or threatened with arrest while reporting an incident to police.[5] A 2016 study of state-level human trafficking cases found that victims were arrested in 59 percent of those cases.[6] In another 2016 study, 91 percent of trafficking victims reported having been arrested; more than 40 percent were arrested nine times or more.[7] Arrest rates are higher in historically marginalized communities. In 2020, for example, Black and Latinx women were 53 percent of the women arrested for domestic violence in Connecticut—but only 25 percent of the state's total population of women.[8]

According to Connie Burk, executive director of the NW Network, an antiviolence organization serving lesbian, gay, bisexual (LGB) and transgender and gender-nonconforming (TGNC) clients, in one year 50 percent of their clients who had contact with police were arrested.[9] A study conducted by the Solutions not Punishment Collaborative in Atlanta found that 38 percent of trans women of color and 26 percent of all trans women who called police for help were arrested.[10] Fear of arrest keeps people from calling police for assistance. In the National Domestic Violence Hotline's survey, 28 percent of those who called police feared doing so in the future because police might be violent toward them, threaten to arrest them, or actually arrest them; 17 percent of those who did not call the police shared the same fear.[11]

Why Do Police Arrest?

Police seem to have three reasons for arresting victims of gender-based violence: for the victims' own good; to compel participation in prosecution; and because they see these victims as perpetrators. In the context of intimate partner violence, police sometimes justify making arrests by claiming that arrest will be helpful, forcing victims to face the seriousness of the violence and encouraging them to seek services.[12] Similarly, law enforcement frequently cites rescue when arresting victims of trafficking. As Ohio attorney general Dave Yost explained, "Arresting the people who are the victims of human trafficking sounds harsh, but the complicated reality is that this often is the best way that law enforcement can help."[13]

Deputy police chief Marc Garth-Green told the Seattle City Council that victims of trafficking might need to be arrested "to disrupt the cycle of violence and abuse.... For people trafficked in prostitution, jail can be a safer place than out on the street."[14] Law enforcement officers use arrest— sometimes repeatedly—to "build trust" with trafficking victims.[15] As one law enforcement officer explained, "You've got to take that girl away from that pimp for a long enough time that she trusts you, and that's not going to happen in 24 hours or 36 hours."[16] Police believe that arrest prompts victims of commercial sexual exploitation to admit to their victimization, enabling them to access the services and supports they need to escape their traffickers.[17]

In some "prostitution diversion" programs, which are specifically designed to prevent people from being prosecuted for sex work–related offenses, police are not permitted to offer trafficking victims and others engaged in sex work services without first making an arrest. In other programs the existence of the program creates an incentive to arrest; police use arrests to bring people to central locations that offer both on-site booking and links to services. Law enforcement's belief that such programs will "save" victims of trafficking from the streets is directly linked to increased policing to fill those programs.[18] Rescue may also be a function of white supremacy. As social science professor Kamala Kempdaoo has argued, white supremacy can be manifested in a desire to help racially marginalized people, which maintains the position and power of whiteness within racial hierarchies.[19]

Some in law enforcement recognize that arresting trafficking victims is a counterintuitive way to provide assistance. As sergeant Kathy Lacey of the Anchorage Police Department has explained, law enforcement's intervention options are limited: "We don't want to punish them. We want to remove them from that situation, and the tools that we have to remove them from that situation are to arrest them and to remove them from that trafficker."[20] Arrest is often described as a minor inconvenience in the service of a larger goal and harmless so long as the person is not convicted and left with a criminal record. What that perspective ignores, however, is the harm caused by arrest. Whatever good intentions law enforcement might have don't keep people who are arrested from pushing back against the coercion implicit in the requirement that they comply with services or face incarceration.

This vision of arrest as helpful, as rescue, is particularly ironic given how often victims of gender-based violence report abuse by law enforcement officers. High-profile stories like that of Oklahoma police officer Daniel Holtzclaw (who was found guilty of raping or sexually assaulting eight different women, some while he was on duty) can make it seem as though violence by law enforcement officers is exceptional. In fact, such violence is an everyday occurrence. Lawyer and organizer Andrea Ritchie collected numerous accounts of police abuse of victims of violence in her book *Invisible No More: Police Violence against Black Women and Women of Color*, including the story of Cherae Williams. Williams called police after being beaten up by her boyfriend. The officers who responded refused to take her complaint, then beat her savagely, breaking her nose, rupturing her spleen, and fracturing her jaw after Williams asked for the officers' names and badge numbers. Williams said that officers "beat me until I was bloody.... They left me there dazed and with a warning. They told me if they saw me on the street, that they would kill me."[21]

Victims of gender-based violence by law enforcement often include officers' own partners; studies suggest that intimate partner violence is more prevalent among police officers than in the general population.[22] Police violence against sex workers is also common. One woman described her interactions with police as "disrespectful. I've had a police officer stick his finger in my pussy. I've had them lifting up my dress. I've had them [say] 'oh you're just a bird bitch, you ain't nothing.' 'You're the scum of the earth, why would you sell your body?'"[23] Police sexually assaulted 26 percent of those surveyed in a study of Alaskan sex workers; 9 percent had been robbed or beaten by police.[24] And 37 percent of young people doing sex work who responded to a Chicago study had been assaulted or harassed by police.[25] Adding injury to injury, victims of police violence are frequently arrested in those encounters.[26]

Law enforcement officers arrest victims of violence to compel their participation in prosecution because they assume that prosecution is beneficial to victims and society. Arresting victims is acceptable when victims disagree with that assessment. Police officers justify arresting victims of intimate partner violence along with their partners because they believe that arrests make victims more likely to assist in prosecution.[27] Similarly, police arrest people who are sold for sex to determine their value as witnesses and "persuade" them to testify. As law professor Sabrina Balgamwalla has written: "Detention, interrogation, and the possibility of pressing charges all serve to compel testimony."[28] Or, as one law enforcement officer explained: "They did [provide information] after they got arrested when we were like, 'Do you want to be a witness, or do you want to be a suspect? Decide.'... And they became cooperative witnesses. Which is what we wanted."[29]

Finally, police arrest victims because they do not see the people they arrest as victims—they see them as perpetrators. Victimization, gender studies professor Julietta Hua has observed, must be legible to state actors before victims are deemed worthy of belief and protection.[30] Like others in the legal system, law enforcement officers have a binary view of the world: there are victims and there are offenders. Officers are conditioned to look for "true," "deserving," or "innocent" victims (the only people worthy of assistance) and rely on stereotypes to make judgments about victimization. To be seen as a victim, a person must conform to those stereotypes. For women, that means presenting in a manner consistent with feminine norms, being helpless and passive, afraid rather than angry, and cooperative with police.[31] The further women stray from these norms, the less credibility they have, and the more likely they are to be arrested.[32]

Victimization is also determined by identity. Again, the further a person is from hegemonic norms centered around race, gender identity, and social class, the less likely they are to have their victimization acknowledged. Women and TGNC people of color are seen as violent, angry, and threatening. When they use violence, that violence is characterized as aggressive rather than defensive.[33] Law enforcement officers use the physical appearances of trans women to justify suspicions about their claims of victimization, questioning why someone they perceive as male wouldn't be able to defend themselves.[34] The operation of these norms makes victims of color, low-income victims, and TGNC victims disproportionately likely to be arrested.[35]

Victims of intimate partner violence are arrested when they affirmatively use force, when they defensively use force, when their partners persuade police that the victim is the aggressor, and when police are unable to determine what has occurred. Laws and policies designed to protect them have increased arrests of victims. The mandatory arrest laws enacted in many jurisdictions have created the same problems for adult victims as they have for young people. When first adopted, feminist scholars cautioned that mandatory arrest policies might increase arrest rates for women.[36] They were correct. As chapter 1 notes, arrest rates increased across the board after jurisdictions adopted such policies, but for women (and more specifically, Black women), more than any other group, without evidence that women had suddenly become more violent.[37] In fact, as criminologist Susan Miller has found, no one in the criminal system believed that women had suddenly become more violent. Instead, they attributed the increases in women's arrest rates to mandatory arrest policies and the training for law enforcement tasked with implementing these policies, which stressed the importance of making arrests rather than using discretion.[38]

The reasons women are arrested vary: because police repeatedly respond to their homes when they fail to leave violent relationships; because they damage property in response to being assaulted; because they are "overly emotional" when they talk to police and are therefore considered not credible; because their partners call police first; and because officers don't know the history of the relationship and therefore lack context for understanding the immediate incident. What is clear, though, is the importance of unambiguously asserting one's status as a victim, staking a claim of victimization, to avoid arrest. An example: Crystallee Crain was assaulted by her ex-husband. Neighbors called the police. When Crain emerged from the bathroom, she found police talking to her ex-husband, who persuaded police that he was the victim. Despite her visible bruises, the police, following the mandatory arrest policy, arrested Crain after she admitted to fighting back to defend herself.[39] Stereotypes drive how women's actions are characterized during arrests. Stereotypes of Black women as angry and therefore dangerous, for example, may explain why police perceive the crimes committed by Black women as more serious than those committed by other groups.[40] Law enforcement protects "true," "innocent" victims; others get arrested.

Mandatory arrest laws are also responsible for an increase in dual arrests, which often involve victims of violence.[41] Dually arrested women frequently seem to be acting in self-defense.[42] Research shows that officers often fail to weigh factors like severity of injury, prior violence, and whether one party was acting in self-defense (all of which could prevent victims from being arrested) before making dual arrest decisions.[43] A study of calls to a hotline in New York City, for example, found that in 60 percent of dual arrests there was a history of one party abusing the other—information that should have prevented police from arresting the victim.[44] The failure to adhere to perfect victim stereotypes drives dual arrest. Low-income women, sex workers, and transgender victims of violence are all disproportionately likely to be dually arrested.[45] Dual arrest cases are frequently dropped, but there is little recourse for wrongfully arrested victims; generally, law enforcement cannot be held legally responsible for such arrests.[46]

To prevent police from mistakenly arresting victims of violence, several states have added primary physical aggressor provisions to their mandatory arrest laws. These provisions require police to determine who is actually or primarily responsible for violence before making an arrest using a number of factors, including a party's history of intimate partner violence; the severity of the injuries inflicted on each party; the potential for future injury to a party; and evidence of self-defense.[47] Research suggests that arrests of victims can be avoided if police follow these laws.[48] The inclusion of primary physical aggressor language has decreased rates of dual arrest in some jurisdictions.[49] But the effectiveness of these provisions varies.[50]

Obstacles to implementing primary physical aggressor provisions include the lack of access to information about the parties' pasts, time constraints, the inability to get information from the victim of violence (because of fear or language barriers, for example), and the inability to assess the dynamics of the relationship at the scene.[51] And primary aggressor laws only protect victims when police properly identify the primary aggressor. When victims are angry or agitated, using alcohol or drugs, admit to fighting back, have been arrested or convicted in the past, are not seen as credible, or their partners are particularly persuasive, they may still be arrested as primary aggressors.[52] Despite the existence of these policies, victims—particularly people of color, people with disabilities, and people with mental illness or substance use issues—are misidentified as primary aggressors.[53]

Victims of commercial sexual exploitation are similarly vulnerable to arrest when law enforcement officers see them as criminals rather than victims. Again, victim stereotypes drive police decision-making. If victims fail to appear sufficiently grateful for their "rescue," don't seem afraid, or are older, nonwhite, or undocumented, police may not recognize their victimization.[54] Officers also misidentify those who use illegal substances or struggle with mental health issues.[55] Studies regularly find significant percentages of victims of trafficking who have been arrested (sometimes multiple times) as offenders rather than identified as victims.[56] One woman, who was arrested five times before law enforcement realized she had been commercially sexually exploited, said, "They were wearing guns and uniforms, and it made me very scared. They didn't tell us anything. They treated us like criminals during the arrest and it was scary."[57] This treatment may stem in part from law enforcement officers' suspicion that victims "are in part responsible for their situations of exploitation."[58] That skepticism is fueled by victims' decisions to return to their traffickers instead of assisting law enforcement, which frustrates law enforcement officers and affects their perception of not only the person who returns but of all victims.

Law enforcement's suspicions about the credibility of rape victims can lead officers to see them as criminals rather than victims. In 2008 eighteen-year-old Marie reported her rape at knifepoint to police in Lynwood, Washington. Detectives seized on an inconsistency in her story and, after receiving a tip describing Marie as attention-seeking, decided she had made a false claim. Detectives asked to meet with Marie at the police station, where they confronted her with the inconsistency and told her they believed she had fabricated the story. Detective Jerry Rittgarn later reported, "Based on her answers and body language it was apparent that [Marie] was lying about the rape." Detectives asked Marie to give them the "true" story. Under pressure, Marie changed her story, saying that she had been raped in a dream but insisting that she believed it had happened. After continued questioning by detectives, Marie wrote a statement saying that she made the story up. But after leaving the police station, Marie repeated that she had been raped and asked to take a lie detector test. Rittgarn responded that if she failed the test, she would be booked into jail and lose her housing. Marie "backed down." Later that month, Marie learned that she had been charged with false reporting, a gross misdemeanor with a possible one-year sentence. Marie ultimately took a plea deal that required her to meet certain conditions and pay court costs but did not leave her with a criminal record. Two years later, police in Colorado arrested the serial rapist who had raped Marie and several other women after Marie initially reported.[59]

In a similar case, a law student in Kansas was raped by a friend of her ex-boyfriend. She reported the rape to police but stressed that she did not want to press charges. The police were skeptical of her claim, suggesting that she was seeking cover because she had cheated on her boyfriend and was remorseful. After three months passed, she was asked to come to the police station to help officers understand an anonymous tip they had received. When the student arrived, however, she was arrested and charged with three felonies, accused of making a false report. The woman later learned that within ninety minutes of making her report, "police had decided she was lying."[60] Officers believed that the student fabricated the rape claim to seek revenge against an ex-boyfriend, to support a "narrative of a woman scorned." She called the experience "every victim's worst nightmare." Prosecutor Charles Branson dropped the case months later. While Branson continued to believe the woman had made a false report, he worried that pursuing the case would dissuade other victims from coming forward.[61]

The Experience of Arrest

Law enforcement arrests victims of violence at times and places when attending to their victimization should be the priority. Illinois recently passed legislation to prohibit police officers from arresting victims on outstanding warrants when officers are dispatched to hospitals to investigate rape and sexual assault. The law was a response to reports of patients being pinned to the ground and handcuffed just after being examined by forensic nurse examiners and being handcuffed to hospital beds and taken into custody before evidence collection had even begun. Police officers responding to calls about intimate partner violence arrested victims for crimes ranging from having an outstanding warrant to having an unregistered dog.[62]

Not surprisingly, knowing that police could arrest them for matters as minor as unpaid parking tickets influenced victims' decisions about seeking medical care. Many survivors regretted seeking medical attention;

some chose not to get care at all. Although some officers were described as reluctant to make arrests, others "tried to hurry nurses, including one who paced back and forth in the triage area saying there were better things to do than to wait on the exam. Another stood on the other side of the curtain in the room as a rape victim was examined."[63] The new law does not require police to refrain from making all arrests, however. Victims can still be arrested for forcible felonies, violent crimes, and violations of parole.[64]

Arrest can be harrowing for victims of violence. Victims describe being confused, offended, shocked, and traumatized. Erica, whose partner self-inflicted injuries that he used to claim she had assaulted him, described her arrest: "So all of a sudden, two cops came running down the hallway, and I remember the leather on their belts. That noise scared me. I remember the leather and the things rubbing on their belt was something, even talking about it now scares me. . . . So the next thing I know, the cop grabs me brutally by the arm and slams me, my face, against the door."[65] Jin, arrested in a trafficking raid, said, "As I was running a police officer struck me in the back of the head with the back of a gun and I fell to the floor and I passed out. . . . I had no idea they were police when they all broke in." Lily was also arrested in a trafficking raid: "They were wearing guns and uniforms, and it made me very scared. They didn't tell us anything. They treated us like criminals during the arrest and it was scary."[66] Police can be abusive during arrests, demeaning, insulting, and physically and sexually assaulting victims of violence. Arrests are particularly fraught for trans victims of violence, who may also be questioned about their genitalia, misgendered, insulted, and strip-searched.[67]

Victims frequently describe coercive interrogations, which can lead to false statements, minimization of abuse, and acceptance of responsibility for someone else's actions. For instance, Jody Boyd remembers that "the two male detectives that interrogated me read me my Miranda rights and asked if I understood what was read. I said no. Instead of explaining them to me he read them over two more times. I still could not comprehend what my rights were. He said until I initialed my name next to my rights I could not see my children, who were sitting in the next room. That is all I could think about and all I wanted."[68] Boyd initialed the form and answered police questions without having counsel present. Information from that interview was later entered into evidence at her trial. Law enforcement officers use other questionable tactics, giving survivors misinformation to make them more likely to talk, promising to let them go if they do talk, and preventing them from talking about their own abuse.[69] During postarrest interrogations, the aggressive tactics used by law enforcement make victims feel nervous and threatened and telegraph law enforcement officers' skepticism about their stories.[70]

After arrest, victims are held in jails for periods of time that can be quite lengthy, particularly if they are unable to post bail—a frequent problem for women.[71] The jails to which victims are initially taken can be frightening places. Irene was relieved when police arrived at her home after her boyfriend strangled her—until they arrested her. It was her first arrest, and she asked police a number of questions. "As a result, she was quickly labeled uncooperative and transferred to solitary confinement. Irene surveyed her dark, dirty surroundings. The thin mattress was filthy, there was blood on the floor, and she listened as the prisoner across the hall banged his head against the cell door."[72] For trans people the fear of being held is compounded when they are placed, as they usually are, in jails with a differently gendered population, where they are misgendered, have their genitals examined, are vulnerable to sexual assault, and are unable to access needed medications.[73] Even if they are quickly released, the experience is traumatic. As Celia, a trafficking victim repeatedly arrested for prostitution, explained: "One never lets go of the fear. Being afraid never goes away. They provoke that."[74]

Arrests are not findings of guilt. But arrests can have a host of negative consequences beyond the trauma of being arrested, the frustration of being identified as an offender, sometimes after years of victimization, and the stigma from publicity around the arrest. Arrests are expensive, even if charges are ultimately dropped. The costs of arrest include cash bail or bail bonds fees, bills for legal representation, monitoring fees for those released under supervision, and decreased income because of lost employment.[75] Being arrested creates a permanent record that can be accessed by the police and, often, the public. Arrest can lead to the denial or suspension of occupational licenses, an inability to access public benefits, and loss of child custody. Child protective services may become involved when parents and primary caretakers are arrested. Employers may decline to hire based on arrest records; arrest can also lead to suspension or termination from a job. The Kansas law student can expect to face pointed questioning about her character when she seeks admission to the bar, given that she was charged with a crime involving dishonesty. Organizations serving victims of intimate partner violence deny services and supports to those they deem offenders, which could include people arrested for violence. Because low-income people of color are disproportionately arrested, these negative effects, which some judges have characterized as punishment, are disproportionately visited upon them.[76]

While some victims describe arrest as positive—for example, as a "wake-up call" or an indication of just how serious the violence against them has become—others learn never to call police for assistance as a result of their arrests. Massage parlor workers in New York City, who are frequently targeted for arrest by police, have said they would rather jump than be arrested, referring to the death of Yang Song, who fell to her death from a window as officers raided the building where she worked.[77]

Arrests are the entry point into the criminal legal system for victims of violence. In many cases they are also the exit point, if prosecutors decline to push cases forward. But for those who are prosecuted, the damage done by arrest is minimal compared to that done by prosecution.

PROSECUTION

As law professor Angela J. Davis has observed: "Prosecutors are the most powerful officials in the criminal justice system, bar none."[78] Prosecutors decide who will be charged, what they will be charged with, whether to recommend diversion from prosecution, whether to ask that a person be detained until trial, whether a plea bargain will be offered (particularly significant because the vast majority of cases end in guilty pleas), who will be required to testify, and based on charging, what the likely sentence will be. Because of the breadth of their power, "prosecutors control the criminal justice system and frequently predetermine the outcome of criminal cases."[79] Prosecutors have almost unlimited discretion in the use of these powers, even when exercising that discretion leads to disproportionately punitive interventions against people of color.[80]

While in theory the primary obligation of the prosecutor is to seek justice, prosecutors often have other, competing goals. Some prosecutors see their mission as securing convictions rather than seeking justice or fail to recognize when those goals diverge. Even prosecutors who describe themselves as "progressive" misuse their power. Understanding how prosecutors decide what they will prosecute "is one of the greatest enigmas of the criminal justice system."[81] In the context of gender-based violence, however, some of the same factors that motivate police to arrest push prosecutors to pursue cases.

Why Prosecute?

Prosecution (potential or actual) is used to "rescue" victims and require them to engage with services, particularly in the trafficking context. Prosecution is seen as "a minimal cost of eradicating trafficking, if not a net benefit to arrestees."[82] The threat of incarceration—the longer, the better—makes victims more likely to comply with prosecutors' demands that they seek services in lieu of prosecution. A similar dynamic plays out in cases of rape and intimate partner violence. Prosecutors use criminal prosecution to "save" victims of violence, even when—or particularly when—they believe victims are unwilling or unable to save themselves. As Honolulu prosecutor Keith Kaneshiro contended, his office did "a lot of things to help victims of domestic violence, even when the victims did not know what's good for them."[83]

Prosecutors bring cases that they think they can win. Criminologists Susan Miller and Michelle Meloy have noted that prosecuting victims of intimate partner violence who use force is easy: victims tend to tell their stories in detail, are less likely to argue that they are innocent, and are often eager to plead guilty.[84] Prosecutors are more likely to pursue cases against people who use weapons or have a prior criminal history, making those cases easier to win. Similarly, in the trafficking context, prosecutors are more likely to go forward in "slam-dunk" cases: "They want it all wrapped up ahead of time before they even charge anyone."[85]

Prosecutors pursue cases against victims when they are unaware or do not believe that the defendant is a victim. At the point of charging, for example, a prosecutor may not know that the defendant was a victim of violence. Past violence may not always be apparent on the face of the case, and the defendant may not be familiar to the prosecutor. In some court systems, technology does not permit prosecutors to access information (which could include the parties' criminal histories, reports from other jurisdictions, and information about civil protection orders) that already exists about the parties' relationship and could be used to evaluate a defendant's victimization claim. If the defendant has never sought assistance, such evidence might not exist. Defendants who have the opportunity to offer evidence of victimization to prosecutors may resist disclosing that information, afraid that such disclosures will endanger them or provide prosecutors with something to use against them.[86]

Even when they do offer that information, prosecutors may not believe it. For instance, federal prosecutors charged Noor Salman with aiding and abetting terrorism because she failed to inform authorities about her husband Omar Mateen's homophobic beliefs and plans. In 2016, Mateen killed forty-nine people in a mass shooting at Pulse nightclub in Orlando, Florida. After the incident Salman described how Mateen had physically abused her and isolated her from her family. Prosecutors questioned her claim of abuse, noting the failure of her family to share that information with the FBI.[87]

Evidence of victimization must be overwhelming to persuade prosecutors that victims should not be prosecuted. Only "true" victims avoid prosecution. Although, as sociologist Kathleen Ferraro has argued, criminalized survivors are "neither angels nor demons," they should be as close to angelic as possible to persuade prosecutors not to proceed.[88] Having a prior criminal record undermines this image, as does infidelity, using illegal substances, and fighting back against a partner.[89] Prosecutor Ellsworth Connelly, for example, saw Sherrie Allery as "a hard drinking, cussing, woman who was out to kill her husband. She wanted to get rid of him. She was a bad wife and a bad mother. She threatened to kill him the night before and did it exactly as she said she would. She yelled about how glad she was that he was dead. Open and shut."[90] Even if Allery's claim that her husband had abused her was true, "'domestic disputes' do not give anyone a right to kill someone."[91]

A prosecutor's decision to bring a case against a victim reflects the prosecutor's belief in the strength of the case and, by extension, their skepticism about the credibility of the victim's claim. When victims become defendants, it is as though a switch flips for prosecutors; the ability to appreciate a defendant's victimization disappears. To bring a case, prosecutors must have a good faith belief that they can prove that case beyond a reasonable doubt. Once the decision to prosecute is made, prosecutors become committed to their case theory and make the facts fit the argument. Prosecutors may dismiss victimization claims out of hand, offer alternative explanations for the victim's actions, or argue that any past victimization is irrelevant to the current case. Prosecutors regularly counter victimization claims by arguing that the defendant was angry or jealous rather than afraid, that the violence they describe is minor, was mutual, or did not occur, that the defendant could have left the situation rather than committing a crime, and that "strong" women (i.e., women who can "hold their own" against their partners) couldn't possibly be abused.[92]

Prosecutors made several of these arguments in Shamika Crawford's case. In 2019 police arrested Crawford after her children's father, Kevin Mayers, filed a vague complaint alleging that Crawford and two men hit and kicked him. Crawford was charged with misdemeanor assault. At her first hearing, prosecutors agreed to her release but asked the court for an order prohibiting Crawford from returning to her home in the Bronx, where Mayers claimed to be living (but was not). Crawford objected to the imposition of the order. Prosecutors countered that "the charges in this case are violent" without stating exactly what Crawford was alleged to have done. The court entered the order. At a later hearing, the prosecutor asked the court to keep the order in place, explaining that there were approximately seventeen prior reports of domestic violence involving Crawford and Mayers. What the prosecutor failed to disclose, however, was that the prior reports named Mayers as the perpetrator and Crawford as the victim. These reports detailed how Mayers had punched and strangled Crawford and beat her with a stick. Crawford was forced to live in her car and at the homes of friends, was separated from her children, and lost her jobs. Having decided that Crawford was the abuser, prosecutors could not see her in any other light. Prosecutors dismissed the charges 123 days after initially charging Crawford, recognizing that they could not make a case against her.[93]

Similarly, prosecutors refused to believe that Kristopher Graber raped Maddesyn George the night before she shot him. As Victoria Law reported, on July 11, 2020, George was hanging out at Graber's house when he began touching her and refused to stop despite her request. After George told Graber to "get the f*** off of me," Graber pulled out his gun, unloaded it, put two bullets back in, and told George that she wasn't going anywhere.[94] Graber raped George with a vibrator. George fled with Graber's money, drugs, and gun after he fell asleep. The next day, Graber, a white man, came looking for George, a member of the Colville Confederated Tribes, on the Colville Reservation in Washington State. Witnesses saw Graber searching for George with a shotgun. Graber found George sitting in a friend's car and reached through the open car window. Afraid that Graber "was going to rip me out of the car and start beating me up," as she had "seen him do . . . to other females," George fired Graber's gun through the window, hitting him in the chest. Graber died from his injuries.[95]

Law enforcement rejected George's sexual assault allegations from the moment they took her into custody. Although George told police that Graber had raped her, they did not take a rape kit (a failure consistent with law enforcement's historical unwillingness to investigate claims of sexual assault by white men against Native women).[96] Instead, George was federally charged with possession with intent to distribute methamphetamine (the drugs George took from Graber's home), second-degree murder, and several related crimes. In pleading after pleading, federal prosecutors rejected George's claim that she feared Graber and acted in self-defense. Prosecutors asserted that George was a drug addict and habitual criminal who robbed Graber and bragged about it later. Prosecutors described Graber as a flawed but "kind and giving" man.[97] A man who would never hurt or rape a woman, notwithstanding his several convictions for offenses related to intimate partner violence, the protective orders filed by multiple women alleging that he had strangled and threatened them, and his reputation for "beat[ing] the living shit out of a woman. He is known for that."[98] Against a backdrop of sky-high rates of gender-based violence against Native women and the huge number of missing and murdered Native women in the United States, prosecutors refused to acknowledge George's victimization.[99]

George was not just a bad victim. She was also, as gender studies professor Luana Ross has written, a "bad Indian . . . shiftless, savage, drunk, immoral, dumb criminal."[100] Prosecutors drew on this trope to discount

George's claims. At sentencing, prosecutors again dismissed George's story of violence, calling the matter "simply a drug trafficking case."[101] Facing the possibility of forty-three years in prison, Maddesyn George pled guilty to voluntary manslaughter. Prosecutors sought seventeen years in prison; George was sentenced to six-and-a-half years.

In some instances prosecutors recognize victimization claims but believe the need to punish outweighs other considerations. The prosecutor in Juanita Thomas's case, for example, failed to win a conviction against Francine Hughes (whose case was the subject of the 1984 Farrah Fawcett movie *The Burning Bed*) three months before Thomas was tried. The prosecutor "swore he would not tolerate 'open season on men.'"[102] Respect for the rule of law is also a priority for prosecutors. After Joann Gilliam lied to a federal grand jury about her boyfriend hitting her with a gun, prosecutors charged her with perjury and obstruction of justice. Prosecutors recognized that she was a victim and that she feared for her life if she testified truthfully. But, as prosecutor Stephen Schenning said, "Just because she's wearing the mantle of a victim that doesn't give her a pass on breaking the law."[103] Similarly, as prosecutor Doug Miles has written about a destruction-of-property case, "While I am sympathetic to Rebecca's situation, I cannot condone her decision to destroy Jack's property. Her prior abuse makes her conduct understandable, but it does not make her immune from the criminal law."[104]

Coerced Participation in Prosecution

Prosecutors' desires to rescue and win can combine in problematic ways for victims of violence. Prosecutors have long contended that to successfully bring cases involving gender-based violence, they need victims to testify. Evidence suggests that prosecutors are more likely to bring trafficking cases, for example, when victims cooperate.[105] But victims are often reluctant to testify. Testifying can be emotionally difficult, requiring victims of violence to relive their trauma and face intense, often hostile, questioning from defense attorneys. Victims who are uninterested in prosecution for whatever reason—because they do not want anyone punished, have other priorities, or want to maintain relationships with their partners—may decline to testify. When persuasion fails, the belief that sometimes "people need protecting even if they don't want protecting" can lead prosecutors to coerce victim participation in criminal proceedings.[106] Prosecutors use subpoenas, material witness warrants, and contempt charges to compel victim testimony.

Prosecutors can subpoena unwilling witnesses to testify, requiring them to appear in court and making it clear that there are penalties for not complying. The failure to appear in court pursuant to a valid subpoena enables the prosecutor to request a material witness warrant. As described in chapter 2, material witness laws empower prosecutors to ask that witnesses whose testimony is deemed essential to the prosecution of a case be arrested and held, sometimes until testimony is given. In many states those detained on material witness warrants are not entitled to constitutional protections, counsel, or compensation for their time. In some cases victims are held in the same prisons as those arrested for crimes against them.[107]

It is impossible to know how often prosecutors use material witness warrants to arrest and hold victims of gender-based violence. Such cases generally only come to light when reported by the media. Jessica Mindlin of the Victim Rights Law Center has stated that while such detentions are relatively rare, prosecutors have "consistently" used material witness warrants to hold victims of gender-based violence in some states, including California, Washington, and Maine.[108] Some prosecutors acknowledge that the aggressive use of material witness warrants is office policy. Prosecutor Kaneshiro, who staunchly defended his office's policy of pursuing any case involving intimate partner violence where he had the evidence to do so, regardless of the victim's wishes, had a woman arrested at her graduation party in order to ensure her testimony, while the man accused of strangling and threatening her with a knife was released on his own recognizance.[109]

The actions of other prosecutors reveal that their office policy is to seek material witness warrants. Reporters in Washington County, Tennessee, identified more than a dozen victims of intimate partner violence who were jailed after they declined to participate in prosecution. Prosecutor Tony Clark defended the policy, saying that prosecutors needed to "send a message": "I'm not going to go back and apologize for what we've done, because I think we were doing the right thing. At some point in time, where do we draw the line in saying that we're just going to dismiss these cases if a victim doesn't appear?"[110] Victims suffer harsh treatment while incarcerated. Donna Oliver, one of the Tennessee victims jailed after failing to appear, described how she was "grabbed by both male and female guards, thrown down, (sprayed), had every ounce of clothing taken from me, even my glasses. . . . My knees were badly bruised. You could see grab marks all over my legs."[111] Correctional officers concurred that they had used force and chemical spray against Oliver. Notwithstanding Oliver's claims, Clark denied that the use of arrest was harmful, stating, "Do I think we're re-victimizing victims? No I don't."[112]

Even in jurisdictions with prosecutors who describe themselves as "progressive" or where prosecutors acknowledge that material witness warrants should be used sparingly, victims of violence are jailed when prosecutors believe that those victims will not appear to testify otherwise. "Progressive" prosecutor Marilyn Mosby authorizes prosecutors in Baltimore to seek material witness warrants (called body attachments in Maryland) in cases involving gender-based violence. Maine prosecutor Maeghan Maloney, who learned about the use of material witness warrants in a training course for district attorneys, said that she wished she did not have to seek the warrants but sometimes had to do so "for the cases where if I didn't use it, I'd be in the position of talking about why [the victim] was killed."[113]

Crystal Rodriguez, for example, failed to appear for her boyfriend Patrick Iraheta's court date, despite signing a subpoena agreeing to appear. Rodriguez told prosecutors she did not want to testify against Iraheta, who "placed his hands on [Rodriguez's] throat, leaving scratches and red marks." Prosecutors believed that they could not prove their case against Iraheta without Rodriguez's testimony. DeKalb County, Georgia, prosecutor Sherry Boston requested a material witness warrant for Rodriguez. Boston justified her action by stating her belief that Rodriguez would be in "grave danger" if the case did not go forward, given the history of violence in the relationship. On the third day of Rodriguez's incarceration, Iraheta posted bond and was released. Rodriguez's release was delayed, however, because of issues with scheduling and with the jail, which failed to send her to a hearing and took four additional days to release her after being ordered to do so. Rodriguez was held for seventeen days. Although that delay "concerned" Boston, she nonetheless continued to justify Rodriguez's detention because "we did think it was necessary to get the testimony." Iraheta later pled guilty, obviating the need for Rodriguez's testimony.[114]

Lawanna Belgard was subpoenaed to testify by Harvey County, Kansas, prosecutors. Belgard failed to appear and was arrested on a material witness warrant. Belgard did not appear because she had not seen the person who seriously injured her since the event and did not want to see the person again. But prosecutors decided that her testimony was essential, and so Belgard was jailed pending her testimony—in the same facility as the person who abused her. "I was in holding the whole time, but I saw my abuser three times.... It brings back all of that stuff. All those feelings and emotions that I have put away. It makes my heart race, even just thinking about it." The president of the Kansas County and District Attorney's Association called jailing victims like Belgard "unfortunate."[115]

Perhaps no prosecutor in America was more committed to the use of material witness warrants than Leon Cannizzaro, the former district attorney for Orleans Parish, Louisiana. As Cannizzaro told the media, "If I have to put a victim of crime in jail, for eight days, in order to ... keep the rapist off of the street, for a period of years and to prevent him from raping or harming someone else, I'm going to do that" and called incarceration "an inconvenience" for victims.[116] Cannizzaro believed that once victims connected with the criminal legal system (regardless of how they connected), they had a responsibility to follow through. "This criminal justice process is not like an invitation to a party, where you have the right to decline to show up."[117] In 2019, Cannizzaro's office asked for eight victims of crime to be jailed. All eight had been subjected to intimate partner violence.[118]

Renata Singleton is painfully familiar with Cannizzaro's determination to prosecute these cases. On November 2, 2014, Singleton's boyfriend, Vernon Crossley, destroyed Singleton's cell phone during an argument. The police arrested Crossley. Shortly thereafter, the Orleans Parish District Attorney's Office contacted Singleton. Singleton informed the office that she was not interested in participating in prosecution. Singleton had three children and a new job. She did not want to spend what little spare time she had on a criminal case involving a man with whom she was no longer involved.[119] Nonetheless, on April 21, 2015, prosecutors delivered two "subpoenas" to Singleton, ordering her to speak with them on April 24, 2015. The documents stated, A FINE AND IMPRISONMENT MAY BE IMPOSED FOR FAILURE TO OBEY THIS NOTICE.[120]

Those "subpoenas," however, were not legally binding documents issued by a court. The documents were fabricated by prosecutors, designed "to coerce victims and witnesses into submitting to interrogations by prosecutors outside of court."[121] After a friend in law enforcement told Singleton that she had not been properly served with a subpoena, Singleton decided not to attend the meeting. On April 24, 2015, prosecutor Arthur Mitchell asked the court to jail Singleton as a material witness. Mitchell told the court that Singleton had failed to appear pursuant to a valid subpoena. Judge Robin Pittman issued an arrest warrant and set Singleton's bond at $100,000. Pittman based Singleton's bond on Mitchell's statements to the court.[122]

On May 29, 2015, aware of the outstanding warrant for her arrest, Singleton went to the district attorney's office and told Mitchell that she would not answer questions without an attorney present. Mitchell responded: "You're the victim. You don't get a lawyer."[123] When Singleton still refused to answer questions, she was arrested, handcuffed, and taken to the Orleans Parish Prison. Singleton had never been arrested before. She was afraid for herself, for her children, who had been left without a parent in the house, and for her new job, which she worried she would lose. Because Singleton could not pay the $100,000 bond set by the court, she remained in prison for the next five days. On June 2, 2015, Singleton finally appeared before a judge—dressed in an orange jumpsuit, shackled hand and foot, chained to the other people appearing before the court that day. She was released on a reduced bond of $5,000 and given a curfew and an ankle monitor. Crossley, who was arrested for destroying Singleton's phone, had a different experience with the criminal system. His bond was initially set at $3,500. Crossley paid the bond and was released on the day that he was arraigned. He pled guilty to two misdemeanors. He did no jail time. And because he pled guilty, prosecutors never needed Singleton to testify against him.[124]

Renata Singleton was not the only victim of gender-based violence subjected to arrest and incarceration pursuant to a material witness warrant in Orleans Parish. The Orleans Parish District Attorney's Office also requested and received a material witness warrant for a victim of child sex trafficking, who was held for eighty-nine days (over the Christmas holiday and into the new year) before seeing a judge. She was finally released after 109 days. The victim lost her housing, began living on the streets, and lost custody of her child as a result of being detained. In another case, a rape victim was held for twelve days before she was taken to court. Prosecutors not only made the initial requests that victims be imprisoned in these cases but also controlled the length of time the victims spent in jail, because they were not brought to court until the prosecutor notified the court that a victim had been arrested and requested a hearing. Although people arrested in Louisiana generally must be seen by a judge within seventy-two hours, no such protections apply to those held under material witness warrants. Lawyers for Renata Singleton estimated that at least fifty victims or witnesses were held for longer than seventy-two hours in a five-year period.[125]

Jane Doe was raped in Harris County, Texas, in 2003. After years of assisting police and prosecutors working on her case, police finally made an arrest in 2015 after DNA linked the suspect to the rape kit Jane Doe provided to police. Throughout those twelve years, Jane Doe lived in the same house and cooperated with police. She was willing to testify against the man who raped her. Sometime after the DNA match was made in 2015, however, Jane Doe was incarcerated in a separate matter. Prosecutors sought a material witness warrant (called a writ of attachment or bench warrant in Harris County) for Jane Doe. As a result of that warrant, Jane Doe was not released from prison on her scheduled release date. Instead, she was detained for nearly three additional months. During that time she was not taken before a judge to explain that she wanted to cooperate with prosecution, provided an attorney, or permitted to post bail.

Jane Doe was not the only victim held on a material witness warrant requested by the Harris County District Attorney's office in early 2016. A woman referred to as "Jenny" in the media and "Jane Doe" in a later lawsuit began testifying against her rapist on December 8, 2015. After breaking down on the stand, she was hospitalized and then, at prosecutors' request, held in jail until the trial resumed. Bail was set at $10,000. On December 18, 2015, Jenny, who lived with bipolar disorder, was mistakenly booked into the Harris County Jail as a perpetrator of sexual assault rather than a victim. She was not assigned to the Mental Health Unit, where she could have received treatment for her bipolar disorder. Jenny was assaulted by another inmate and denied a transfer to another part of the jail after that assault.

On January 8, 2016, Jenny experienced a psychiatric episode during which she begged God to rescue her. A guard responded by punching her in the face during an ensuing physical altercation. Jenny was slammed to the floor and handcuffed. The guard who punched Jenny asked prosecutors to file felony assault charges against her. On January 11, 2016, about three weeks after being booked into the Harris County Jail, Jenny resumed her testimony in the rape trial. Three days later, she was released from jail and the charges against her were dropped. District attorney Devon Anderson justified the decision to hold Jenny: "If nothing was done to prevent the victim from leaving Harris County in the middle of trial, a serial rapist would have gone free—and her life would have been at risk while homeless on the street. . . . There were no apparent alternatives that would ensure both the victim's safety and her appearance at trial."[126]

Brian Balzer was a correctional officer at Coffee Creek, Oregon's state prison for women, where he repeatedly coerced Brandy Buckmaster, incarcerated at Coffee Creek, into having sex with him. After Buckmaster's release Balzer was arrested and charged with custodial sexual misconduct and supplying contraband to incarcerated people. Balzer was released on $2,000 bail. Buckmaster testified against him in the grand jury and planned to testify at trial. But after Buckmaster, who had a history of drug addiction, relapsed, prosecutors were concerned that she would not appear as a witness at Balzer's trial. Prosecutor Dan Hesson sought to have her detained, arguing that Buckmaster "was complicit in perpetuating the illicit relationship between she and the defendant" and had "led a life of crime." He was granted a material witness warrant. Buckmaster returned to jail, where prosecutors did not provide her with any support services and she struggled to meet her basic hygiene needs. In response to questions from the media, Hesson would not characterize Buckmaster as a victim and said of the warrant: "It is a terrible idea that she is in jail, but I can't find a better alternative."[127] Buckmaster spent fifty days in jail before testifying against Balzer, who was found guilty of custodial sexual misconduct.[128] Balzer was sentenced to sixty days in jail.[129]

Material witness warrants are regularly used in sex trafficking prosecutions. Prosecutors generally ask for material witness warrants in two kinds of cases: when victims are hard to reach and when victims do not want to testify because they fear retaliation, don't trust prosecutors, or want to avoid the trauma of testifying. Prosecutors elide the damage they do by using material witness warrants to hold victims of commercial sexual exploitation by blaming defendants in trafficking cases for any harm done. As prosecutors argued in one court pleading, the victim was "re-victimized because she had to be held so that she could be present to testify at the defendant's trial." Any damage done to the victim occurred only because her unwillingness to testify forced prosecutors to ask to have her held.[130]

Asking for material witness warrants has many benefits and few downsides for prosecutors. Prosecutors are generally immune from liability for requesting warrants, even when they make false or misleading statements to judges about witness availability to support those requests. In *Flagler v. Trainor*, for instance, prosecutor Matthew Trainor told the court that Stephanie Flagler was not responding to his calls and was avoiding being subpoenaed to testify and asked that the court issue a material witness warrant. But Flagler argued that Trainor never contacted her or attempted to subpoena her and that she had confirmed she would testify the day before she was arrested pursuant to the material witness warrant. The US Court of Appeals for the Second Circuit held that even if Trainor had in fact lied to the court about Flagler's willingness to testify, that conduct came squarely within his "'function' as an advocate" and was therefore immunized. The court noted that while prosecutorial immunity could leave a "genuinely wronged defendant without civil redress against a prosecutor whose malicious or dishonest action deprives him of liberty," "society has found more benefit in insulating the exercise of prosecutorial discretion."[131]

Similarly, in *Adams v. Hanson*, the US Court of Appeals for the Sixth Circuit held that a prosecutor was immune from liability for making allegedly false statements to support a material witness warrant. Prosecutor Karen Hanson subpoenaed LaTasha Adams, who was six months pregnant and under a doctor's care for a high-risk pregnancy, to testify against the father of one of her children in a racketeering case. When Adams met with Hanson pursuant to that subpoena, she told Hanson she did not want to testify. Hanson requested and was granted a material witness warrant. Hanson never told the court that Adams had met with her pursuant to a subpoena, which demonstrated Adams's willingness to comply with a court order (making incarceration unnecessary). Adams spent twelve days in jail without being brought before the court. She was held in isolation for twenty-three hours each day. Adams claimed that "she was never given an opportunity to obtain counsel or post bond, and that she was never advised of the basis of her detention, of any right to be represented by counsel, or of any right to a hearing."[132] Like the Second Circuit, the Sixth Circuit noted that arguments supporting requests for material witness warrants fall within the prosecutor's role as advocate for the state, even when the prosecutor's statements are false. The Sixth Circuit instead chided the trial court for failing to give Adams an opportunity to be heard or to set bail before issuing the warrant.[133] A judge made essentially the same ruling in Jenny's case in Harris County, Texas.[134]

Prosecutors can request that victims of violence be held in contempt and jailed when they refuse to testify. The District Attorney's Office in Boulder, Colorado, made such a request in May 2021 after the victim in a strangulation case refused to testify, citing her Fifth Amendment right against self-incrimination even after being granted immunity from prosecution. The woman was held in jail overnight. The next day, when she again refused to testify, prosecutors dropped the case. Although prosecutor Anne Kelly said incarcerating victims should be rare, she believed it was justified in this case: "we felt it was in the community's best interest and the victim's best interest to hold him accountable.... The respect for a victim's wishes is at the forefront, but in domestic violence cases the analysis is much more complicated than that."[135]

The Violence Against Women Act (VAWA) could serve as a check on these kinds of prosecutorial practices. Jurisdictions receiving funding through VAWA Services, Training, Officers, and Prosecutors (STOP) grants are prohibited from using grant funding to force victims to participate in prosecution. The threat of losing approximately $216,000 in STOP grant funding may have persuaded prosecutor Clark to stop using material witness warrants in Washington County, Tennessee.[136]

In some jurisdictions prosecutors have disavowed jailing victims of violence. Kim Ogg, who unseated Harris County DA Anderson in 2016, has promised never to ask for a material witness warrant for a victim, as has Jason Williams, who replaced Cannizzaro as Orleans Parish DA in 2020.[137] Moreover, Ogg supported Jenny's Law, enacted in 2017, which requires that anyone subject to a material witness warrant has a right to an attorney and a hearing both before the warrant issues and after the witness has been jailed.[138] But these practices continue in many jurisdictions—a function of the uncritical reliance on the criminal legal system to address gender-based violence. Little wonder, then, that some victims of gender-based violence feel that being a witness is worse than being charged with a crime.[139]

Charging, Bail, and Plea Bargaining

Prosecutors have unfettered discretion in deciding whether, who, and what to charge. That discretion gives prosecutors the opportunity to consider several factors, including a prior history of victimization and a defendant's claims of self-defense, before making charging decisions. The American Bar Association's standards for prosecutors state that prosecutors should file criminal charges "only if the prosecutor reasonably believes that the charges are supported by probable cause, that admissible evidence will be sufficient to support conviction beyond a reasonable doubt, and that the decision to charge is in the best interests of justice."[140] Probable cause is a fairly low threshold—prosecutors must believe that it is more likely than not that a crime occurred. "So," despite the American Bar Association's admonition, Angela J. Davis has contended, "frequently prosecutors will bring charges that they know they cannot prove beyond a reasonable doubt, just to give themselves leverage in the plea bargaining process."[141]

Prosecutors frequently overcharge, both vertically (bringing the most serious charges possible) and horizontally (bringing as many charges as possible), to increase the chances of forcing a plea bargain.[142] In the context of prostitution diversion programs, which often involve victims of commercial sexual exploitation, overcharging enables prosecutors to require more intensive and intrusive services as a condition of a plea bargain.[143] For people charged with killing abusive partners, overcharging can convince them to plead guilty to lesser charges even if they have viable claims of self-defense.[144] Prosecutors can also decide to reduce charges—

something they do much more frequently for white women than Black women charged with offenses involving intimate partner violence.[145]

Overcharging justifies prosecutors' requests for substantial—or no—bail. Bail is, in theory, intended to ensure that a person charged with a crime returns to court to face those charges. But in practice, bail is often used to keep those charged with violent crimes incarcerated until they are tried, with prosecutors arguing that the defendant is likely to flee, poses a danger to others, or is likely to reoffend.[146] Those requests may be motivated by assumptions that the person charged is guilty of the crime—despite the presumption of innocence that the defendant is still entitled to at that stage of the proceedings—and may help convince defendants to plead guilty.[147] In trafficking cases, bail is also used to "protect" defendants from what the legal system perceives as their poor decisions. Victims of trafficking held on bail are "safe" in that they cannot return to traffickers (who may also be their intimate partners)—even if they are assaulted in jail or otherwise harmed by being held.[148] There is often no mechanism for factoring a defendant's previous victimization into the court's determination about whether a person should be held.[149]

For example, Manhattan prosecutors asked for Tracy McCarter to be held without bail after McCarter was charged with murder. James Murray had abused McCarter for years before the night that Murray came to her apartment drunk, demanded money for alcohol, and assaulted McCarter. McCarter picked up a knife to defend herself, stabbing her husband in the chest. McCarter screamed for help, called 911, and attempted to stop the bleeding. Despite McCarter's six years of residence in New York, prosecutor Sara Sullivan argued that McCarter was a flight risk because she had family in Texas and had worked as a traveling nurse. Prosecutors also justified their request based on the strength of their case: McCarter admitted to stabbing Murray. Prosecutors contended that McCarter was not a victim of violence. They alleged that she had previously been violent toward Murray, although a police report from that incident states that it involved a verbal argument, that Murray was too drunk to stand when police came, and that he was not physically injured. Prosecutors argued that McCarter was not afraid of Murray and stabbed him either because she was jealous and angry about his relationships with other women or because she was trying to prevent him from stealing her purse.

Defense attorneys repeatedly asked the court to set bail, arguing that Murray had abused McCarter for years, abuse that intensified when Murray was drinking, and that McCarter's skills as a nurse were necessary during the COVID pandemic. McCarter volunteered to wear an electronic monitoring device to address concerns about flight. Nonetheless, prosecutors continued to oppose McCarter's request for bail, saying that there had been no change in circumstances and that "the argument the defendant is a victim of domestic violence is not new."[150] Despite one judge's "concerns about whether this woman is a victim of domestic violence and whether this is not part and parcel of a long history in which she felt some need to defend herself," courts denied bail until journalist Victoria Law began reporting the story, leading to more widespread coverage, and the antiviolence community expressed outrage and support for McCarter.[151] McCarter was released on electronic monitoring after spending six months on Rikers Island. Initially confined to her home, McCarter was later permitted to be outside seven hours per week.

Like Tracy McCarter, Naomi Freeman spent six months in jail before being released. Unlike McCarter, Freeman had to post substantial bail to do so. In July 2015, Freeman's boyfriend, John Perry, pulled her out of her minivan by her hair, threw her to the ground, and repeatedly punched her. When a bystander pulled Perry away, Freeman got back into the van and, as she attempted to drive away, allegedly ran him over deliberately. Freeman ran away from the van. Perry died from his injuries. Freeman's bail was initially set at $500,000 and later lowered to $350,000, the lowest the judge said could be set for first-degree murder. Freeman, unable to pay, went to jail. She was pregnant at the time and suffering from lupus. She left two children at home. Over the next six months organizers with the Chicago Community Bond Fund created a fund specifically dedicated to bailing out Freeman. Just before Christmas 2015, donations from 345 individuals enabled Freeman to post bail, "seek pregnancy-related care, and give birth to her baby without handcuffs, shackles or jail guards."[152] Ultimately, and despite their assertion that Freeman could have driven away from Perry, prosecutors offered Freeman a plea deal—plead guilty and be sentenced to time served. Rather than leave her three children behind again, Freeman took that deal.

Naomi Freeman's case illustrates the connection between bail and plea bargaining. As law professor Marc Howard has written: "When defendants are held for lengthy periods in pretrial detention or unable to post bail, they face extraordinary pressure to accept any agreement that will return them to liberty (and thereby perhaps allow them to keep a job, or to maintain custody of their children)."[153] But even in cases that don't involve bail, plea bargaining is the norm. As many as 95 percent of criminal cases are resolved through plea bargains. Plea bargains allow prosecutors to control huge caseloads, avoid lengthy trials and the risk of losing, and ensure that punishment is meted out to those they believe to be guilty. For defendants plea bargains "reduce uncertainty and risk" by guaranteeing shorter sentences than they might receive if convicted of more serious charges. Recognizing that pleas are a valuable commodity, prosecutors often engage in "hard bargaining," overcharging initially and threatening to add additional charges and seek longer sentences if the defendant declines a plea. As in other areas, prosecutors have broad discretion in plea bargaining; courts have not forbidden the use of hard-bargaining tactics.[154] Judges reinforce the pressure to plea bargain by meting out "trial penalties," imposing harsher sentences on those who are convicted after exercising their right to trial. In courtrooms where trial penalties are well known, defendants often opt for plea bargains rather than chancing a longer sentence.[155]

Research on criminalized survivors establishes that women take pleas. Significant numbers of women plead guilty in cases where they might have credible defenses.[156] They take pleas so that they can go home to and maintain custody of their children, keep their employment, and maintain financial stability. They plead so that they can be eligible for diversion programs that provide them with services in lieu of incarceration and criminal records. They plead because they cannot afford to pay for representation through trial. They plead to avoid having to talk publicly about their victimization. They take pleas because they think that they will not be believed. They plead to avoid more serious charges or mandatory sentences and because they do not understand the ramifications of taking a plea. They plead to protect their children from having to testify or from facing long sentences of their own.

Rebekah Charleston pled guilty because she feared for her life. Charleston was trafficked for the first time at seventeen and met her second trafficker just before she turned eighteen. The trafficker provided her with a place to live and a feeling of security and told her that he loved her. But after she turned eighteen, he began selling her for sex and violently abusing her and his other victims, beating one so badly that she required facial reconstruction surgery after she escaped. Charleston had no resources and no control over any facet of her life. She was sold daily, for up to twenty hours per day. After each "date," Charleston's trafficker or one of her "wife-in-laws" took the money she collected. In 2006, Charleston was arrested and charged with conspiracy to commit tax evasion. Prosecutors believed that she and three others were running a prostitution ring and charged them with tax fraud for failure to pay taxes on their earnings. Charleston's trafficker hired and paid for an attorney for her. The attorney met with her for less than five minutes and never discussed the case with her. He negotiated a plea deal that protected her trafficker's businesses. Her trafficker said that he would kill her if she incriminated him in any way. Charleston took the plea.

The interrelationship between overcharging and plea bargaining is at the heart of one of the best-known cases involving a criminalized survivor. Marissa Alexander turned down the prosecution's plea offer of three years imprisonment. Convicted after a trial in 2012, she was sentenced to twenty years in prison. After Alexander's conviction was overturned on appeal in 2013, prosecutor Angela Corey announced her intention to retry Alexander on three counts of aggravated assault and seek consecutive rather than concurrent sentences—sixty years, rather than twenty. Alexander pled guilty to the three counts and was sentenced to three years imprisonment, plus an additional two years of house arrest and monitoring.[157]

Culpability Inflation

Survivors can be prosecuted for the bad acts of their abusive partners or traffickers, in a move that gender studies professor Alisa Bierria and organizer Colby Lenz have described as "culpability inflation."[158] The prototypical example of culpability inflation is "failure to protect": holding abused parents criminally responsible for harm done to their children by their abusive partners. "Failure to protect" is a crime of omission—that is, parents are punished for not meeting their obligations to their children.

When a child is abused by a parent or another caregiver and the state believes that the nonabusive parent failed to take reasonable action to prevent that abuse, that parent can be held criminally liable. Failure to protect strips mothers of their maternal status and transforms victims of violence into perpetrators, as culpable for a child's injuries as the person who inflicted those injuries. As the prosecutor in Pauline Zile's case argued to the jury, "During 7-year-old Christina Holt's terrifying last weeks of life, Pauline Zile wasn't a mother; she was a co-conspirator."[159]

Bierria and Lenz argue that prosecuting parents for failure to protect is a method of maximizing punishment, ensuring that the largest number of people experience the longest period of incarceration.[160] The penalties for criminal failure to protect can be substantial. In six states the nonabusive parent can be sentenced to life in prison; in other states the maximum penalty is ninety-nine years.[161] Intimate partner violence problematizes what constitutes reasonable action in a failure-to-protect case. The inability to recognize the ways that intimate partner violence might prevent a parent from seeking help or otherwise constrain a parent's actions can make it look as though the parent has the capacity to act and has chosen not to do so. Protective actions that a parent may have taken are characterized as too little, too late, insufficient to meet the duty to protect. Bierria and Lenz explore these ideas through the cases of Tondalo Hall and Kelly Savage.

Tondalo Hall met Robert Braxton Jr. when she was sixteen years old. The couple had two children before Hall was nineteen. Braxton abused Hall throughout their relationship. Braxton, angry that Hall worked while he stayed at home with the children, threatened her regularly, telling her that "if you put yourself in a man's position, then you deserve to be hit."[162] Braxton isolated her from her family and community. He hit her. He strangled her. He threatened to have her children taken away if she tried to leave him or reported his abuse to anyone. Nonetheless, Hall was secretly saving money to move herself and their children away from Braxton. Hall was unaware, however, that Braxton had also harmed their children. When she noticed that her infant son's leg was swollen, she immediately took him for medical treatment. Doctors found that the child had a broken leg and that both he and his baby sister had broken ribs. In the initial investigation Hall tried to take responsibility for the children's injuries, afraid of what Braxton would do if she revealed his history of violence. But prosecutors recognized that Braxton, not Hall, had harmed the children and charged Braxton with child abuse. They charged Hall with permitting child abuse, despite their acknowledgment that she had not injured the children and despite the steps she took to make them safe.[163]

In a similar case, twenty-two-year-old Kelly Savage was charged with first-degree murder for aiding and abetting her husband, Mark Savage, in the death of her four-year-old son, Justin. The charge was based on Kelly's decision to leave Justin at home with his father while she ran errands. Those errands were part of a safety plan Kelly had developed with a domestic violence hotline. She planned to board a bus and leave her husband the next day. Prosecutors called her first husband, Michael Alvarado, as a witness. He testified that he too had abused Kelly, but that she was "strong"; the jury laughed when Alvarado described "slapping [Kelly Savage] up the side of her head."[164] Prosecutors argued that Kelly caused her own abuse, "manipulat[ing] the men in her life into repeatedly beating and raping her."[165] Because Kelly Savage did not leave or call the police in response to her husband's abuse, prosecutors contended, she had "directly 'aided and abetted'" him in Justin's death.[166]

Prosecutors also use felony murder and accomplice liability laws to hold survivors criminally responsible for the acts of others. Sociologist Lora Bex Lempert found that 60 percent of the women sentenced to life in Michigan were convicted for homicides they did not commit. Most of those women's crimes were connected to their intimate partners, "whose violent choices, directly or indirectly, resulted in the women's sentences of life imprisonment."[167] Felony murder imposes responsibility for a murder on anyone involved in the commission of a felony that results in someone's death—regardless of whether the defendant caused that death, intended that death, or could foresee that death could occur.[168] More than forty states have felony murder laws. In some states felony murder is punishable by death. Felony murder laws enable prosecutors to extend culpability for murders to the abused partners of the people who actually commit those murders. In California researchers found that 72 percent of women incarcerated for felony murder had not killed anyone; most of those women were subjected to intimate partner violence by the actual killers.[169] The felony murder rule disproportionately affects Black people.

About 40 percent of those convicted of felony murder in California are Black.[170] In Cook County, Illinois, 81 percent of those sentenced under the felony murder rule are Black.[171]

When Eraina Pretty was sixteen, she met Ronald Brown, then twenty-one. Early in their relationship, Brown lavished love and attention on Pretty, something she had not experienced before. But over time, Brown changed. He became controlling, demanding to know where she was and forbidding her from leaving her apartment in Baltimore. He physically abused Pretty, once kicking her in the leg until she believed her leg was broken. Pretty feared Brown.

Pretty worked part-time as a cashier in a store owned by Louis Thomas. After Thomas sexually assaulted Pretty, she stopped going to work. When Brown asked why she was not working, Pretty told him what had happened. Brown told Pretty that he would rob the store in retaliation but needed her help to gain entry. Pretty opposed the plan, but Brown insisted that she accompany him, knowing that Thomas would open the door for her. Pretty, afraid of Brown, did as she was told. When Brown told her to help tie up Thomas and another man in the store, Eugene Cole, she did that too, promising Thomas and Cole that nothing would happen to them if they followed Brown's instructions. After the men had been restrained, Brown told Pretty to go to the front of the store. Instead, she ran away. As she did, she heard gunshots. Brown shot and killed Louis Thomas and wounded Eugene Cole. Eraina Pretty—who was afraid of Ronald Brown, had not wanted to go along with the robbery, and had not been present when the shots were fired—was charged with first-degree felony murder.

Rudeara Bailey was a thirty-three-year-old mother of two when her boyfriend, Clifton Dobbins, robbed and killed Helen Dyott in Bailey's apartment. Bailey did not know of Dobbins's plan to rob Dyott before the incident and only learned what Dobbins had done when Dobbins asked her, while they lay in bed with his arm around her neck, if she believed he could kill someone. She said that she did believe it, knowing that he had been violent toward her in the past. Dobbins disclosed that he had killed Dyott and told Bailey she had to help him clean the apartment to hide the evidence. He threatened that if she did not help him, or if she tried to go to the police, he would kill her and her children. Several days later, when Dobbins was arrested on other charges, Bailey, believing herself safe, went to police and told them everything she knew about the murder. She showed them the places she had cleaned, led them to the murder weapon, and agreed to testify at Dobbins's trial. Bailey told police that she was afraid of Dobbins. The police characterized her as helpful and very emotionally upset about the crime.

Five months later, Bailey was arrested and charged with first-degree felony murder—not because police considered her a suspect but at the insistence of prosecutors, who contended that she was in the apartment when the murder occurred. At trial, Bailey (and other witnesses) denied that she was present. She admitted that she had cleaned up after the crime and had initially withheld information from police but provided that information as soon as Dobbins was incarcerated and she was safe to do so. Bailey also stood up to Dorchester County (Maryland) prosecutor Michael Maloney on the stand. Maloney asked, "You think it's just an over zealous [sic] prosecution case here against you, don't you?" Bailey responded, "It makes me wonder why it took you so long to arrest."[172] But her willingness to fight for herself may have undermined her claim of victimization—certainly a woman willing to stand up to a zealous prosecutor wouldn't have been afraid of her boyfriend. Bailey was convicted and sentenced to life in prison.

Other forms of accomplice liability are used to hold victims of violence responsible for the actions of those who abuse them. Ramona Brant, for example, was involved with a man whom she believed was the man of her dreams until he became abusive during Brant's first pregnancy. She left him, but he begged her to return and promised to change. And for a while, he did change—until Brant became pregnant again. Then the abuse became "one hundred times worse." Brant told no one what was happening and was afraid to leave, lest he make good on his threat to take the children from her if she reported the abuse. Brant knew that her partner was a drug dealer and sometimes went with him to pick up packages or sent messages over the phone. In 1993 her partner was arrested and offered a plea that would protect Brant from prosecution. Her partner rejected the deal, saying that "if he couldn't have me, nobody else would." Brant was charged with conspiracy, and although everyone agreed that she had never bought or sold drugs, she was found guilty of conspiracy to distribute cocaine and cocaine base and sentenced to life in federal prison.

The jury did not hear evidence of her partner's abuse of and control over her.[173]

Criminalized survivors can be charged as accessories as well. After her abusive husband was incarcerated, Aminah Elster started a new relationship. When her husband was released, he found Elster and threatened to kill her if she didn't give him her boyfriend's location. Elster's brother-in-law killed the boyfriend. For revealing his location, Elster was convicted of being an accessory to murder and sentenced to fifteen years to life.[174]

While there is a rich history of prosecuting sex traffickers in the United States dating back to the Mann Act, which prohibited "white slavery," the modern anti-trafficking movement is relatively recent—and very focused on carceral responses to trafficking. Following the lead of the anti-domestic violence movement, the nascent anti-trafficking movement advocated strongly for robust criminal interventions and vigorous prosecution of those laws. In 2018 the US Department of Justice awarded $77 million in grants to combat trafficking, the majority of which went to law enforcement. The prosecution of trafficking victims for crimes related to their own trafficking has been a consequence of that carceral bent.

In 2019 law professor Kate Mogulescu received a packet of letters from a group of women incarcerated in the Federal Correctional Institution in Tallahassee, Florida. The women had found each other in prison and learned that they shared a common story: many of them were young (in their late teens or early twenties when convicted), they were victims of commercial sexual exploitation, and all of them were prosecuted for sex trafficking. These cases present in several ways. Some women are minimally involved in trafficking. Some are compelled to participate by their own traffickers, who try to distance themselves from illegal activity by having their victims post ads, collect money, or recruit and manage others. Some are involved in abusive intimate relationships with their traffickers, which complicates their ability to distance themselves from illegal activities. Some try to protect other victims in ways that prosecutors characterize as "grooming." Prosecutors are often reluctant to believe that victims of trafficking are forced or coerced into their crimes, discounting their victimization even when they clearly meet state and federal definitions of trafficking victims. Prosecutors and courts are left decide who "deserves" leniency when they are prosecuted.[175]

Prosecutors decided that Desalashia Williams was one of the unde-serving. Williams met Jeremy Grant in 2013, after a lifetime of physical, emotional, and sexual abuse at the hands of family members and roman-tic partners. Williams was convinced that this relationship would be dif-ferent. But while Grant was initially caring and loving, he soon became abusive. Grant regularly threatened, hit, and pushed Williams. On one occasion he threw her down the stairs and out of a window. Williams was deeply afraid of Grant by 2014, when he began selling minors for sex.

Williams was initially unaware of Grant's activities. When she asked him about the girl who had been hanging around their home and had recently disappeared, Grant told Williams that he had been selling the girl and that she should not ask about his business. In the summer of 2014, when Grant brought in two additional girls, Williams knew what he was doing but was too afraid to report him. She believed he would make good on his threats to kill her if she did. She did what she could to help the girls—filled out job applications with them, took them to church, took one girl to her grandmother's house, and consistently, but unsuccessfully, encouraged them to leave Grant. When Grant ordered Williams to take the girls to have their hair and makeup done, she tried to make it like an outing for the girls, to show her support for them. As Williams said, "They were trapped, just like me."

Grant began to use Williams's social media accounts and email addresses to conduct his trafficking business. He threatened to beat Wil-liams if she used them without his permission. He began forcing Williams to collect money from the men who bought the girls, distancing himself from the transactions. Those were the only times that Williams touched money during that period, and she immediately gave the money to Grant. His control over Williams was total. If Williams refused to assist Grant or questioned what he was doing, he beat her, on one occasion breaking her leg. Grant repeatedly warned Williams that if she turned him in, he would kill her and her family. Williams believed these threats; Grant had, in the past, threatened to shoot Williams's father if he intervened in their relationship.

By December 2014 all the girls Grant was selling for sex had escaped. Grant then began to sell Williams, once forcing her to have sex with sev-eral men in their apartment. The second time Grant attempted to prostitute Williams, she was arrested. Fearful of Grant's threats, Williams did not initially tell police that she had been forced into prostitution, only coming forward with that information after Grant had been arrested. Despite the years of abuse she had endured at Grant's hands, his control over her, and the fact that Grant had trafficked her, Williams was charged with conspiracy to engage in sex trafficking. Williams pled guilty and was sentenced to thirteen years in federal prison.

Defenses

The defenses available to criminalized survivors rely on the same stereotypes and assumptions about victims of violence that preclude police and prosecutors from seeing those charged with crimes as victims. In some jurisdictions, for example, having been a victim of trafficking is a defense to prosecution for prostitution. But defendants must be able to persuade courts or juries that they are in fact victims to avail themselves of the defense. Providing that proof may come at a substantial risk to the victim. Representative Amy Volk of Maine sponsored legislation establishing a sex trafficking defense to prostitution but was clear about her expectations for those who sought to use the defense: "If you can show us you're a victim by turning in your pimp, we won't prosecute you."[176]

SELF-DEFENSE

Proving self-defense could prevent prosecution and punishment of people who use violence to protect themselves. To successfully argue self-defense, a person must show that they used force in response to a reasonable fear of imminent or immediate serious bodily harm or death and that the amount of force used was proportionate to the threat posed. They may also have to prove that they did not use force first and attempted to retreat or flee before using force. The concept of "reasonableness" often has both subjective and objective components: the person must prove that they subjectively believed that an imminent threat of death or serious bodily harm existed at the time they acted and that a reasonable person assessing the situation would share that belief. If a person who uses force can establish these elements, their use of deadly force is legally justifiable, the equivalent of a finding that no crime has been committed.

But self-defense has long been complicated in cases of gender-based violence, particularly for women who kill their partners. At common law a woman who killed her husband could be convicted of petit treason, eliciting more serious punishment than if she had killed anyone else. Killing in response to a husband's physical abuse did not excuse the conduct, because husbands had the right to physically discipline their wives. Past violence was not relevant to a claim of self-defense.[177] By the late 1970s defense attorneys representing women who killed their partners regularly advised them to claim temporary insanity rather than self-defense.[178] Self-defense was regarded as especially inappropriate in "nonconfrontational" cases. As law professor Ellen Yaroshefsky has explained: "In 1980, the claim of self-defense in a case where the aggressor was not in the act of attacking the woman was regarded as simply not viable."[179]

Women faced a number of obstacles in making self-defense claims. Self-defense law contemplated two men of similar size and strength facing each other in a fair fight. The law failed to account for size and strength differentials between men and women, which sometimes made it appear that women had used disproportionate force, especially when women used weapons to make up for those disadvantages.[180] By looking only at the specific incident in the case, self-defense law precluded women from explaining how a history of abuse affected their perceptions of the imminence or immediacy of death or serious bodily injury. This issue often arose in cases where a woman acted after an abusive incident or when the person killed was sleeping (although most cases where women argue self-defense involve killings during a confrontation).[181] Similarly, without context, the reasonableness of the woman's perception of the level of danger might be questionable. In many jurisdictions the person using force was required to retreat from the danger if at all possible, even if that threat came from within the person's home.

Bringing a successful self-defense claim was a particular challenge for Black women, whose victimization is often minimized and who appear to racist judges and jurors as "just another violent black person, shooting it out."[182] In a 1978 article activist and author Assata Shakur described Lucille, a Black woman convicted of killing her partner despite "medical records which would prove that she had suffered repeated physical injuries as the result of beatings by the deceased," including a mutilated

arm and a partially severed ear.[183] "The District Attorney made a big deal
of the fact that she drank," Shakur wrote. "And the jury, affected by t.v.
racism, 'law and order,' petrified by crime and unimpressed by Lucille as
a 'responsible citizen,' convicted her."[184] The failure to understand the relationship between intimate partner violence and women's use of force led
judges and juries to reject women's self-defense claims. A 1990 study of
women subjected to abuse who killed their partners found that the majority had been convicted because they could not establish the elements of
self-defense.[185] Offering evidence of battered woman syndrome (BWS)
was meant to solve that problem.

BATTERED WOMAN SYNDROME

As articulated by psychologist Lenore Walker in her 1984 book, *The Battered Woman Syndrome,* BWS consisted of two elements: the cycle of violence and learned helplessness. Walker's cycle of violence theory posited
that intimate relationships marked by violence followed predictable patterns: a tension-building phase, leading to an acute battering incident,
followed by a honeymoon period. Walker argued that the cycle repeated
itself, with the time between incidents growing shorter and the incidents
of violence becoming more serious, until a victim either left the relationship or was killed.

"Learned helplessness" borrowed from psychologist Martin Seligman's
work demonstrating that dogs became conditioned to respond passively
to repeated physical harm if they perceived that there was no escape from
that harm. Walker applied this theory to women subjected to abuse, arguing that women, like dogs, could be conditioned to believe that escape
from violence was impossible. Bringing these two theories together,
Walker suggested that conditioning kept women in abusive relationships,
even as they perceived the danger increasing, until they had no choice but
to use deadly violence to prevent harm to themselves or their children.
Walker later expanded and refined the theory, combining some features
of post-traumatic stress disorder and some factors from her own research
to redefine BWS.[186]

Criticism of BWS quickly emerged. BWS was not supported by Walker's
own research.[187] The description of battered women as passive to the
point of nonaction was a caricature that did not accurately depict many,

even most, women subjected to abuse.[188] BWS failed to reflect the experiences of tough women, confident women, independent women, working women, women who were angry rather than (or in addition to) fearful, women who fought back against their abusers, women who failed to present as traditionally feminine. BWS excluded Black women stereotyped as angry, assertive, and strong.[189] The theory was also internally inconsistent—how could extreme passivity explain the very active step of killing a partner? And describing the experience of being battered as a syndrome suggested that victimized women were mentally ill or emotionally unstable, undermining arguments that a woman's actions in defending herself were reasonable.

Given the shortcomings of BWS, lawyers and advocates sought a different way to present evidence about intimate partner violence to courts. In 1996 the National Institute of Justice and the National Institute of Mental Health recommended that professionals stop using the term "battered woman syndrome."[190] Many experts began using the phrase "battering and its effects" instead, moving away from the individual pathology suggested by the term BWS toward a broader consideration of the social context of intimate partner violence.[191] By then, though, several states had enacted laws allowing defendants to introduce evidence of BWS (in some places, battered spouse syndrome), language that still appears in state laws. Even in jurisdictions that did not use the language of BWS, "lawyers, judges and juries, in practice, are making sense of the social phenomena that the law is being applied to in exactly the same way, arriving at similar outcomes."[192]

BWS is not a defense. It is a mechanism for bringing expert testimony on the impact of intimate partner violence on the defendant into the courtroom to explain elements of self-defense, including imminence, reasonableness, and proportionality. By 1996 every state allowed the introduction of evidence about a history of intimate partner violence in the context of a self-defense claim, and state courts found that defense counsel's failure to introduce such evidence was grounds to reverse convictions.

Prosecutors are happy to use BWS to explain why victims might recant prior statements about violence but vigorously refute evidence of abuse when victims become defendants. Prosecutors characterize these defendants as angry, jealous, unfaithful, hard partying, and profane. Relying on the language of coercive control, lawyer and psychologist Karla Fischer has argued, prosecutors use "any perceived autonomy, independent activities, or open conflict between the decedent and the defendant to argue that the defendant was not battered. She was not 'really' battered if she had her own checking account, worked outside the home, purchased a gun at a pawn shop, or lived in her own apartment."[193]

Prosecutors turn attempts to explain the history of abuse against criminalized survivors, as prosecutor Michel Paulhus did in Sylvia Flynn's case: "It's an insult to the ones who truly are battered and live like that and suffer.... Sylvia Flynn is not a battered woman. She's a woman scorned, and that's why John Flynn is dead."[194] Even defense attorneys can be dismissive of their clients' claims. For example, Janea recounted that her public defender noted she had "no police reports or other evidence to prove that she had been a victim of domestic violence" before reminding Janea that "she could have left at any time."[195]

A ruling allowing the introduction of evidence of battering or a finding of BWS is not tantamount to an acquittal. Judges and juries can still reject that evidence, decide that other factors are more important, or use the evidence to support a finding of imperfect self-defense, which reduces a charge of murder to manslaughter.

STAND YOUR GROUND

Some criminalized survivors have argued that in using force against their partners, they were simply standing their ground, as they were legally entitled to do. But courts and prosecutors have largely rejected those arguments, contending that Stand Your Ground laws—laws that permit the use of deadly force in self-defense even when the defendant could have retreated—do not apply in cases involving gender-based violence. Stand Your Ground laws, enacted in various forms in at least thirty-four states, confer immunity from prosecution: if you establish that you were standing your ground, you avoid prosecution altogether. But as law professor Mary Anne Franks has observed, Stand Your Ground laws were not written to benefit women with self-defense claims: "One self-defense rule for men, another for women."[196] That was certainly Marissa Alexander's experience. Despite being in her home, where she had a lawful right to be (and her husband did not), Alexander was denied the right to claim immunity under Florida's Stand Your Ground law.

Stand Your Ground didn't protect Brittany Smith either. Smith was raped by an acquaintance, Todd Smith, after allowing him to come into her Stevenson, Alabama, home during a snowstorm. Todd threatened to kill Brittany and her family if she told anyone about the rape. But Brittany was able to pass a note to a cashier at a gas station, saying that if she was found dead, Todd Smith had killed her. Brittany later texted her mother, instructing her to call the cashier at the gas station, and sent her brother to talk to the cashier as well. When her brother learned what had happened, he went to Brittany's house with a gun and confronted Todd. Todd attacked Brittany's brother. Brittany grabbed the gun and told Todd to let her brother go. Todd responded that he would kill both Brittany and her brother. Brittany fired a warning shot, and when Todd still wouldn't let go, she fired two more shots. When Todd collapsed, Brittany called 911, saying that a man who tried to kill her had been shot and asking them to send an ambulance "because I don't want this man to die."[197] Brittany and her brother administered CPR, but Todd Smith died just as police arrived at the scene. Brittany told police what had happened and showed them her injuries. A forensic examination found bruises and bite marks all over her body as well as evidence that she had been strangled.

Initially, Brittany Smith and her brother told police that her brother had shot Todd Smith; they did not believe that a woman defending herself from rape could get a fair trial. Two days later, Brittany was arrested for murder. At a 2020 hearing, she claimed that she was standing her ground, as permitted by Alabama law, when she shot Todd Smith. But Judge Jenifer Holt found that Brittany's use of deadly force was not warranted because the judge did not believe—despite the rape, the note Brittany had passed to the cashier (which was entered into evidence), the cashier's testimony about Brittany's fear, the thirty-three wounds forensic nurses documented from the attack, and testimony that Todd Smith was strangling Brittany's brother when she fired—that Brittany was at risk of harm. She was denied immunity.[198] Facing life in prison, Brittany Smith pled guilty to murder.[199]

Ky Peterson's lawyer didn't even inform him that he could argue Stand Your Ground. Peterson, a Black trans man in rural Georgia, was raped twice before the night a stranger propositioned him as he walked home. Both times he reported the rapes to police. Both times police did little to nothing in response. Peterson began carrying a gun after the second rape. On October 28, 2011, Peterson was hit from behind and knocked unconscious. When he awoke, the man who had approached him earlier was "on top of him, naked and spitting homophobic slurs...as he forced himself inside Peterson." Peterson shot his attacker, then moved the man's body. Police, believing that Peterson killed the man during a robbery, arrested him the next day. A forensic exam supported Peterson's rape claim. Peterson's actions were covered by Georgia's broad Stand Your Ground law, which permits the use of deadly force based on a reasonable belief that such force is necessary to prevent death, bodily injury, or a forcible felony, like rape. Peterson's lawyer believed Peterson's claim that he was defending himself. "But [just because] I believe you, that doesn't mean that we're going to win in front of a jury."[200] Peterson, fearing that he would receive a life sentence or the death penalty, pled to involuntary manslaughter and was sentenced to twenty years imprisonment. He was released in the summer of 2020.

There are victims of violence who can satisfy judges and juries that they acted in self-defense. Breanna Sullivan, for example, endured four years of violence before shooting her husband of four years. Sullivan had extensive documentation of her injuries, including medical records from hospitalizations and photographs of black eyes and bruises. Her husband was criminally charged three times for abusing Sullivan. Sullivan was initially charged with murder and ultimately tried for voluntary manslaughter. She argued self-defense and was found not guilty. But Sullivan recognizes that she is "a very rare statistic. On one side of it, fighting back it's still very often the victim ends up killed, when you do try to fight back. Even if you don't, most of the women I've been able to connect with who have been through something like me, they didn't get the not guilty."[201] Or as one woman convicted of killing her rapist explained: "I was mad as hell because I was being raped and I took the life of the man who was raping me. The state paid me back by taking my life away."[202]

DURESS

Tanisha Williams was twenty years old, a victim of repeated sexual, physical, and emotional abuse, the mother of two young children, and unhoused when she met Patrick Martin. Williams had been doing survival sex work; Martin offered her a place to live in exchange for sharing the bills. What Williams did not know was that Martin planned to sell her for sex. When she refused, Martin began beating and strangling her, taking her money, and forcing her to care for his house and his children. Martin always carried a gun, and Williams feared he would use it. But Williams did not want to go back to sleeping in cars. She decided to stay with Martin and endure his violence until she saved enough money to move out.

On December 29, 2002, Kevin Amos came to Martin's Saginaw, Michigan, apartment. Believing that Amos had looked at him disrespectfully, Martin punched and pistol-whipped Amos, who lost consciousness. Martin ordered Williams to tape Amos's mouth and nose closed. When Williams began to scream, Martin picked her up and slammed her against the wall, cracking the drywall, then cut off her airway with his fist. He ordered her to either "get down or lay down," which Williams understood to mean comply with his order or be killed. Martin agreed with her assessment: "At that time, [Williams] was terrified.... I told them, 'If you don't do it, I'ma do you.' So they did it but it was out of fear." Or, as Williams said, "Because I ain't have no choice but to do it."[203]

The case went cold for seven years. But in 2009, Williams decided to tell the truth. Hoping to give Amos's family closure, Williams told police everything she knew about the crime. Martin was convicted of first-degree murder and sentenced to life in prison. Williams testified against Martin at trial.[204] Williams believed that police and prosecutors would understand that she had only complied with Martin's orders because she knew he would kill her if she did not. What Williams did not know was that even though she acted under duress, that explanation would not protect her from a murder conviction. Duress excuses criminal actions taken because the person was under threat of imminent death or serious bodily injury, had reason to believe that the threat was real, and could not otherwise avoid the harm. But in most states, including Michigan, duress does not apply to intentional murder. As the prosecutor in Williams's case argued,

> She testified that she's under that duress, we'd call it, the threats. You'll find the judge will instruct you that's not a defense to homicide. The law does not allow one person to sacrifice the life of an innocent to save their own.... The law says, no, you can't do that. You've got to resist. You've got to—you've got to take your chances. Yeah, she was threatened, but I don't think it's that simple with her either.[205]

Duress is available as a defense to other crimes, however, and criminalized survivors frequently commit other crimes under duress. Women who commit economic crimes, for example, often attribute those crimes to the demands of male intimate partners.[206] Criminologist Beth Richie has argued that criminality under duress operates as a survival strategy for Black women subjected to abuse.[207] But criminalized survivors may find it difficult to persuade prosecutors and courts that their victimization should excuse their actions when innocent third parties (as opposed to their abusive partners) are injured.

Prosecutorial Misconduct

Prosecutors' desire to win cases can sometimes lead them to engage in questionable, even unethical, behavior. In its ruling denying Jodi Arias's appeal of her 2013 conviction for killing her former partner, the Arizona Court of Appeals highlighted repeated instances of problematic behavior by prosecutor Juan Martinez: "He bullied witnesses and Arias herself, suggested that a psychologist had romantic feelings for Arias, appealed to the juror's [sic] passions and fears." Martinez also changed the facts of the case in ways that made "the crime seem colder, crueler, more heinous—aggravating factors that would allow for a death sentence."[208] The Arizona Court of Appeals found a pattern of intentional misconduct and referred Martinez to the State Bar of Arizona for discipline. But it upheld Arias's conviction, finding that Martinez's actions did not justify granting Arias a new trial.[209] Martinez was later disbarred.[210] Arias is serving life in prison without the possibility of parole.

The prosecutorial misconduct in Juanita Thomas's case was even more egregious. Thomas's boyfriend, Willie Hammond, had been abusing her for years. In the year before his death, Hammond strangled Thomas with a bicycle chain, kicked her, and punched her in the head. On July 28, 1979, Hammond hit Thomas and tried to force her to perform oral sex on him. When she refused, Hammond reached for a letter opener on the dresser. Thomas grabbed a butcher knife from under the bed and stabbed him repeatedly. Thomas was found outside her Lansing, Michigan, home, bloody and in her underwear, crying. Hammond was dead. Thomas was convicted of first-degree murder.

Prosecutors must provide the defense with exculpatory evidence—evidence that is favorable to the defendant—before trial. The prosecutors in Thomas's case not only failed to turn over the evidence (a bloody screen that undermined the prosecution's argument about how the crime was committed) but, knowing that police had destroyed the evidence, argued that the lack of evidence proved Thomas's guilt. Prosecutors also failed to disclose that Thomas's boyfriend had a significant criminal record, which would have supported Thomas's argument that defending herself was reasonable given his history of violence. Based on this misconduct, as well as other issues at trial, Thomas sought a new trial. Thomas and prosecutors ultimately reached an agreement. In exchange for dismissing her motion for a new trial, Thomas pled guilty to second-degree murder and was resentenced to thirty to fifty years with credit for time served and released on parole after eighteen-and-a-half years in prison.[211]

The two most likely outcomes for survivors who are prosecuted are acquittal and conviction. But even if a case results in acquittal, arrest and prosecution do real harm: pretrial detention, the cost of defending against criminal charges, the social stigma attendant to prosecution, job loss, separation from children, trauma, and stress. For those convicted of crimes related to their own victimization, the costs are much higher.

4 Punishment and Sentencing

Over the course of their nineteen-year relationship, Scott Shanahan blackened Dixie Shanahan's eyes, beat her (with his fists and with other objects) until she was bruised and bleeding, dragged her by her hair, threw her down the steps of their home, stuck her head in a toilet, poked her in the eye until it bled, threatened to shoot her, tied her up and left her for days in their basement (on multiple occasions), ran over her legs with a lawn tractor, smashed her head into a door (twice), slammed her head into the window of their car, and humiliated her in front of their friends. During Dixie's second pregnancy with their daughter Ashley, Scott tried to beat her into miscarrying after she refused to have an abortion. During her third pregnancy, in August 2002, Scott swore that he would kill the baby one way or another.

On August 30, 2002, Scott Shanahan beat Dixie Shanahan while Ashley watched. When Dixie tried to run to the car, Scott took her car keys, pushed her to the ground, and dragged her by her hair back into the house. He jammed two shotgun shells into his shotgun and told Dixie that he would kill her that day. He took the phones and the shotgun into their bedroom. Dixie went into the bedroom to use the phone. When Scott moved toward her, Dixie grabbed the shotgun, closed her eyes, and fired, killing him. After less than a day of deliberation, a jury convicted Dixie

Shanahan of second-degree murder. On May 10, 2004, Judge Charles L. Smith III sentenced her to fifty years' imprisonment—the mandatory minimum sentence in Iowa for second-degree murder.[1]

For some criminalized survivors of gender-based violence, "the process is the punishment."[2] Interacting with the criminal legal system can exacerbate the trauma that victims have experienced and undermine efforts to heal. As psychologist Judith Herman has noted, "If one set out intentionally to design a system for provoking symptoms of traumatic stress, it might look very much like a court of law."[3] For those convicted of crimes related to their own victimization, however, the process is just the beginning. Conviction requires some sort of punishment, and that punishment can range from serving a sentence in the community under minimal supervision to life imprisonment or death. "Perfect victims" may be able to use their experiences as victims to justify less stringent punishment. But those claims are much harder to make at the point of punishment, both because of external constraints (like mandatory sentences) and because a finding of guilt often serves as a negative verdict on the credibility and strength of victimization narratives. As a result, victims of gender-based violence frequently find themselves incarcerated and subjected to other forms of punishment that not only fail to acknowledge their experiences of victimization but often exacerbate their trauma.

WHY PUNISH?

Criminal punishment is usually justified on one (or more) of four grounds: rehabilitation, incapacitation, deterrence, and retribution. Rehabilitation is meant to remake the person into a law-abiding citizen. Incapacitation removes the person from society so that they cannot do additional harm. Deterrence prevents people who might offend from engaging in harm because, having seen what the punishment has been or will be, they understand the potential negative consequences of their actions. And retribution, the oldest moral underpinning for punishment, is intended to ensure that those who commit crimes receive the punishment they deserve. Punishment settles the score between the person who commits a crime, their victim, and the wider society.

Punishing survivors of gender-based violence is difficult to justify using these theories. In an era in which prisons barely meet people's basic human needs and substantive programming is scarce, few argue that punishment rehabilitates. Nonetheless, in sentencing eighty-year-old Lavetta Langdon for the murder of her husband after fifty years of torture and despite his recognition that she had "lived in hell," Judge David Urbom sentenced Langdon to eight to ten years' imprisonment to "rehabilitate" her.[4] For criminalized survivors, relying on rehabilitation is particularly inapt. Crimes committed by criminalized survivors are often specific to their victimization. The problem is not with the person who commits the crime, but with the harm they are experiencing.

Justifying punishment using rehabilitation reinforces outdated stereotypes suggesting that gender-based violence is linked to some deficiency or infirmity in the victim. Rehabilitation also assumes that the person convicted of a crime does not appreciate that their actions were problematic; rehabilitation is meant to change the person's underlying values. Criminalized survivors understand that they may be technically guilty of crimes. What they dispute is the failure to recognize the context for those crimes and to apply the law—and the values underlying the law—appropriately. As one woman convicted of killing her husband explained, "I'm not asking to be found not guilty, because I am guilty, I took his life, I did it. . . . I am definitely guilty of taking his life, I mean, if I was found not guilty, they'd have to look for who did it, right, I mean someone's got to be guilty. And I certainly take responsibility for what I did, I have no problem with that, but I certainly don't deserve 18 to 20 years for it."[5] Faced with the same situation again, many would be forced to make the same choice.

Incapacitation is generally linked with incarceration (although house arrest and electronic monitoring are forms of incapacitation) and assumes that because people have committed crimes in the past, they are likely to do so again unless removed from society. But many criminalized survivors have never offended previously, and most (including those who have been convicted of serious violent crimes) will not reoffend. Incapacitation is therefore unlikely to prevent offenses by these people. What incapacitation does do is deprive society of the many other functions performed by these people—as parents, caregivers, workers, and members of communities—while at the same time imposing the costs of their incarceration on taxpayers.

Deterrence is no more persuasive. The evidence for the deterrent value of punishment is inconclusive, particularly when the sentence involves incarceration. Sentencing people convicted of violent crimes to prison may have no greater impact on recidivism after release than sentencing someone to probation.[6] Incarceration may instead spur offending by exacerbating preexisting mental health conditions or trauma and making it difficult for people to find legal employment after their release.[7] For the criminalized survivor being punished, deterrence is largely unnecessary: that person is unlikely to find themself in the same situation again. Other survivors, perceiving immediate danger to themselves or their children and no other clear or effective options, are unlikely to be deterred from acting by the abstract threat of punishment or the knowledge that another person has been punished for taking similar action.

Which leaves retribution. Retribution motivated the judge in the case of Barbara Jean Gilbert, who killed her husband after fifteen years of abuse. The judge handed down the maximum sentence of incarceration—even though the probation department asked for probation, citing her "exemplary" conduct, and prosecutors did not ask for prison time. The judge explained his decision: "You have snuffed out a life.... Therefore the court has the right to inflict pain and deprivation on you."[8] But what does a criminalized survivor deserve, particularly when the victim of the crime for which the person is being punished has inflicted immeasurable damage on that person? Retributivists stress that the punishment must be proportionate to the crime. To determine proportionality, context is essential. A proportionate response should factor in the harm already suffered by the person being punished. As Darcy K. WarBonnett has observed, prior to entering prison she was already serving a life sentence by virtue of having been abused by her partner. "We are incarcerated not AS punishment, but evidently for MORE punishment."[9] Retributivists also argue that punishment restores moral balance. That balance is necessarily different, however, when the victim of a crime has abused the person convicted of that crime. The moral balance has already shifted away from the victim because of their earlier actions.

Even if none of these rationales for punishment is satisfied, society may still seek to punish those who commit crimes. Punishment reinforces the value of and respect due community norms. Directing hostile feelings toward those who have committed crimes allows members of society to vent their frustrations and feel in control, while at the same time believing they are right. To the extent that punishment fulfills those needs, "punishment pleases."[10] The need to assert community norms and control motivates community members to call for harsh punishment of criminalized survivors. As one newspaper columnist wrote after Dixie Shanahan was sentenced: "Open a loophole for one woman to kill an abusive spouse and pretty soon you've got dozens of dead husbands."[11]

SENTENCING

Criminal punishment is effectuated through sentencing. If charging begins the process of stripping victim status from a criminalized survivor, sentencing usually cements it. Even if the survivor's story of abuse is initially viewed as partially or wholly credible, the acceptance of the state's version of facts in a plea bargain or the finding of guilt by a judge or jury marks the rejection of the survivor's claim. In a system anchored to the victim/offender binary, there is simply not room for two victims. To acknowledge the victimization of a criminalized survivor also means acknowledging that the person will be abused twice—once by the perpetrator of gender-based violence and again by the state.

Sentencing actualizes the state's position that a criminalized survivor is no longer a victim, using degradation of the survivor to reinforce the point. In Cook County, Illinois, criminologist Nicole Gonzalez Van Cleve watched as an elderly woman holding the pole of an oxygen tank "shuffled into open court in jail-issued slippers." When Van Cleve asked what the woman had done, the prosecutor answered, "She shot her husband in the ass, and the prick died on her." The woman told the judge that her husband had abused her and she could not take any more. She had meant to hurt but not kill him. Van Cleve watched as the judge excoriated the defendant, telling her that she was a "*bad ... bad* woman" and responsible for the abuse. "The judge berated her in a manner so harsh it appeared to reenact the domestic abuse that I read in the case file; this time the judge was the public abuser and, incidentally, the judicial arbiter." The judge did not simply punish the woman. He humiliated and degraded her. In this process, Van Cleve explained, "the defendant is not a victim; she is not frail; she is not to be sympathized with nor indulged with respect and decency. Instead, she should be seen and called out publicly as the 'lower species' that she is revealed to be."[12]

To send that message to others, judges tell criminalized survivors, "'I'ma make an example of you.'"[13] Prosecutor Angela Marsee and Judge Ray C. Elliott clearly sent this message to Tondalo Hall. Chapter 3 described how Hall was prosecuted for failing to protect her children from their father's abuse. Hall agreed to testify against their father, Robert Braxton, and in October 2006 she entered a guilty plea. The plea did not guarantee her a particular sentence, but Hall believed that she would receive a sentence equal to or less than Braxton's. Hall and Braxton were held in the same jail before and during Braxton's trial. Braxton sent Hall threatening letters while in jail. One letter contained an outline of his hand and said, "Since I can't do it, here's my hand & slap yourself."[14]

Hall asked that she not be transported to court with Braxton, who threatened her during those rides. Her request was ignored. During her testimony at Braxton's trial, Hall was visibly nervous. Marsee attempted to question Hall about an incident where Braxton strangled Hall. But Hall was not permitted to testify about that incident because Marsee failed to comply with procedural requirements that made such testimony admissible. In the middle of the trial, concerned about the strength of their case, prosecutors offered Braxton a plea deal. Braxton pled guilty to abusing the children and was sentenced to eight years' imprisonment, with all but the two years he had already served suspended. Braxton was immediately released from jail on December 8, 2006.

Hall's sentencing hearing was held eight days later. At sentencing, Marsee argued that Hall was responsible for the state's inability to prove its case against Braxton. "As this court is well aware," Marsee argued, "the case against [Braxton] fell apart in part because of her minimizing and denying what happened in that household.... He definitely should have received a more significant sentence, but because of her minimizing and continuing to protect herself and protect him, that had a real impact on what we were able to do with him in the jury trial."[15] Marsee contended that Hall chose Braxton over her children—despite Hall's efforts to leave Braxton, her visible fear of Braxton, and her requests that she be protected from Braxton during his trial. Marsee asked the court to sentence Hall to life in prison. The same evidence of victimization that the state sought to introduce at trial, it ignored at sentencing.

Elliott similarly discounted Hall's fear, attributing her discomfort in court primarily to the experience of testifying, and only secondarily to Braxton's abuse. Elliott focused on his belief that Hall had been "less than truthful" in her testimony:

> There would be certain questions that would be asked of her where she would look over at the defendant and make direct eye contact with him prior to her taking a moment or two to respond. That tells me something, based on my years of experience. Was she scared of him? Probably. But again, even weighing that factor into the equation, I'm of the opinion she was less than candid. I think, in my opinion, she lied on some issues under oath.[16]

What the judge refused to see was the relationship between Hall's fear of Braxton and her "less than candid" testimony, because for Elliott (as well as for Marsee) there could only be one victim—the children. Elliott sentenced Hall to thirty years' imprisonment. Like Hall, half of the women convicted of failure to protect in Oklahoma between 2009 and 2018 were abused by the same person who injured the child. In 25 percent of those cases, they received longer sentences than the people who inflicted the harm.[17]

Discretion in Sentencing and Mandatory Minimums

Judges can send such messages because they often have enormous discretion in sentencing. While prosecutorial charging decisions have a significant impact on the sentences ultimately available to a judge, once a person has been convicted, sentencing is usually the province of the judge. Judges can consider a variety of factors, including conduct for which the person was not convicted or was acquitted, the number and type of charges brought by the prosecutor, statements from victims, recommendations from prosecutors and probation or parole officers, and, in some jurisdictions, agreements made pursuant to plea bargains. Judges also bring their own backgrounds, life experiences, perspectives, and biases to sentencing decisions. In a very few states judges can consider whether the person acted in response to chronic or severe intimate partner violence inflicted by the victim.[18]

In cases involving criminalized survivors, judges sometimes struggle to find what they believe to be just sentencing outcomes, recognizing both that the person has been convicted of a crime and that the crime took place in a particular context. In a case involving an eighteen-year-old woman who killed her partner after enduring more than two years of abuse and, on the evening of his death, an attempted rape, Judge Daniel Angiolillo considered the following factors in sentencing: the defendant had no prior criminal record, was doing well in school, and was remorseful; the victim's history of domestic violence against the defendant and evidence of "battered woman's syndrome"; the victim's family's desire for a prison sentence; the testimony of family and community about the victim's good character.[19] Though he could have sentenced her as a juvenile, preventing her from having to go to prison, Angiolillo sentenced her to 1.5 to 4.5 years in state prison. At the end of the day, as San Joaquin County Superior Court judge Bernard Garber recognized in sentencing Jessica Samson, a survivor of intimate partner violence who stabbed her partner, "What is justice? Justice is going to be the best thing I can come up with."[20] Garber sentenced Samson to four years' imprisonment.

Judicial discretion can produce inconsistency in sentencing, with judges "rarely see[ing] eye-to-eye."[21] The evidence on whether women are sentenced more harshly than men for the same crimes is mixed.[22] But criminalized survivors (like Tondalo Hall) convicted of felony murder or accessory liability sometimes receive sentences longer than those who actually commit the crime.[23] Studies also suggest that victims of intimate partner violence receive longer sentences than other women charged with homicide.[24]

Sentencing guidelines can provide judges with discretion to recognize victimization. Sentencing guidelines set a range of appropriate punishment—a span of months of incarceration, for example. But that discretion may be limited. A judge who departs from the guidelines must provide a justification for a sentence above or below the guidelines. That range is typically much higher for certain kinds of crimes. The zeal for harsher punishment in cases involving sex trafficking, for example, led Congress to enact a ten-year to life sentence for some forms of trafficking. With "upward departures" based on the age of the victim and other factors, sentences can be much higher. The guidelines enable prosecutors to lock criminalized survivors of sex trafficking accused of the same offenses as their traffickers into long sentences by charging them with more serious crimes, using the leverage created by those charges to secure plea bargains, and arguing for sentencing enhancements that add additional time to the base sentence.

Mandatory minimum sentences deprive judges of any discretion to show mercy based on mitigating factors. Mandatory minimums require judges to give the same minimum sentence to every person convicted of a particular offense, regardless of the underlying facts. As Representative Mark Green of Tennessee argued in the context of sex offenses, mandatory minimums are necessary to prevent judges from "coddling" those convicted of sex offenses and "ignor[ing] the rights of the law-abiding public."[25] Mandatory minimum sentences increase prosecutorial control over the sentencing process. By charging someone with a crime that carries a mandatory minimum, a prosecutor can deprive a judge of discretion from the outset of a case.[26] Mandatory minimum sentences also give prosecutors leverage by creating incentives for defendants to plead to reduce charges with long mandatory minimums to lesser charges carrying shorter, and possibly discretionary, sentences.[27]

Mandatory minimums prevent judges from factoring a history of abuse or duress into sentencing decisions. In Dixie Shanahan's case, for instance, Iowa's fifty-year mandatory minimum sentence for second-degree murder meant that Smith could not sentence her to probation or suspend her sentence of incarceration, alternatives that he believed just given the lifetime of abuse she had endured. At sentencing, he said, "This matter is a tragedy in every sense. You've suffered abuse, one person is dead and now you're looking at almost a lifetime of jail. None of that is necessary." Smith called the fifty-year sentence legal but wrong.[28] Ashley Barnett had been sexually abused, neglected, physically abused, and commercially sexually exploited by the time she was convicted of conspiracy to commit sex trafficking of a minor and sex trafficking of a minor, crimes in which her role was minimal. At sentencing, Judge Anne C. Conway recognized this history of victimization, stating, "I thought in a lot of ways Ms. Barnett is a victim too, victim of society." Conway sentenced Barnett to the statutory mandatory minimum sentence of ten years' imprisonment, saying that the sentence was longer than she would have otherwise imposed and that "the Court would have considered a sentence below the mandatory minimum had I been free to do so."[29]

Domestic Violence Survivors Justice Act

In 1998, New York passed a statue enabling judges to impose shorter sentences on some criminalized survivors. But that law, known as Jenna's Law, was ineffective—the number of people it applied to was limited, it precluded judges from ordering alternatives to incarceration, and oddly, in some cases, it resulted in longer sentences for criminalized survivors—and rarely used.[30] Hoping to address the problems with Jenna's Law, in 2009, New York's Coalition for Women Prisoners, an alliance led by formerly incarcerated women, began advocating for a law they called the Domestic Violence Survivors Justice Act (DVSJA). The act was designed to provide relief to victims of intimate partner violence sentenced to long terms of incarceration for crimes related to their victimization as a result of New York's stringent mandatory sentencing laws and to prevent others from receiving similarly onerous sentences.

Despite consistent opposition from the New York District Attorneys Association, the New York legislature overwhelmingly passed the law ten years later. Under the DVSJA a sentencing judge can—but is not required to—determine whether a defendant was a victim of domestic violence at the time of the offense and if the abuse was a "significant contributing factor" in the crime. If so, the judge can find that the mandatory sentence is "unduly harsh" and impose a shorter sentence than otherwise required by law. The DVSJA does not apply to aggravated, first-degree, and some forms of second-degree murder.[31] Advocates hoped the law would blur the bright line between victim and offender, showing judges that defendants can be both, and estimated that close to five hundred people could potentially benefit from the DVSJA's initial sentencing provisions each year.

Taylor Partlow was the first person to seek relief under the law. Partlow was convicted of first-degree manslaughter after stabbing her boyfriend to death. Multiple witnesses testified that Partlow's boyfriend had dragged her by the hair, punched her, and strangled her. Witnesses saw Partlow with a black eye immediately after her boyfriend's death. But New York Supreme Court Justice Russell Buscaglia declined to apply the DVSJA at Partlow's sentencing, stating, "The abuse, No. 1, was not substantial abuse and not a significant contributing factor to your behavior." Buscaglia agreed with prosecutors that Partlow had "other options."[32] Buscaglia sentenced Partlow to eight years in prison.[33]

Nikki Addimando was the second person to seek relief under the law. Described as "the freaking poster child for the DVSJA," Addimando presented evidence at trial that her partner, Christopher Grover, had abused her for years.[34] Police, medical professionals, victim services agencies, and child protective services workers in and around Duchess County, New York, all had records documenting Addimando's abuse. Photographs showed Addimando with bruises. Medical records detailed gruesome injuries caused by repeated sexual assaults and, in one instance, being burned with a hot spoon. The defense introduced photographs that had been posted to Pornhub. In those photos, which Addimando testified were taken by Grover, Addimando was "naked, bound, hunched, restrained, and gagged."[35] On the night she shot Grover, Addimando testified, Grover had cleaned his gun, put several bullets in, and showed her a diagram of the brain, noting where he could shoot to kill her or permanently impair her speech and memory. He sexually assaulted her. Then he ordered her to sleep with him on the couch. When she pulled away, the gun fell to the ground. Addimando took the gun and pointed it at Grover, who said, "Here's what you're gonna do. You're gonna give me the gun. I'm gonna kill you. I'm gonna kill myself. And then your kids will have no one."[36] Sure that Grover would kill her, Addimando pulled the trigger.

Prosecutor Chana Krauss attacked Addimando's credibility and character. The prosecutor argued that Addimando's narrative of abuse was inconsistent. Krauss suggested that the many injuries seen in photographs of Addimando could have been "self-inflicted" or the result of "foreplay with any one of her other sexual partners." The prosecution's expert, Dr. Stuart Kirschner, testified that Addimando was "inviting abuse" by sending "condescending" text messages to Grover. The jury found Addimando guilty of second-degree murder, apparently agreeing with Krauss that Addimando "just wasn't a victim."[37] Judge Edward McLoughlin also agreed. Asked to apply the DVSJA in Addimando's case, McLoughlin declined. He found that the evidence of abuse offered by Addimando was "undetermined and inconsistent" and that Addimando could have utilized the "tremendous amount of advice, assistance, support, and opportunities to escape her alleged abusive situation" rather than killing Grover.

The court noted that professionals, friends, and family could have assisted Addimando and mentioned Addimando's failure to confide in law enforcement about her abuse when the opportunity arose. The court held that "the questions and inconsistencies that remain regarding the defendant's alleged abuse and abusers, do not amount to sufficient proof that the alleged abuse was a significant contributing factor in the defendant's act of murder." McLoughlin suggested that Addimando's claims of abuse were not credible because Grover did not fit the profile of a "typical abuser." Although Addimando "may have been abused in her life... the choice she made that night, and the manner in which the murder occurred, outweighs her undetermined abusive history." Even if the court believed Addimando's claims of abuse, McLoughlin found, Addimando "had a myriad of non-lethal options at her disposal" and could have "safely" escaped Grover.[38]

At sentencing, Addimando told the court:

> I wish more than anything this ended another way. If it had, I wouldn't be in this courtroom, but I wouldn't be alive either, and I wanted to live. I wanted this all to stop. I was afraid to stay, afraid to leave, afraid that nobody would believe me, afraid of losing everything. This is why women don't leave. I know that killing is not a solution and staying hurts, but leaving doesn't mean living. So often we end up dead or where I'm standing, alive but still not free.[39]

Notwithstanding her statement, McLoughlin repeated his belief that Addimando had options other than killing Grover, noting that she had independent income, family, a car, a job, and friends and therapists willing to help her. McLoughlin believed that Addimando could have left the home when Grover was at work, sleeping, or when pointing the gun at him. Before sentencing her to nineteen years to life in prison, he called Addimando a "broken person" and concluded: "When you boil it all down, it comes to this, you didn't have to kill him."[40]

Following McLoughlin's decision, New York legislators expressed concern that if the ruling was upheld, "it may become almost insurmountably difficult for most survivors of domestic violence to gain the intended benefit of the Act."[41] A little over a year after she was initially sentenced, an appellate court reduced Addimando's sentence, finding that the substantial evidence that Grover had abused Addimando was a significant contributing factor to the crime and that McLoughlin's suggestion that Addimando could have left the apartment reflected "antiquated impressions of how domestic violence survivors should behave."[42] Prosecutor Robert Tendy disagreed with the appellate court's decision, stating that the court "believed all the defendant's uncorroborated claims about Mr. Grover . . . the one who was really the abused in this case." The court resentenced Addimando to 7.5 years in prison.[43]

It is hard to know what impact a similar law in Illinois, which allows judges to consider how domestic violence might "excuse or justify the defendant's criminal conduct" during sentencing, has had, because those cases are not tracked. But given the stereotypes and misconceptions that judges continue to hold about intimate partner violence, that impact has probably been limited. As attorney Gail Smith lamented, "While we won some change in sentencing laws, we have not won the change in the culture that we would need to have for women not to be punished when they act to save their lives."[44] Nonetheless, other states are considering such laws. For example, 70 percent of Oregon voters expressed support for a law modeled after the DVSJA, enabling judges to consider domestic violence as a mitigating factor in sentencing and allowing judges to impose less stringent sentences than required by Oregon's mandatory minimum sentencing scheme.[45] Oregon's District Attorney's Association opposes the measure, however, arguing that such legislation is unfair to victims of crime and that the legislature should uphold the mandatory minimum sentencing scheme that voters enacted in 1994.[46]

Extreme Sentencing

Between 1984 and 2012 the number of life sentences imposed in the United States increased 469 percent; the number of life-without-parole sentences ("a sentence that does not even exist in most other democracies, because it is considered inhumane") increased almost 400 percent between 1992 and 2012.[47] The Sentencing Project has called life sentences "the lifeblood of mass incarceration."[48] Life sentences are directly responsible for a significant percentage of the growth of the prison population in the United States. One in fifteen incarcerated women is serving a life sentence; one in nine Black women in prison has been sentenced to life. The number of women serving life and life-without-parole sentences has increased dramatically in recent years, growing 20 and 43 percent respectively between 2008 and 2020. During the same period the number of women imprisoned for violence increased by 2 percent.[49]

Life sentences, especially life-without-parole sentences, function as a "death penalty in slow motion" or "death by incarceration."[50] As Cynthia Cupe, incarcerated at the Edna Mahan Correctional Facility in New Jersey, has written: "You are alive but you are no longer allowed to live, at least not in the terms most would consider living life. You are alive but what kind of quality of life under oppressive circumstance can anyone have."[51] Significant numbers of criminalized survivors are sentenced to life. Of forty-two criminalized survivors convicted of murder in a California study, all but two received life sentences. Six were sentenced to life without parole. Thirty-four were sentenced to indeterminate terms ranging from seven to fifteen years to life; all had served at least twenty-five years at the time the study was conducted.[52]

In theory, life sentences are meant for the most dangerous, least redeemable people. But as one incarcerated woman noted, "Lifers are in some sense stereotypes. Not everybody is a cold-blooded murder [*sic*]. Some people just got caught up and a lot of women are in here behind a man."[53] That is particularly true for those sentenced to life in prison for felony murder or for being accessories, like Eraina Pretty and Rudeara Bailey. Judges use life sentences to make examples of criminalized women. Nancy Seaman was convicted of killing her abusive husband by a jury who did not see her as "a meek, howling woman waiting for the next beating." But the sentencing judge believed she had been abused and instructed her to use her life sentence to help others: "The lesson you have to teach is to get help and get out."[54]

Being sentenced to life is a uniquely disorienting experience. Criminalized survivors who receive life sentences have to "adjust to being incarcerated, and being incarcerated for the rest of their lives."[55] Some women believe that death would be preferable to life in prison. Twenty-eight years into her life sentence for felony murder, Eraina Pretty wrote to then-governor Robert Ehrlich to ask that if he would not grant her clemency, he consider killing her by lethal injection. She wrote: "I can no longer endure the suffering, mainly of slow death." Some criminalized survivors are sentenced to death. Of the fifty-two women on death row as of May 2020, 81 percent are survivors of physical and/or sexual abuse; 21 percent are incarcerated for killing their intimate partners. At least four women were abused by their victims; an additional twelve women were abused by a co-defendant.[56]

Lisa Montgomery was abused by everyone she should have been able to trust: her mother, her stepfather, her husband. When Montgomery was a child, her mother and stepfather beat her and held her under cold water in the shower, duct-taped her mouth closed if she talked out of turn, and left her strapped in her highchair for hours if she failed to finish her food. Montgomery's stepfather began raping her when she was eleven. Her mother knew about the rapes but didn't report them and blamed Montgomery for the abuse. The stepfather slammed Montgomery's head against a concrete floor while raping her and allowed other men to rape her, sometimes as barter for services. When Montgomery told her cousin, a sheriff's deputy, that she had been gang raped by her stepfather and his friends, her cousin drove her home and said nothing. No teacher, no counselor, no law enforcement officer ever intervened to protect her. Montgomery's mother pressured her into marrying her stepbrother, who beat and raped her, when she was eighteen. Montgomery had four children, then was sterilized against her will. She suffered from permanent brain damage because of her mother's alcohol abuse during her pregnancy. Over time, Montgomery developed bipolar disorder with psychotic features, complex post-traumatic stress disorder, and dissociative disorder directly linked to her experiences of trauma.

By the time that Montgomery killed Bobbie Jo Stinnet, she had endured every form of abuse imaginable. But the crime was horrible—Montgomery cut Stinnett's abdomen open and removed her eight-month-old fetus, then tried to pass the child off as her own. The picture prosecutors drew of Montgomery as a "bad mother"—one who didn't cook or clean and whose home was dirty—combined with the defense's failure to introduce evidence of her trauma or connect it to the crime, led to the imposition of the death penalty.[57] Despite her mental illness (and despite Supreme Court precedent prohibiting the execution of people who are mentally ill), the United States executed Lisa Montgomery on January 13, 2021.

INCARCERATION

Most criminal convictions—around 70 percent—result in some prison time, despite the lack of evidence that incarceration prevents future offending.[58] Judges sentence people to incarceration in part because few alternatives to incarceration exist once a person has been convicted. Incarceration falls disproportionately on Black people, particularly Black women, who are almost twice as likely as white women to be sentenced to prison.[59] Black women made up 45 percent of the prison population at the Maryland Correctional Institution for Women in July 2018 but accounted for only 30 percent of Maryland's population. Lesbian and bisexual women are also disproportionately represented in prisons. They are three times as likely as heterosexual women to be incarcerated and account for as much as 42 percent of prison populations, while only making up about 3 percent of the general population.[60]

American prisons have been described as the "harshest and scariest places in the democratic world."[61] That's by design: former Massachusetts governor William Weld once said that prison should be a "tour through the circles of hell."[62] Recollections of their first moments in prison are strikingly similar across the narratives of incarcerated people: coming in shackled, being photographed and fingerprinted, having to strip and being invasively searched, showering while correctional officers watch, receiving institutional clothes and bedding, and finally, losing your name and becoming a number. One woman described the process as "an assembly line. Each person had a job to do. You go in there, you weren't a person anymore, you weren't human anymore, they could care less."[63] Another saw it as "transformation"—"an agency taking away your sense of self in the dehumanizing process that comes with incarceration."[64]

Some women describe the experience as becoming the property of the state—so much so, they claim, that if they are caught giving or getting tattoos, they are sanctioned for "destruction of state property."[65] For transgender women housed in men's facilities, incarceration can also mean being stripped of all vestiges of femininity. Paula Rae Witherspoon remembered: "Then I was forced to strip off my clothes, bra, panties, and stand nude in front of them while I changed clothes. This generated a lot of 'cat calls,' whistles, and more lewd comments. The floor Sgt got so mad he pulled me out, emptied the barber shop out, and ordered the barber to 'skin him like and [*sic*] onion and cut those DAMN NAILS.'"[66]

Newly incarcerated people are bombarded with the noises and smells of prison. They have no privacy. They are anxious about the environment and about following the prison's rules. They are grappling with what it means to lose their freedom. And they are beginning to confront the other losses that incarceration brings: loss of identity, personal space and effects, privacy, day-to-day family life, their health, and ultimately, people they love to death.[67] Coming to prison is traumatic for almost everyone. Incarceration itself is a form of violence. As Angela Y. Davis and Cassandra Shaylor have written, "Prisons are places within which violence occurs on a routine and constant basis; the functioning of the prison depends upon it."[68] Over the past thirty years, sociologists Meredith Huey Dye and Ronald Aday argue, prisons have only become more punitive, a result of what they call the "penal harm movement."[69]

Incarceration is that much more traumatic for people who have experienced abuse. Being incarcerated can trigger post-traumatic stress disorder and cause mental health problems. Criminalized survivors frequently recognize the tactics used to maintain order and control within the prison. After being sent to solitary confinement when a correctional officer felt insulted, organizer and formerly incarcerated survivor Monica Cosby realized "what was happening to me inside (the prison) was what happens in violent relationships."[70] The irony of incarceration is that at the point at which victimization claims are acknowledged the least, the potential for increased trauma is the greatest.

Conditions of Confinement

The conditions of confinement in most prisons make it clear how little incarcerated people are valued. People are crammed into facilities designed to house a fraction of the population incarcerated within. lois landis, incarcerated in Wisconsin, described how seven hundred women were housed in a unit designed for eighty-five. Storage closets were turned into cells and "women are packed together like mares in a hot, stifling cement stable."[71] Overcrowding taxes resources and the physical plant of the facility and increases the potential for conflict. Incarcerated people live in facilities with limited light and plentiful mold, where temperatures are often at extremes. Marcia Powell died in an Arizona prison of organ failure after being left in an open cage outdoors for four hours.[72] Jane Dorotik, formerly incarcerated in California, and Kwaneta Harris, imprisoned in Texas, both endured stifling summer heat in prisons with no air conditioning.[73] Harris described how incarcerated people share their cells with birds, bats, rodents, roaches, and snakes; at night "we place earplugs in our ears to prevent baby roaches from entering."[74] At Florida's Lowell Correctional Institution, incarcerated people reported worms crawling out of bathroom sinks and toilets. Inspectors found black larvae in the sinks and drains full of bugs. Incarcerated people working in the kitchen at Lowell "tied the bottom of their pants legs or tucked them in their boots to keep the mice from crawling up their legs."[75] Prisons are noisy: "raised voices, clanging metal doors, loud announcements, alarms, barked orders."[76] Those noises can trigger post-traumatic reactions.

Food in prison is both inadequate and inedible. The portions are small, overly processed, high in cholesterol, fat, and sodium, low in fiber, fruits, and vegetables, and often full of chemicals.[77] In some prisons no fresh meals are provided during the weekends. In her diary, Carrie Roache, incarcerated at Scott Correctional Facility in Michigan, described feeling very sick for several weeks, then realized, "I've been hungry, that's all. I got some extra food and when you eat and you've been so hungry for so many days you can tell the difference."[78] Other basic human needs are rationed as well. Roache noted in her diary: "I have no blanket. I have no coat. I wake up and can't sleep at night because I'm cold. I have no walking shoes. I have only two sets of clothes. I have to wear dirty clothing."[79] In Texas, Harris explained, "Everyone receives 5 tampons, 6 rolls of T.P., 1 pack of pads monthly. Every 4-6 months we receive 1 toothpaste and 1 toothbrush. That's all you get if you're indigent without outside support."[80] In Michigan, Glenda Gale asked a correctional officer for toilet paper; the officer responded, "What for?"[81]

There is no privacy in prison. Incarcerated survivors are observed while showering, using the toilet, and eating. Correctional officers can come into their living spaces at any time and "rifle through, touch, search, handle, discard, and break" people's possessions.[82] Conditions are worse for those who are being closely monitored. After Lisa Montgomery's death warrant was issued, she was transferred to "a cold, single cell with constant bright lights." Male guards watched her use the toilet. Her belongings and clothing, including her bra, underwear, and socks, were taken from her. She was given a "loose fitting gown with Velcro straps" known as a suicide smock to wear, and later, after being told to "be a good girl, now," a pair of mesh underwear, a crayon, a piece of paper, and socks.[83]

Conditions are also worse during lockdowns. At various points during the COVID-19 pandemic, incarcerated people in many states have been confined to their cells for up to twenty-three hours per day, allowed out only to shower or, if lucky, use the phone (but not both). All activity in the prison—education, religious services, other programming, employment, visitation—stopped. Food quality declined even further, as kitchens and commissaries closed: "'One peanut butter and jelly sandwich with sour macaroni salad' for dinner in Pennsylvania, a 'hard hot dog weenie' in Texas, 'expired milk' in Kansas."[84] Women quarantined in the Dallas County Jail went more than a week without getting a change of clothing. On day ten the women "decided to take off the crusty, stained uniforms they had been wearing for a week and a half without a wash. Some women wore just their bras and underwear; others were naked." The women were given fresh uniforms thirteen days after they were quarantined.[85]

When conflict occurs, incarcerated people cannot simply walk away. "The 12-foot chain-link fence, topped by razor ribbon and concertina wire, that surrounds the perimeter of the facility" is a constant reminder that no matter what happens in the prison, criminalized survivors cannot leave.[86]

Treatment by Correctional Officers

Correctional officers have almost complete control over the lives of incarcerated people. "You got to eat when they say eat; you got to go to bed when they say go to bed."[87] Studies have repeatedly found that correctional officers describe women as problematic prisoners: "emotional, manipulative, impulsive, and resistant to taking orders."[88] Correctional officers respond to incarcerated women differently than they do men, punishing them more frequently and more severely for lesser offenses. Women are ticketed for "disrespect," "reckless eye-balling," "derogatory comments," "disruption," and "insolence." A Scrabble board becomes "contraband."[89] Women of color and lesbians, bisexual, and trans women are punished most severely.[90] Punishment for infractions includes the loss of good time credits (which can mean longer sentences), loss of privileges, and restriction to cells or placement in solitary confinement. In 2015 women at Logan Correctional Center in Illinois lost the equivalent of ninety-three years in good time credits as a result of discipline. Between 2016 and 2018 loss of good time credits resulted in an additional 1,483 years served.[91]

Abusive, humiliating, and degrading treatment by correctional officers retraumatizes incarcerated survivors. Such treatment is widespread. In New York's Bedford Hills women's prison, for example, 74 percent of criminalized survivors had witnessed physical, sexual, or verbal abuse by staff; 53 percent had experienced such abuse; and 51 percent had witnessed or experienced racist behavior by staff.[92] Esther, incarcerated in Michigan, said correctional officers "scream at you like you're a dog and they're training you."[93] A Department of Justice investigation of Edna Mahan found that correctional officers regularly referred to incarcerated women as "'bitches,' 'hoes,' 'assholes,' 'dyke,' 'stripper,' 'faggot-assed bitch,' 'motherfuckers,' and 'whores'" and made comments about the women's appearances, sexual preferences, and sexual histories.[94] While supervising women working in the fields in Texas, Harris reported, correctional officers refer to the women by their convictions: "'Dope fiends hoe this row,' 'Baby killers carry the cabbage bags.'"[95] This kind of verbal abuse forces criminalized survivors to relive their trauma. As Melly explained, "That [disrespectful speech] is a rape of my spirit. You come into my cell and terrorize me. You rape me every single day [with the demeaning attitude.]"[96] A woman incarcerated at Bedford Hills said, "Some officers like to abuse their power as an office[r]. In some cases, it reminds us of our abusers and how we got here."[97]

Physical violence is routine in prison as well. Some of that violence is state-sanctioned. Joe Vanderford, a trans man at Minnesota's Shakopee Correctional Facility for women, described how an officer "emptied a whole can of mace in the chow hall on a woman he said stole milk" without regard to the impact on the people around her.[98] Other times, that violence far exceeds the amount of force correctional officers are permitted to use. Correctional officers reportedly broke the neck of Cheryl Weimar, a woman incarcerated at Lowell. Weimar was experiencing psychological distress and needed medical care. Instead, correctional officers "slammed" her to the ground and "dragged" her to a wheelchair "with her head bouncing along the ground."[99] In January 2021 correctional officers at Edna Mahan left one incarcerated woman with a broken eye socket and a trans woman in a wheelchair after being kicked and punched repeatedly.[100] The trans woman, Rae Rollins, was hospitalized with a concussion caused by correctional officers pushing her into a wall a month after she shared her story about correctional officers' abuse.[101] While twenty-two correctional officers and nine supervisors were suspended after the incident, Rollins's mother feared that "the ones who are left are going to retaliate.... I am definitely afraid for her life."[102] Rollins was later transferred, first to a men's prison, then to a prison out of state.[103]

Sexual abuse of incarcerated women by correctional officers is also rampant. Again, some of that violence is state-sanctioned. Incarcerated people regularly endure invasive strip searches. Described as "sexual assault by the state," such searches usually involve bending over and spreading a person's buttocks so that correctional officers can look for contraband.[104] These violations are only condoned, Angela Y. Davis has argued, because the people being searched have been convicted of crimes: "Society assumes that this kind of assault is a normal and routine aspect of women's imprisonment and is self-justified by the mere fact of imprisonment. Society assumes that this is what happens when a woman goes to prison."[105]

Strip searches are regularly conducted after incarcerated women have visits. During the early part of the COVID-19 pandemic, that policy was applied to remote visits in some facilities, despite the impossibility of passing contraband during such visits. As Tracy McCarter recounted: "At Riker's I had to submit to a FULL BODY strip search w/ cavity search just to get on a COMPUTER to see my family BEFORE & AFTER each televisit."[106] In a women's prison in Michigan, strip searches were conducted "in an unmistakably gendered manner."[107] After visits women were required to sit naked in a chair, pull their knees to their chests, and spread their genitals. Menstruating did not exempt incarcerated women from this practice. One incarcerated woman, Louise, "told my family not to come anymore. I have been raped too many times that [the chair] was horrific for me."[108] Incarcerated women report guards groping rather than searching them and inserting objects into their vaginas during searches.[109]

At Lincoln Correctional Center in Illinois, correctional officers engaged in a "training exercise" forced a group of incarcerated women to strip naked and stand facing the wall of the prison's gymnasium, shoulder to shoulder, for more than an hour, then publicly strip-searched the women while male correctional officers, trainees, and civilians watched. The women were told to raise their breasts, lift their hair, cough and squat, and spread open their buttocks and vaginas. Women who were menstruating were forced to remove their tampons. After the search they were not given anything to stanch the blood and "were left to bleed on themselves for several hours, soaking through their clothes and getting blood on their legs and feet."[110] During the search correctional officers screamed obscenities at the women, insulted them, and threatened to put them in segregation. Correctional officers called the women "dirty bitches" and told them, "You all are fucking disgusting," "I can't believe women smell like this," and "No man wants to be with you because you smell like death."[111] The entire exercise lasted five to seven hours. The women were not permitted to sit down or use the restroom during that time. Some women had seizures. Others "soiled themselves."[112] Willette Benford was one of the women searched. "Nearly 10 years later, my wrists and hands still swell as a result" of being handcuffed behind her back for close to six hours. The prison conducted a second, nearly identical training exercise almost two years later, involving some of the same women, including Benford. "The shame of those days stayed with me for years."[113]

Some correctional officers use strip searches as punishment. "When one official was mad, I suddenly could not squat low enough or cough deep enough to please her. I had to do it over and over again. All naked, of course. It's all about control and intimidation."[114] Strip searches are demeaning for all incarcerated people but are particularly traumatic for criminalized survivors. Laura Whitehorn described being "forced to stand still and allow men to touch my body in ways that would have automatically provoked me to fight back if I had been outside of prison."[115] A criminalized survivor described strip searches as the "downgradingest, hurting-est," depriving her of dignity and self-worth. "I lost something there."[116]

Correctional officers make transgender women vulnerable to sexual assault by placing them in cells where they are likely to be raped. As Kim Love explained,

> The COs use the transgendered prisoners to keep the violence rate down.... If you look like a female, they'll put you in a cell.... They told me that's gonna be your husband, and that's where you're going to be and you're going to love him. And I did my time with him.... Without the sexual tension being brought down, the prisoners would probably overturn that place.... They use us.[117]

Love only left the cell when her cellmate "walked me, like a dog." She could talk to other trans women but was not permitted to make eye contact with anyone else. Correctional officers reinforced this control over Love, telling her—under her cellmate's orders—that she was not permitted to talk to other people while her cellmate was at work. In other contexts this would be called trafficking. As Love observed, "Correctional officer, they're basi-cally pimpin'." [118] If these women try to defend themselves, they are often charged with assault and sent to solitary confinement. One study found that 59 percent of trans women incarcerated in men's prisons in Califor-nia had been sexually abused.[119] Trans men are also vulnerable to sexual abuse. Pinky Shear, formerly incarcerated in Georgia, heard a prison offi-cial tell a trans man "he got raped cause he needed to be reminded that he was 'born with a pussy...that's what pussies are for.' "[120]

Other forms of sexual abuse are illegal but common. Incarcerated peo-ple have a right under the Eighth Amendment to be protected from sexual abuse. As the US Court of Appeals for the Eleventh Circuit explained in *Sconiers v. Lockhart*, "Some things are never acceptable, no matter the circumstances. Sexual abuse is one."[121] The Prison Rape Elimination Act requires prisons to implement standards to prevent the sexual abuse of incarcerated people and makes eligibility for federal funds contingent upon the adoption of and adherence to those standards. Nonetheless, recent Department of Justice investigations of Edna Mahan, Lowell, and the Julia Tutwiler Prison in Alabama found evidence of "severe and preva-lent" sexual abuse ranging from oral, anal, and vaginal rapes, to coerced sex in exchange for contraband, to groping, rubbing up against, and watching incarcerated people while they used the toilet and showered.[122]

Incarcerated women have filed lawsuit after lawsuit documenting pervasive sexual abuse by correctional officers.[123] In 2020 fourteen women sued the United States for sexual abuse committed by correctional officers at Federal Correctional Complex Coleman, alleging that they were "coerced and threatened...lured into private offices or remote sheds with no surveillance cameras, or stalked relentlessly by corrections officers until they had no choice but to submit." Victims of sexual assault were told to take birth control and given morning-after pills.[124] At least three officers admitted to engaging in "sexual conduct" with women incarcerated at Coleman.[125] Five correctional officers from Chittenden Regional Correctional Facility in Burlington, Vermont, have been charged with sexual misconduct since 2011.[126] The California Department of Corrections and Rehabilitation fired at least six male correctional officers who sexually abused incarcerated women between 2014 and 2018.[127]

A 2012 report from the Bureau of Justice Statistics found that 4 percent of heterosexual, 8 percent of lesbian, and 8 percent of bisexual incarcerated women had been sexually victimized by correctional officers.[128] Nearly all of the women surveyed at the Central California Women's Facility reported sexual abuse or harassment.[129] That abuse is not limited to correctional officers. In 2019 nine women filed suit against John Thomas Dunn, a therapist who worked at Missouri's Chillicothe Correctional Center, alleging that he sexually assaulted them. When one of the women reported Dunn's behavior to authorities, she was asked, "Why would he go after you when there's young, beautiful women on this camp?"[130]

While abuse is widespread, redress is limited. The first step for many incarcerated people is the prison grievance process. That process, however, is widely seen as ineffective and unlikely to result in meaningful protection. Correctional officers refuse to provide those seeking to grieve with the appropriate forms, deny receiving forms, or "lose" them. Even if they can make claims, incarcerated people often lack proof beyond their assertions, and officials are unlikely to find them more credible than the correctional officers they accuse.[131] The reporting process can be as traumatic as the sexual assault. At Edna Mahan, for example, a person reporting sexual assault is taken to the medical unit in handcuffs and shackles, scanned for contraband, strip-searched, and placed in solitary confinement until they are interviewed about the incident. They are likely to lose their housing and their jobs.[132] Given these obstacles, few women—as few as 8 percent—formally report being assaulted.[133] Nationally only about 12 percent of all claims of sexual victimization by correctional staff are substantiated.[134] Black women are less likely than white women to have their reports of sexual violence by correctional officers investigated. When they are investigated, those investigations are less likely to result in substantiated claims, suggesting that "Black women's reports, particularly, may not be taken as seriously for the decision to investigate and the process of investigation."[135]

If they are arrested, few officers are held criminally accountable for sexually assaulting incarcerated people. When cases go to trial, the inherent suspicion of the credibility of incarcerated people undermines their claims. While civil claims are possible under the Eighth Amendment, incarcerated people must prove that they faced a substantial risk of serious harm, that prison officials knew that a substantial risk of harm existed, and that officials were "deliberately indifferent" to that harm. Often prison officials either lack the requisite knowledge or are immune from suit. In *Tangreti v. Bachman*, for example, Cara Tangreti was repeatedly sexually assaulted by three correctional officers, all of whom were fired and criminally prosecuted. Tangreti sued prison officials, alleging that they were deliberately indifferent to the substantial risk that she would be sexually abused. Although the court conceded that the sexual abuse Tangreti experienced was severe, it found that state officials (including the commissioner of corrections, the state Prison Rape Elimination Act (PREA) director, and the prison's warden) were not subjectively aware of, and therefore not deliberately indifferent to, her abuse.[136]

Raising allegations of sexual assault makes incarcerated people vulnerable to retaliation. Correctional officers can make the lives of those who report sexual abuse "a living hell"—"tearing up" people's rooms, arbitrarily creating restrictions, denying visitation, and sending those who report to solitary confinement.[137] During investigations, incarcerated women are pressured to recant and their motivations for reporting are questioned. Even while investigators from the Department of Justice were on site at Lowell, officers warned incarcerated women of the negative consequences of disclosing sexual abuse.[138] An incarcerated woman told the Department of Justice team that she had been repeatedly sexually harassed by a sergeant at Lowell but feared reporting because it could mean losing visits with her son. The next day the team learned that she had been placed in solitary confinement. The woman's mother called the prison; she said that "she feared for her daughter's life because the sergeant made threats against her daughter when he found out her daughter talked to Department personnel."[139]

Stacy Barker, incarcerated in Michigan, repeatedly filed grievances and lawsuits against the state: for educational parity, for visitation rights, and about the sexual assault of incarcerated women. In response, "she was placed in solitary confinement, chained down naked, threatened, raped, denied visits with her daughter, and subjected to humiliating extra vaginal and anal searches by guards."[140] Tracy Nadirah Shaw was raped by a correctional officer for four years but did not report the rapes; her rapist threatened to harm her family if she did. Only seven years later, after that correctional officer sought a position as the manager of her unit, did she report. She was transferred to a prison six hours away from her family and told that her claim was not only unfounded but frivolous.[141] Pinky Shear has written about being raped by a correctional officer in Georgia, who told her, "If you say anything, you will never see your kids again. I will kill you. We know how to make accidents happen here."[142]

Abuse by correctional staff retraumatizes criminalized survivors. That abuse is impossible to avoid. "Unlike women on the outside," criminologist Laura Bex Lempert has written, "there is no place that imprisoned women can go to escape predatory, unprofessional officers. They are literally and figuratively locked in to interactions with officers who can and sometimes do assault them—physically, verbally, and emotionally."[143] The failure to provide redress sends incarcerated survivors a message about their worth: "It's just something that happened to an already abused woman. Done. I didn't/don't matter."[144]

Solitary Confinement

Disobeying a correctional officer's orders, fighting, and even minor violations of prison rules like "singing during count, singing in the lunchroom, putting someone's bag lunch on the floor, braiding someone's hair, walking backwards on the sidewalk in the courtyard, having talcum powder in their shoes, loitering, passing food, and ... eating someone's piece of cake in the lunchroom when it was offered to them" can land a person in solitary confinement.[145] Solitary confinement has been described as "inhumane" and "a form of torture." Faith Haines, incarcerated at Edna Mahan, called it "a place ... designed to break us emotionally and physically."[146]

Nonetheless, American prisons regularly use solitary confinement, even for those who have prior histories of victimization. Also known as restricted housing, administrative segregation, or protective custody, solitary confinement is generally understood to involve locking an incarcerated person in a small cell for as many as twenty-three hours per day, with extremely limited contact with other individuals or the outside environment. People held in solitary are often restricted from engaging in programming or exercise, lack access to reading and writing materials, and have little privacy, particularly in institutions where solitary confinement cells are monitored by video. In the poem "Barbwire," AjeeDaPoet described solitary as

Skin itch
Overheated
Freezing
Immune system sick
Same small space
Eat, piss, and take a shit
Nowhere in this does the spirit of humanity fit
The "bing" where life in the mental no longer sings
The "hole" was solely designed to destroy the human soul

Where prison guards become control gods
No way to escape
Women are beat, belittled and raped
More than any other
Solitary confinement is hell's dungeon for people of color...[147]

Between 18 and 20 percent of incarcerated people spend time in solitary confinement during a given year.[148] Pregnant people, people with mental illness, transgender women, LGB individuals, and victims of sexual assault by correctional officers are all likely to spend time in solitary. Women are often sent to solitary confinement for minor infractions. Black women are sent to solitary confinement at disproportionate rates.[149]

Prolonged stays in solitary confinement are especially destructive. Recognizing the harm caused by extended segregation, in 2015 the United Nations adopted the "Nelson Mandela Rules," international human rights norms on the use of solitary confinement. The rules prohibit holding people in solitary for more than fifteen days. The United States has failed to follow those rules. In 2016, the US Department of Justice recommended that incarcerated people be held in solitary confinement for no longer than ninety days and only for repeat serious offenses.[150] But Kwaneta Harris has been in solitary confinement in a Texas prison continuously since 2015. Harris shot and killed her abusive boyfriend. While in prison, she was accused of forging a judge's signature to decrease her sentence and placed in segregation pending a hearing on that accusation. As of April 2021, Harris had been in segregation for almost two thousand days. She is not the longest resident. Harris reported that another woman in her unit had been there for twenty-six years as of 2021. Harris has called her experience "forever punishment."[151]

Spending time in solitary confinement exacerbates trauma and pre-existing mental health conditions. Solitary is used to retaliate against incarcerated people who report abuse or mistreatment and makes people vulnerable to abuse by correctional officers. Because people in solitary are usually kept apart from the rest of the prison, officers can use excessive force, restraints, chemical agents, and sexually and emotionally harm incarcerated people without being seen. An observation aide at Women's Huron Valley Correctional Facility in Michigan described seeing a woman with a history of mental illness being held in solitary, naked, with her hands cuffed behind her back, ankles cuffed with handcuffs, the cuffs attached to each other with a chain, forcing her into a backbend position. When the aide asked how long the woman would be kept in that position, she was told "2 hours or longer if she doesn't learn to behave."[152]

Solitary is used as "protective custody" for transgender women in men's prisons. Most transgender people in the United States are held in prisons consistent with the sex they were assigned at birth. Because transgender individuals are at high risk of sexual and other forms of abuse in prisons, however, prison officials place them in segregation for their own "protection." The potential for abuse of trans individuals by correctional officers in such settings is high. And in segregation, transgender people may be deprived of essential medical care and access to other prison services, like law libraries, that would help them secure the right to such care.[153] Daisy Meadows, a trans woman who has spent substantial time in solitary, says that she "would rather be raped every day than be in the hole."[154]

Prison Health Care

Prison is hard on people physically and mentally, particularly for those with health issues related to past victimization. Experiencing violence is linked to a variety of chronic health problems, including gastrointestinal conditions, chronic pelvic and back pain, depression, sleeping and eating disorders, and stress and anxiety disorders. The chronic stress associated with intimate partner violence may even decrease the length of telomeres in the cells of women who experience such abuse, accelerating the aging process at the cellular level and contributing to poor health outcomes.[155] Incarceration decreases a person's life expectancy.[156] Prison health care does little to alleviate those problems.

Simply getting access to health care in prison is a substantial challenge. The process of asking to be seen by medical staff for regular care can be onerous. If a correctional officer gives a person an appointment at sick call, it might still be hours before the person is seen. It can take months to see a doctor, even for people with chronic conditions. In an emergency it can be difficult to convince correctional staff that the need for care is real. Correctional officers accuse incarcerated people of "malingering" and responses range from indifference to threats. Some correctional systems require copays for medical care. Even a five-dollar copay can be prohibitive for an incarcerated person. Carrie Roache, for example, was forced to decide between paying five dollars to see a doctor, who might not do anything for her condition, and using that same five dollars for aspirin and food.[157] Medications are sometimes delayed, and pain medication is almost always denied, even for those healing from surgery or fighting life-threatening illnesses, out of suspicion that a person is a "drug seeker."[158]

For trans individuals, getting access to gender-affirming health care is challenging at best. In most prison systems trans individuals must have a diagnosis of gender dysphoria before they can access hormones and other needed care. "In this process," writes Jennifer Gann, imprisoned at Salinas Valley State Prison, "you may run into roadblocks and obstacles, such as an unsympathetic psychologist or psychiatrist."[159] Victoria Drain found herself "in an intense battle with administration in order to be allowed to receive my hormone therapy. Because I am forced to file paperwork and grievances in order to see the proper doctors to begin this process, I am oftentimes disrespected by staff and labeled by officers as a 'problem.' In turn, they do everything in their power to make life as difficult as possible, as if it wasn't bad enough already."[160]

As a result of the poor health care provided by many prisons, even relatively minor conditions can become life-threatening. Kelly Savage-Rodriguez was incarcerated in a California prison when her tonsils became infected. Savage-Rodriguez repeatedly asked to have the problem addressed, but correctional officials ignored her until she became very ill. "They were willing to let me die" from tonsillitis, Savage-Rodriguez said. Upon her return from surgery, Savage-Rodriguez was strip-searched and made to cough and squat, even though doing so threatened to pull out her stitches and cause significant harm. The failure to provide routine care in a timely manner can have disastrous consequences. Connie Hanes described how she watched as a woman with asthma asked to see a doctor. Correctional officers wouldn't give her a pass. The woman had a heart attack. "She died before they could even get her to the clinic."[161]

Life-threatening but potentially treatable conditions become de facto death sentences in prison. As Geneva Phillips, incarcerated in Oklahoma, reported:

> [People] have been turned away, filed sick call after sick call only to be told "It's nothing" or "There's nothing wrong with you." These women have then gone on just to later find out that they have Stage 4 brain cancer (denied medical parole, died in prison), Stage 4 colon cancer (medical parole granted four hours before death, died at hospital), and a twenty-five-year-old who collapsed, went into a coma and died at the hospital (granted medical parole the same day she died).[162]

At the Federal Correctional Institution in Aliceville, Alabama, three women died of medical neglect between 2018 and 2020. Hazel McGary waited for eight months to see a cardiologist. She experienced fatigue, was confined to a wheelchair, and regularly fell out of bed. On March 18, 2019, McGary's roommate found her on the floor and called staff, who took her away. McGary died that day of a blood clot that started in her leg and traveled to her heart.[163]

The COVID-19 pandemic made the limitations of prison health care abundantly clear. Prisons were overwhelmed with infected people unable to socially distance; they were denied masks and other protective equipment. People with health conditions that made them more susceptible to COVID worried about how contracting the virus would affect them. Lulu Benson-Seay wrote to her sister from Bedford Hills on March 20, 2020, asking for help. "I cannot afford to get this virus. It may kill me." On April 28, 2020, Benson-Seay died of COVID-19.[164]

When she began to have trouble breathing, Schwanika Patterson asked to see a doctor. Correctional officers "called at least seventeen times," but no one answered. Patterson was later taken to see a nurse, given a breathing treatment for asthma, and returned to her unit at Bedford Hills. She was not tested for COVID until two days later, then moved to a different room. Patterson said, "I felt like I was dying, and nobody was helping me."[165] After Demetria Mason tested positive, she was moved to "a large, open dormitory filled with approximately sixty-five others. It smelled of mildew and bologna. . . . One woman was vomiting blood, and 'the staff just told her it's part of the virus.'"[166] Many incarcerated people, like Benson-Seay, chose not to disclose that they were experiencing COVID symptoms for fear of where they would be sent.

Mental health care in prisons is similarly limited. Substantial numbers of incarcerated people live with mental illness. A study in the Oklahoma Department of Corrections found that between 62 and 69 percent of incarcerated women had major psychiatric issues, including mood disorders, psychotic disorders, and post-traumatic stress disorder.[167] As Amber Rose Howard, the statewide co-coordinator for Californians United for a Responsible Budget, noted: "If you don't already have struggles with mental wellness, you're definitely going to get some mental health issues when you're locked in a cage, when you're shackled at your wrists and at your ankles, when you're made to pull your pants down and cough and squat in front of several sheriffs at a time."[168]

Prison health care providers often fail to treat these conditions in any meaningful way. Disability Rights Maryland documented how Wexford Health Sources, a private contractor providing health care in Maryland's prisons, failed to provide treatment plans, psychosocial interventions, or cognitive therapy for individuals with mental health issues at the Maryland Correctional Institution for Women (MCI-W). The one thing Wexford did provide was psychotropic medications. Those medications were administered in the infirmary, a setting tantamount to segregation or solitary confinement, despite clear best practice guidance from the Society of Correctional Physicians, among others, that the use of segregation poses a serious risk of harm to individuals with mental illness. Some prisons also use tools like five-point restraints (straps that hold down a person's arms, legs, and midsection) and chemical sedatives to control incarcerated people with mental illness, even when such practices would be illegal if used in psychiatric hospitals.[169]

Incarcerated people, particularly incarcerated women, attempt and complete suicide at disproportionately high rates. Past physical and sexual victimization predicts the risk of suicidality.[170] Prison mental health care providers do not recognize or appropriately treat at-risk people. Suicidal people are often placed in observation cells to monitor their behavior. Such cells feature "suicide-proof design, social isolation, the removal of personal property and constant observation by officers." Although intended to be therapeutic, the use of observation cells has been linked to diminished mental health for those caged in them.[171] At Camille Griffin Graham Correctional Institution in South Carolina, women who sought mental health services because they were suicidal were punished to dissuade them from asking for help again. Mental health staff at the prison ordered that the women be fed "nutraloaf" (a variety of foods blended and baked into a loaf), have their mattresses removed from their cells, and be denied feminine hygiene products, forcing them to bleed on themselves. Suicidal women told the therapist who exposed the practices that they hid their symptoms rather than seek staff help.[172]

At MCI-W a young woman in segregation attempted suicide by tying a sheet to a vent in her cell after getting no response to requests for help. Less than six weeks later, Emily Butler hung herself using a sheet tied to the vent in her segregation cell after asking unsuccessfully to talk with a mental health professional. Butler's history of depression, bipolar disorder, and post-traumatic stress disorder were known to the prison. She was not screened for mental health issues before being placed in solitary confinement. "Ms. Butler was declared dead around 11:00 a.m., but her body lay on the floor in the middle of the segregation unit for hours.... Emily Butler was only 28 years old when she died."[173]

Reproductive health care is similarly lacking in prisons. Around 4 percent of people admitted to state prisons are pregnant when they arrive.[174] Despite the substantial number of pregnant people in prisons, few prisons have policies addressing the care of pregnant people. When policies do exist, they are often disregarded or violated.[175] Pregnant people are sometimes confined to infirmaries to receive care, in conditions that approximate solitary confinement. In some states a stay in the infirmary precludes an incarcerated person from accessing the commissary, which keeps pregnant people from being able to supplement the meager rations they receive.[176] Pregnant people in some states are shackled during transport as well as during and after labor. Shackling during childbirth is extremely traumatic and may trigger post-traumatic stress reactions in people who have histories of victimization. In extreme cases pregnant people are denied care while in labor, forcing them to deliver without medical assistance. An incarcerated woman at the Taycheedah Correctional Institute in Wisconsin was placed in segregation after she refused to have labor induced. Several days later, the woman repeatedly informed the medical staff that she was in labor but was told she was not "in immediate need of medical attention." The woman delivered her child by herself in the segregation unit. Correctional staff said she had "pushed that baby out on purpose, just to get out of segregation."[177]

As criminalized survivors age, their health care needs become more acute. A 2014 study of incarcerated women found that incarcerated women aged fifty and over had, on average, four chronic medical conditions, histories of victimization, and high rates of mental health challenges and took five medications daily.[178] Head injuries associated with intimate partner violence may lead to earlier cognitive decline. Past injuries and the passage of time can result in impaired mobility for older incarcerated people, who struggle to move around prisons. "There's people who have walkers and they live up on a tier. They have to go up the stairs. There was one woman would throw her walker up and then go up the stairs."[179]

The Eighth Amendment requires that the government provide incarcerated people with adequate health care. The failure to do so is considered cruel and unusual punishment. Confronted with evidence of substandard medical care, states have agreed (after being sued) to improve the quality of care incarcerated people receive. But those agreements can be hollow promises. In 2012 incarcerated people at Fluvanna Correctional Center for Women in Virginia filed suit alleging that the private health care companies contracting with the state at the facility had failed "to provide necessary and appropriate medical care" and had provided "deficient medical care." The suit alleged that people without medical training were assessing whether people needed medical appointments, requests for emergency care were ignored, people regularly received incorrect or no medication, and prison treatment providers failed to provide the care ordered by doctors outside the prison.[180] In 2016 the parties settled, agreeing to revised policies for medical care and improvements to the host of problems identified in the lawsuit. As of 2021, the independent monitors charged with overseeing the changes report that "medical care remains spotty" and incarcerated people continue to be denied needed medical treatment.[181]

Prison Is Gendered Violence

Prison replicates the gender-based violence that criminalized survivors experienced before being incarcerated. Because prison is a total control institution, incarcerated people are deprived of the ability to make even the most basic choices in their lives: what and when to eat, when to shower, what to wear, how to spend the day. Incarcerated people have to ask permission to turn lights off. They have to ask for more toilet paper. They are isolated from family and friends. Transgender people are denied access to gender-affirming clothing, accessories, and medical care; wearing clothing or grooming oneself in a manner consistent with one's gender identity can lead to discipline.[182] Although the criminal legal system ignores the victimization claims of incarcerated people, "these are women who are victims as surely as anyone is a victim. And now they are twice victims."[183]

To be fair, some victims of violence describe incarceration in neutral, even positive terms. Prison can be a "safe place, a temporary refuge from their violence-filled lives."[184] Some prefer incarceration to the "prison" of violent relationships. As one woman explained, "I would rather do life than to be in the house with that man."[185] Adalynn said, "The day I lost my freedom is the day I gained my freedom.... I've been in this facility for five years and have done more in those five years with myself than I did in that twenty-five years of marriage."[186] Incarceration can give people access to resources that they were unable to secure in the community, providing them with educational opportunities and spurring sobriety and personal growth.

But the parallels between prison and past victimization make it difficult for victims of gender-based violence to heal. As Diane explained, "From the walls that surround you in gray to the hard bed you sleep on, to the blue uniforms that you wear, to the food that you eat, it is all a form of demeaning you socially, personally because they want to break you down. But there's no building you up. You've already been broken, so now they break you down further."[187] When accosted by correctional officials, searched, restrained, or put into segregation, victims of gender-based violence default to the responses they have used in the past: fighting back, fleeing, or shutting down, all of which could result in discipline.[188] For Marcia Bunney, "refusal to tolerate abuse by prison officials was a central component in my agenda of personal healing and growth." But her skill in using her mechanism for resisting—the prison grievance system—led to her transfer to another prison. Bunney wrote,

> It is difficult for a woman who has suffered abuse to achieve a meaningful degree of insight and healing in the prison environment. Conditions within the institution continually reinvoke memories of violence and oppression, often with devastating results. Unlike other incarcerated battered women who have come forward to reveal their impressions of prison, I do not feel safer here because "the abuse has stopped." *It has not stopped.* It has shifted shape and paced itself differently, but it is as insidious and pervasive in prison as ever it was in the world I knew outside these fences.[189]

Or, as one incarcerated woman asked, "How can I be a rape 'survivor' if I have to continue to go through the motions over and over?"[190]

Immigration Detention

Gender-based violence is driving migration to the United States.[191] As they attempt to make their way to the United States, people are frequently physically and sexually abused.[192] By the time they reach the United States, significant numbers of people seeking entry have experienced some form of gender-based trauma. When they are detained for violations of immigration law, undocumented survivors of violence experience the worst facets of incarceration. Undocumented people who enter or attempt to enter the United States in violation of immigration laws are incarcerated in detention facilities that are the same as, as bad as, or in some cases, worse than American prisons.

About half of the undocumented people detained in the United States are housed in prisons and jails. Detained people in these facilities are treated just like incarcerated people: dressed in prison uniforms; handcuffed, shackled, and chained; given meager and inedible food; placed in solitary confinement and locked down for up to twenty-three hours a day. The Department of Homeland Security's Inspector General found that guards failed "to grasp the difference between running a prison and an immigration detention center."[193] Indeed, many of the guards are former correctional officers. The detention facilities maintained by US Customs and Border Protection are not much better. Undocumented people call them *hieleras* (ice boxes) and *perreras* (dog kennels).[194] Detainees have been forced to clean the facilities where they are being held without pay or face punishment including solitary confinement—a practice that constitutes human trafficking.[195]

Detained people lack access to adequate medical care. A 2019 study found that of fifty-two deaths in immigration detention facilities since 2010, twenty-three involved substandard medical care.[196] Women detained at the Karnes County Residential Center in Texas and the Baker County Detention Center in Florida reported that they were not receiving treatment for cancer. Suzanne Moore's breast cancer recurred after the Baker County facility failed to provide her with the tamoxifen she needed to keep it in remission.[197] Reproductive care is severely limited, and miscarriages are common. Despite the requests of pregnant women for help when they began bleeding, "immigration authorities ignored them for hours, leaving them to bleed and miscarry in their cells, and only bringing them to a hospital after it was too late."[198] The women were told they were "lying" or "being dramatic."[199]

The one surgery readily available seems to be unwanted and unauthorized sterilizations. Nurse Dawn Wooten called the Irwin County Detention Center in Georgia "an experimental concentration camp" and a gynecologist working there "the uterus collector," noting that between October and December 2019 five women had been sterilized without a clear understanding of what was being done to them and without their consent. At least nineteen women would come forward with similar complaints.[200]

Sexual violence is common in immigration detention facilities, and women, LGB, and TGNC people are at disproportionate risk. Just as in other prisons, guards in detention facilities prey upon detained people. Over a twenty-six-month period between 2014 and 2016, detained people lodged 1,106 reports of sexual abuse. Only 2.4 percent were investigated.[201] Guards forcibly rape and sexually assault detained individuals and coerce them into sex with promises to provide basic human needs, like clean clothing, soap, and money, or to release them from detention.[202] Using jails and prisons to house detainees contributes to their victimization. Detained people in these facilities are subjected to strip searches, for example, because "it's a jail, so we have to strip search. Perhaps it's not appropriate for these women, but we have to follow the rules."[203] Those who report or complain about abuse face retaliation, including threats, further violence, placement in solitary confinement, and immediate deportation, notwithstanding the strength of their claims for asylum or other immigration relief.[204]

Trans individuals are uniquely vulnerable to abuse in detention facilities. Trans women often flee their home countries after being subjected to gender-based violence—rape, sexual assault, and harassment based on gender identity. Monserrath López left Honduras after being beaten and forced to perform oral sex on four men, after which one of the men cut her hair off and told her how he would torture her and kill her: "We're going to cut you up.... Even your family won't be able to find you."[205] López requested asylum and was sent to a men's detention facility in Texas, where she was sexually and verbally assaulted, denied access to hormone replacement therapy, and threatened with solitary confinement. Even in units specifically meant to provide care to transgender individuals, Human Rights Watch found that trans women detained in ICE facilities were misgendered; violently strip-searched by male guards; denied access to routine, emergency, and gender-affirming medical services, including hormone replacement therapy; verbally and sexually abused; and placed in solitary because of their gender presentation or because they reported abuse.[206]

Detention retraumatizes victims of violence—not just as a result of physical and sexual assault but also because of the tactics used to control those housed in detention facilities: "restricting mobility; keeping women and children in cold *hieleras*; keeping lights on at all hours; disrupting sleep with bed checks; insults and humiliation; withholding information; ever-changing rules and expectations; restricting access to support; isolating women from one another, from their own children, and from the community; intimidation; and threats."[207]

Detention has been linked to self-harm, suicide, depression, and anxiety. Detainees report persistent fear, difficulty sleeping, hypervigilance, and feelings of shame and guilt, in part linked to the perception that they are incarcerated. As one woman explained, "I ran away, fearing for my life, and here I am in jail. What did I do wrong?"[208]

SPECIAL PUNISHMENT

In lieu of or in addition to incarceration, criminalized survivors convicted of particular crimes receive punishment specific to those crimes. For criminalized survivors of sex trafficking, that punishment is registration as a sex offender; for those who fight back against their intimate partners, offender intervention; and for undocumented criminalized survivors, deportation. Each of these punishments reinscribes the people affected as perpetrators of crime, further negating their histories of victimization.

Registration as a Sex Offender

LeeAnn Adkins was twenty-five when she was convicted of sex trafficking a minor. Adkins, a victim of commercial sexual exploitation herself, felt protective of the younger women she met engaging in survival sex work. She wanted to help. She took these women "under her wing... showing them how to make money and stay safe while doing it." Adkins "let another person into an apartment to shower and clean up because she was high, homeless and had nothing. I introduced her to one date, who paid her $40.00. I held the money for her while she took the date and gave it to her after." For the rest of her life, as a result of that transaction, Adkins will be labeled a "sex offender."[209]

Sex offender registries monitor and track people convicted of sexual offenses after their release into communities. Such registries have a long history: California enacted a law in 1947 requiring those convicted of sex offenses to register with local police.[210] Washington State passed the first law requiring people convicted of sexual offenses to register with the state in 1990. Four years later a provision of the Violent Crime Control and Law Enforcement Act, the Jacob Wetterling Crimes Against Children and Sexually Violent Offender Registration Act, mandated that each state establish a registry. In 1996 the federal Megan's Law added a public notification component to registries, requiring that states provide online access to registries and make information available to the public, but allowed states to determine to whom, under what circumstances, and about which people notification was required.

By 1999 every state, the District of Columbia, and some US territories and tribal jurisdictions had enacted sex offender registry notification laws. In 2006, Congress passed the Adam Walsh Act (also known as SORNA, the Sex Offender Registration and Notification Act), which created new sex offenses, increased penalties for sexual offenses, established a federal registry, set minimum standards for notification, and required that states include children as young as fourteen on their registries. And as a result of 2016's International Megan's Law, the passports of those on the registry are required to include a "unique identifier." As of 2020, approximately nine hundred thousand people had registered with state, federal, and territorial registries.[211]

Sex offender registry notification laws generally include registry and notification requirements, residential restrictions, provisions about monitoring, and sanctions for failing to comply with the law. Once in the community, a person convicted of a sex offense is required to register pursuant to state and federal law, providing any information required by law. People on the registry must share work and school addresses, physical descriptions, social media and email information, and descriptions of their vehicles with law enforcement. That information must be updated at least annually, and often more frequently, in addition to whenever it changes. Federal law requires that law enforcement notify the public about persons convicted of sex offenses living in the area. Notification is often posted online and includes at least the person's name, photograph, physical description, age, and information about the conviction. Some states also include home addresses, vehicles, and other information. In some places those on the registry are required to reimburse the state for the costs of notification—for example, ads in local newspapers or cards sent to everyone within a set distance of the person's home.[212]

The notification requirements "are interwoven with a web of restrictions. Depending on where he lives, a person with a sex-related offense may be prohibited from working as a retail clerk, fishing in a public park, volunteering at a polling place, putting up Halloween decorations, or... living with his own children."[213] The most common restrictions involve housing. Most states delineate where those convicted of sex offenses can live, creating buffer zones around "schools, parks, daycare centers, school bus stops, or other places commonly frequented by children."[214] Those buffer zones range from 500 to 2500 feet. The larger the buffer zone, the fewer places available for those convicted of sex offenses to live. In some communities the buffer zones are so comprehensive that there are few, if any, legal residences for those convicted of sex offenses. In 2014 Milwaukee's statute forbidding those convicted of sex offenses from living within two thousand feet of a park, daycare center, or school left them with only fifty-five legally available places to live in the city.[215]

Such laws render significant numbers of people on the registry houseless. In *Doe v. Miami-Dade County*, four men alleged that Miami-Dade's prohibition of those convicted of sex offenses from residing within twenty-five hundred feet of a school excluded "nearly all available and affordable housing in the County."[216] Registrants living in Miami-Dade were forced to live in makeshift outdoor campsites, moving around as the county shut the sites down using various laws, including those prohibiting public camping. Communities have also used zoning to exclude people on the registry. In Los Angeles, for example, rezoning undeveloped land as "pocket parks" prevented people on the registry from living in nearby communities.[217] Even if they can find housing, residency restrictions mean that people may be forced to live in locations far from available employment. Some state laws place restrictions not only on residency but also on working or "loitering" near schools and other places where children might be. Such restrictions preclude registrants from taking jobs that require them to travel within or through restricted areas, attending family gatherings, seeking medical care, and engaging in other activities for fear that they might violate the law.[218]

Other restrictions severely limit the day-to-day lives of people on the registry. Restrictions and outright bans on cell phone, computer, and internet use, for example, make it impossible for those on the registry to engage in activities ranging from shopping to communicating with loved ones to seeking and keeping employment. Several states require people convicted of sex offenses to wear monitors that allow law enforcement to track their whereabouts; Georgia recently struck down a law requiring that such people wear monitors for the rest of their lives.[219] Former New York governor Andrew Cuomo repeatedly endorsed banning those convicted of sex offenses from public transportation. New York has several especially intrusive requirements, requiring those on the registry to agree that they will not have pets, "cross-dress or participate in sexual fetishes," or have "medical procedures meant to enhance ... sexual functioning."[220] People on the registry in New York are required to notify their parole officers when they begin intimate relationships and to notify the other party—in front of the parole officer—of their criminal history.[221] Restrictions are also imposed by private actors. Some social media platforms ban people on the registry; people on the registry have been forced to sue to get access. A man in Milwaukee sued Wisconsin's Children's Hospital after they refused him access to his seriously ill son because of his registration.[222]

Registration, notification, and restrictions might be warranted if there was evidence that they contributed to public safety in some way. But there is no such evidence. Registries were originally justified by contentions that rates of recidivism were particularly high for those convicted of sex offenses. The data do not support those contentions. In fact, recidivism rates for those convicted of sex offenses are fairly low.[223] And the restrictions commonly found in SORN laws do little to prevent violence. Residency restrictions, for example, do not decrease recidivism but are correlated with higher unemployment, housing instability, and the inability to access services—all of which contribute to reoffending.[224] Registries fail to prevent violence, law professor Allegra McLeod has argued, because they fail to reach the settings where the greatest harm is done: "families, schools, churches, prisons, and the military."[225] Registries impose needless costs upon both the individuals registered and society because they target those who are least likely to reoffend.

Registries are effective in one sense—they are uniquely proficient at shaming and endlessly punishing those convicted of sex offenses. Registration and notification laws serve as a kind of condemnation: "Such punishment is best understood not as conveying blame or resentment for what an offender has done, but rather as conveying contempt for who he is."[226] Journalist Judith Levine and gender studies professor Erica R. Meiners have asserted that the laws create "a permanent class of criminal pariahs.... So radical is the marginalization of the large and varied category of persons labeled 'sex offenders' that their existence has been called 'social death.'"[227] Because of the reach of online information, those on the registry are "no longer simply shamed in the public square of one's own community; they are shamed in the eyes of their country, their state, their nation—and in our global economy, the world."[228] Once registration information is placed online, that information is there forever—for employers, landlords, community members, and anyone else to see.

A provision of Alabama's registry and notification law stamped the words "CRIMINAL SEX OFFENDER" in red on registrants' driver's licenses. Every time a person on the registry showed that license as identification, they were forced to reveal their status. A man who challenged the law, whose conviction was by then twenty-five years old, explained, "I have never felt so embarrassed and ashamed in all of my life. I would not wish showing this [branded identification] on my worst enemy."[229] A federal court struck down that provision as unconstitutional but upheld other parts of the registration and notification law. Being on the registry makes people vulnerable to violence. In South Carolina a murder suspect explained that he used the sex offender registry to target victims, telling them "I'm here to kill you because you're a child molester."[230] That violence and harassment impacts those convicted of sex offenses, their families, and even their neighborhoods. Proximity to a person convicted of a sex offense can decrease their neighbors' property values.[231]

The US Supreme Court has refused to recognize that registry and notification laws constitute punishment. In *Smith v. Doe* the Court held that Alaska's registration and notification act was nonpunitive in its intent and effect, distinguishing its provisions both from incarceration and from the shame-based punishments used in colonial America. The Court explained that while the dissemination of accurate information about a person's criminal history might "cause adverse consequences for the convicted defendant, running from mild personal embarrassment to social ostracism," it did not constitute punishment.[232] But eight state supreme courts—including Alaska's—and one federal circuit court have disagreed, finding the provisions of state registration and notification laws so onerous that they are punishment beyond the sentences originally imposed.[233]

Registries were created because, as Senator Charles Schumer opined, "sexual offenders are different.... No matter what we do, the minute they get back on the street, many of them resume their hunt for victims, beginning a restless and unrelenting prowl for children, innocent children to molest, abuse and in the worst cases, to kill."[234] Even if evidence supported that claim, registration and notification laws are casting a much wider net, capturing a variety of people whose convictions have been labeled sex offenses—including survivors of commercial sexual exploitation like LeeAnn Adkins. After serving seven years in federal prison, Adkins described registering as "the most degrading and embarrassing part of my sentence.... This label I have been given has so negatively impacted my life that some days it's hard to even get out of my bed."

Three days after she left prison, Adkins called 911 on herself. Her daughter had set up Facebook and email accounts for her, which she was required to report to her parole officer. The officer had made it clear that the failure to report this information would result in a felony charge. Adkins repeatedly called the office in a panic and when she could not reach anyone, called 911. The 911 operator assured her that weekends did not count and that she could report on Monday. "Living in constant fear of making a mistake," Adkins has written, "or forgetting to report a change made it impossible to sleep for the first 3 or 4 weeks home. Because of the fear, I still do not really do anything online." At Halloween, Adkins was told that she could not decorate her home or pass out candy; at Christmas, that she could not have a nativity scene in her yard. Her parole officer warned her against going to her daughter's softball games. Although Adkins was not prohibited from doing so, the officer worried that if other parents knew about her status, she might not be safe.[235]

People are usually placed on the registry without an individualized assessment of the risk they pose to the community. Crystal Snyder is an exception. Snyder was convicted in federal court of conspiracy to engage in sex trafficking and required to register in New York. Snyder challenged her level-two risk designation, arguing that her involvement in the crime did not warrant such a designation. The court agreed, finding that Snyder had been trafficked as a minor, and

> while she later took on some "management" responsibilities by "training" other girls, answering phones, and making appointments, at the same time, she continued to be exploited by that industry.... There was no evidence or indication that the defendant recruited the identified victim, or any victims, or that she engaged in any acts or conduct to coerce the victim, or any victims, to engage in prostitution.[236]

Recognizing her status as a victim and her minimal role in the conspiracy, the court declared Snyder a level-one. Instead of having to register for life (with a possibility of petitioning for relief after thirty years), Snyder was required to register for twenty years.

Being on the registry makes criminalized survivors vulnerable to abuse and exploitation. Their names and identifying information are publicly available to everyone—including the people who trafficked them. They are constantly under surveillance, allowing law enforcement to search their contacts and communications without a warrant or subpoena. Parole officers can demand access to information that can be used to prosecute other cases, making people involuntary witnesses. Any mistake they make, however minor, can land them back in prison.[237]

Approximately two hundred thousand people have been forced to register because of crimes they committed when they were children.[238] Adolescents involved in survival sex often use the "buddy system" to stay safe. But working with a minor can mean being prosecuted for a sex offense and, if convicted, being placed on the registry.[239] And once adolescents are forced to register, they become more vulnerable to being trafficked. As Emma McLean-Riggs, a staff attorney with the Colorado Juvenile Defender Center, has explained, children convicted of sex offenses are often removed from their homes. Without a place to live or income, they routinely become romantically involved with people who traffic them.

Despite the lack of evidence that registries make society safer, and the evidence that in fact they may make communities less safe, the use of registries is spreading to other types of convictions. Five states have created "violent offender" registries; others have methamphetamine, drunken driving, and career offender registries. Few of them impose requirements as onerous as sex offender registries, but they are nonetheless intrusive, requiring people to update addresses and posting their information online. States are also considering creating domestic violence offender registries.[240] Such registries would expose criminalized survivors of intimate partner violence to the same vulnerabilities currently faced by criminalized survivors of trafficking.

Offender Intervention Programs

Most criminal cases involving intimate partner violence are prosecuted as misdemeanors. Offender intervention programming is frequently used to resolve those cases. In many jurisdictions people accused of intimate partner violence are given the opportunity to enter prosecution diversion programs and/or to avoid incarceration by agreeing to enter intervention programs. For incarcerated people, participation in an offender intervention program may be a condition of probation or parole. Most offender intervention programs rely on the Duluth model, developed through the Duluth Abuse Intervention Project and based on the theory that people use intimate partner violence to assert power and control over their intimate partners. The research on offender intervention programs shows that treatment has a modest, if any, impact on recidivist violence.[241]

Standard offender intervention programs fail to capture the unique dynamics present when a criminalized survivor uses violence against a partner, making these programs both "potentially revictimizing and traumatizing" and "ineffective."[242] Standards for intervention programs rely on a model developed for treating heterosexual men. Women, LGB, and TGNC people are regularly placed in groups designed for men who use violence and in groups with men who use violence against their partners. Programs that focus on the specific incident that led to intervention and fail to consider the entire context of the relationship miss how criminalized survivors' victimization histories contribute to the incident for which they have been referred. Providers "struggle with the ethical implications of providing court-ordered services to women who are often abused themselves" and "may be unaware of how to provide gender-informed intervention services to these women."[243] In states that have designed programs specifically for women who use force, many simply add a section on victimization and alternatives to violence and conflict resolution to existing curricula for men. The best of these programs recognize that they are being asked to treat victims of violence and orient themselves accordingly. Criminalized survivors assigned to such programs report getting some benefits from participation.[244]

But even the best programs can pose significant risks to criminalized survivors. Siting treatment programs within the criminal legal system leaves victims vulnerable to further punishment if they fail to finish treatment. Knowing this, their partners or former partners may find ways to interfere with their successful completion of the program. The partners of women in one program refused to give them money for transportation; left them without childcare; threatened to call their probation officers with allegations of abuse if they didn't buy or sell drugs for the partners; and did call probation officers to allege abuse after self-inflicting wounds. Ex-partners had their new girlfriends call probation officers to make false claims and successfully used participation in the program to argue that a woman should lose custody of her child.[245]

Deportation

Undocumented criminalized survivors complete one punishment only to face another. Undocumented survivors convicted of certain crimes, including crimes involving intimate partner violence and trafficking, can be subject to deportation. Amreya Shefa, for example, was convicted of manslaughter and sentenced to five years in prison after she stabbed her husband as he attempted to rape her. In 2018, Shefa was taken directly from prison to Minnesota's Kandiyohi County Jail and placed in immigration detention. Released from detention in late 2020, as of 2021, Shefa continued to fight her deportation. Ny Nourn, placed in detention after her parole from a California prison in 2017, would have been deported but for Governor Gavin Newsome's decision to grant her a pardon.

It is impossible to know how many survivors have been deported because of criminal convictions, but the consequences for those survivors can be dire. Nourn, for example, would have been deported to Cambodia, a place where she has never lived (she was born in a Thai refugee camp) and has no support. Shefa would be deported to Ethiopia, where retaliatory violence against women who kill their husbands is a real possibility and death threats have sent her family into hiding.[246] Gabby Solano was twenty-six when her abusive boyfriend and his friends forced her to drive them away from a car theft. While at a stoplight, one of her boyfriend's friends killed a pedestrian. Her boyfriend demanded that she conceal the crime, and afraid of what he would do if she told anyone, she did. Solano was charged with felony murder and was not permitted to introduce expert testimony on domestic violence at trial. She was convicted and sentenced to life without parole. After twenty-three years of incarceration, Solano was released and immediately moved to detention. Facing the prospect of being held indefinitely, Solano chose instead deportation to Mexico, a place she left as a child and where she has no family or community.

COLLATERAL CONSEQUENCES AS PUNISHMENT

Punishment does not end when a person is released from prison. As formerly incarcerated activist Susan Burton wrote in her memoir, "A criminal history [is] like a credit card with interest—so what if you paid off the balance, the interest still kept accruing. And accruing and accruing and accruing."[247] Criminalized survivors endure the collateral consequences of convictions in every facet of life. Some of those consequences are mandated. Those convicted of crimes are barred from voting in many jurisdictions, for example. Other consequences are permitted: employers and landlords are allowed to discriminate against those with criminal convictions. And still others are facilitated; imposing consequences is made easier by the existence of online databases containing criminal records.[248] The consequences are both formal—almost fifty thousand state and federal statutes and regulations impose collateral consequences on those convicted of crimes—and informal.

Criminalization creates significant barriers to finding and keeping employment. Some jobs, including childcare and the armed services, are completely barred for those with felony convictions. In Illinois people convicted of sex offenses cannot get teaching licenses. In Tennessee people convicted of felonies or misdemeanors involving "moral turpitude" cannot become beauticians. Other banned professions include "accountant, police officer, architect, barber, roofer, plumber, interior designer, land surveyor, and farm labor contractor."[249] Some convictions make attaining licensure and certification in fields like law, social work, and medicine much more difficult. Even when a conviction is not technically a bar to work, it can be an impediment nonetheless. In states that have passed "ban-the-box" laws, which prohibit employers from asking about a person's criminal history on an initial job application, employers are still able to look into a person's criminal history before offering the person employment. Whether that happens at the beginning of the process or the end, Vanda explained, "as soon as they see that prison or ex-felon, you're out. They're not even gonna look at your application. So you don't stand a chance, actually."[250]

When Kim DaDou Brown was released from prison in New York after seventeen years of incarceration for killing her boyfriend in self-defense, she had two bachelor's degrees. She took a job delivering pizza, the only work that she could find.[251] Even after years of employment, a criminal record can be used to justify termination of employment, as in Angel's case: "Angel had done everything 'right' following her convictions: she left her trafficker, focused on her education and career, and started a family. Yet years later, when leadership at the data-entry company Angel worked at changed hands, her past convictions resurfaced and caused her to lose a job at which she thrived."[252] According to a 2016 survey, 73 percent of trafficking victims reported losing or being denied employment because of their criminal records.[253] Those burdens disproportionately fall on formerly incarcerated Black women, whose unemployment rates are higher than any other group.[254]

A criminal conviction makes it difficult to find and keep housing as well. Public and federally subsidized housing are unavailable to some people convicted of crimes. Although stable housing is essential for those leaving prison, finding landlords willing to rent to people with criminal histories is hard. Landlords frequently conduct online background checks of potential renters, revealing their criminal records. As a result of this legal discrimination, formerly incarcerated people are almost ten times as likely to be unhoused, with Black women again disproportionately disadvantaged.[255] Among respondents to a 2016 survey, 58 percent of trafficking survivors faced barriers to accessing housing because of their criminal histories.[256] Those convicted of crimes are ineligible for public benefits, including Temporary Assistance to Needy Families and the Supplemental Nutrition Assistance Program.

Health care providers also discriminate against formerly incarcerated people. In a survey of formerly incarcerated New Yorkers, 40 percent reported being discriminated against because of their criminal record.[257] "[A] criminal record," sociologist Reuben Jonathan Miller has written, "separates people accused of a crime from the life-giving institutions of a free society."[258] In some cases there are legal avenues to remove these barriers, but formerly incarcerated people may need access to lawyers to pursue them. The inability to meet basic human needs—income, housing, food, health care—can drive formerly incarcerated people to commit crimes just to survive.

Easy access to online information about formerly incarcerated people exacerbates these problems. Some of that data is free. Some is inaccurate. Renata Singleton, held as a material witness, has been listed as a suspect in a crime on a publicly available website. Reams of data about people with criminal records—including birth dates, home addresses, and physical characteristics—are available to "anyone with thirty dollars, a credit card, and enough curiosity to look."[259] Data about juvenile, sealed, vacated, and expunged cases (which should not be publicly accessible) sometimes appear online as well. Such data make it possible to exclude those with criminal convictions from a variety of online spaces; for example, Tinder, Match, and other online dating apps ban those with felony convictions from using their services.[260] Criminologist Sarah Lageson has described public access to this trove of data as "digital punishment."[261] That punishment extends well beyond a person's period of incarceration. And it can make formerly incarcerated people vulnerable to abuse. Kiara, a criminalized survivor of trafficking, described how employers and landlords used information about her prostitution arrests to attempt to coerce her to have sex with them.[262]

Federal courts in the United States are split on the question of whether the collateral consequences that attach after conviction constitute punishment that should be considered in determining a sentence. But US District Court Judge Frederic Block made his position clear in *United States v. Nesbeth*. "There is a broad range of collateral consequences that serve no useful function other than to further punish criminal defendants after they have completed their court-imposed sentences."[263] Those collateral consequences ensure that people convicted of crimes continue to suffer, regardless of how they came to commit those crimes in the first instance and regardless of whether the justifications for punishment support such suffering. And those consequences fall disproportionately on women of color. As one woman explained, she "worked twice as hard before, [but] now I have to work four times as hard because [after incarceration] I had an *extra* stigma attached to me."[264]

Dixie Shanahan was released from prison in 2019. Since her release, she has earned her bachelor's degree, found employment, reconnected with her children, and become a grandmother. She is thriving despite years of abuse, first at the hands of Scott Shanahan and later in prison. Shanahan is lucky. She was released before serving all of the time required by the fifty-year mandatory minimum statute, because Governor Tom Vilsack commuted her sentence. Once survivors of gender-based violence are convicted, their hopes for early release (particularly for those serving long sentences) rest with judges, parole boards, governors, and presidents, via resentencing, parole, commutation, and pardon.

5 Reconsideration and Clemency

By the fourth and fifth times she went up for parole, Eraina Pretty understood what was expected of her. She expressed her genuine remorse for the death of her former employer—a man who sexually assaulted her—though she had not killed him. She downplayed the abuse she had experienced at the hands of the man who did. She described the many things she had accomplished since coming to prison at age eighteen, including completing her bachelor's and master's degrees, mentoring other incarcerated women, and working steadily at a variety of jobs within the prison. And although the Maryland Parole Commission twice recommended that Pretty be paroled, Maryland's governors denied her release both times. It was not until the onset of COVID-19 that she was released—not on parole but under court rules enabling judges to reconsider long sentences for elderly incarcerated people in light of the pandemic. After forty-three years of incarceration, at age sixty-one, Eraina Pretty was free. Criminalized survivors like Pretty have limited options for release from incarceration, and Pretty used them all: second-look sentencing, parole, and clemency.

COURT-BASED REMEDIES

Once trial judges impose sentences, the ability to reconsider those sentences years later is limited. But second-look legislation specifically permits reconsideration of long sentences in particular circumstances. Most versions of second-look legislation require incarcerated people to petition courts for resentencing; in some states prosecutors can make that request. Judges are required to consider a range of factors, including the nature of the crime, the person's growth while incarcerated, whether the person accepts accountability, and the safety of the victim and the community, before resentencing. In jurisdictions where second look is prosecutor-driven, just as in jurisdictions where individuals make the request, judges are under no obligation to grant reduced sentences.

Second-look legislation comes with a variety of restrictions. The laws have largely been focused on those sentenced as juveniles. In Florida, for example, people sentenced to long terms of imprisonment before age eighteen can ask the court to review their sentences after periods of time ranging from fifteen to twenty-five years, depending on the crime.[1] In the District of Columbia, however, the second-look law applies to "emerging adults": those convicted before the age of twenty-five.[2] In addition, second-look legislation may not be retroactive. Oregon's second-look law only applies to juveniles sentenced after January 1, 2020.[3]

A few states have enacted second-look legislation specifically for victims of gender-based violence. In 2001 and 2004, California amended its habeas corpus law to permit survivors of domestic violence to seek reversal or modification of a judgment, a new trial, reduction of charges, or a reduction of sentence in cases where evidence of violence was not introduced at trial if that evidence would have led to a different outcome. As of 2011, nineteen survivors of domestic violence had been released through the California Habeas Project.[4] In 2015, Illinois passed a law allowing survivors of domestic violence whose felony convictions were related to that violence to seek resentencing if no evidence of the violence was presented at sentencing, they were unaware that introducing evidence of domestic violence might be relevant to sentencing, and the evidence is so conclusive that it would likely change the sentence the trial court imposed.[5]

Similarly, recognizing "the harsh effects of lengthy, mandatory sentences for victims of domestic violence where that violence was a significant contributing factor to their criminal behavior," in 2019 New York enacted the Domestic Violence Survivors Justice Act (DVSJA), described in chapter 3.[6] In addition to allowing for consideration of domestic violence at sentencing, the DVSJA enables incarcerated people sentenced to a minimum of eight years to ask for resentencing if they were victims of domestic violence at the time of the offense, that violence was a significant contributing factor to the crime, and the sentence imposed is unduly harsh given the nature and circumstances of the crime, as well as the history, character, and condition of the petitioner. New York's Coalition for Women Prisoners estimated that approximately 360 incarcerated people were eligible for resentencing under the DVSJA.[7]

Some victims of gender-based violence have benefited from second-look sentencing. Keiana Aldrich, whose case was described in chapter 2, was sexually abused by prison staff and retaliated against when she filed complaints. She attempted suicide several times, including once while locked down because of the COVID-19 pandemic. After that attempt her lawyer approached the Sacramento County District Attorney's office and asked them to reconsider Aldrich's sentence. Prosecutors agreed to join the request for reconsideration, based on Aldrich's "upbringing, the circumstances of the crime as well as her rehabilitation efforts while incarcerated." Despite opposition from the man who attempted to buy her, a judge agreed that continued incarceration was unwarranted and released Aldrich after eight years.[8]

In May 2021, Betty Jean Broaden was released from prison in Louisiana after serving almost forty years. Broaden shot a man in self-defense when he attempted to rape her in her home. At trial, "prosecutors attacked her for failing to run out of her own house," although the law did not require Broaden to flee. New Orleans DA Jason Williams created a civil rights division after taking office in January 2021; that division filed a joint motion with Broaden's attorneys asking that her conviction be overturned. Williams explained, "Even a very conservative prosecutor, if they look at all of these facts, would not have charged her but for the sexism that permeated the initial investigation. . . . You don't see many stand your ground claims that are as clear as this one." Prosecutors also noted that racism likely affected law enforcement's reaction to Broaden's initial self-defense claim.[9]

At sixteen Patrice Smith was sentenced to twenty-five years to life for the murder of Robert Robinson. Fifteen-year-old Smith met seventy-one-year-old Robinson in 1998. Robinson took Smith out to eat and bought her presents—a winter coat, boots—then began giving Smith money to have sex with him and with his friends. Robinson asked Smith to strip for him and to bring him other girls. Robinson threatened to tell Smith's father about their "relationship" knowing that Smith's father had warned her not to spend time with Robinson. On the night he was killed, Robinson demanded that Smith have sex with him. When Smith declined, Robinson told Smith she would have to repay him for everything he had given her, slapped her, and threatened to shoot her. Robinson and Smith began physically fighting and fell to the floor. Thinking that he was going to retrieve his gun and shoot her, Smith strangled Robinson with a telephone cord.[10]

In 2020, Patrice Smith asked Judge Sheila A. Ditullio, who imposed the original twenty-five to life sentence, to resentence her. Prosecutor John Flynn, a supporter of the DVSJA, disagreed with its application in Smith's case, arguing that Robinson was killed during a robbery planned long before the night of the crime. "This law should not help out Patrice Smith, bottom line," Flynn stated.[11] Ditullio disagreed. In her ruling on Smith's application, Ditullio noted that at the time of Smith's original trial in 1999, the court did not understand "how profoundly the trauma of sexual abuse and exploitation affects a victim's behavior and choices," providing "a new lens through which to view and assess a defendant's criminal conduct." What was presented as a "sexual relationship" in 1999 was now understood as rape. Smith was not a consensual participant or a prostitute but a sexually exploited child and a victim of sex trafficking.

Ditullio stated: "The 'full picture' here is one of a sixteen-year-old female who had been raped, abused, and coerced by a man fifty-five years her senior, who had exploited and coerced her through escalating offers of money and gifts for sex and by threatening to expose the relationship to her father." But for "the illicit and abusive relationship Robinson cultivated, [Smith] would not have gone to his home and reacted the way she did." Ditullio noted that "the DVSJA was never intended to hold a defendant blameless for her actions or excuse her criminal conduct. . . . Patrice Smith stands convicted of robbery and murder. Nothing in this decision changes that." Nonetheless, "our system also allows for mercy—mercy where the defendant herself is a victim, and where her victimization fueled the crime for which she was convicted."[12] After considering Smith's age at the time of the crime, the abuse Robinson inflicted, and Smith's accomplishments while incarcerated, the court found the sentence unduly harsh and resentenced Smith to twelve years' imprisonment—nine years fewer than she had already served. Smith was the third person resentenced under the DVSJA, the first resentenced for murder.[13]

Resentencing under a similar law has been rare in Illinois. Rachel White-Domain, director of the Women and Survivors Project at the Illinois Prison Project, knows of only two women of the dozens who have applied who have been resentenced.[14] "Despite good intentions," she said, "the law failed to provide an effective avenue for release for incarcerated survivors."[15] In New York fifteen people had benefited from the resentencing provisions of the DVSJA as of June 2021. Obstacles to more widespread use of the law include judicial skepticism, the requirement that a person have two pieces of evidence of their abuse, and the discretion built into determinations of what constitutes substantial abuse and whether that abuse was a significant contributing factor to the crime. After a judge refused to sentence Nikki Addimando under the DVSJA, advocate Kim DaDou Brown vowed to "fix" the law.[16] But how much changing the law would make a difference is open to question. As law professor Kate Mogulescu, who represented Patrice Smith, has observed, the criminal legal system "goes to great lengths to preserve the status quo. Anytime you are trying to infuse an updated way of thinking or a different way of understanding people's experience, there is a lot of resistance."[17]

PAROLE

Most criminalized survivors seek early release through the parole system—if parole is an option. There is no constitutional right to discretionary (based on an individual determination of suitability for release) parole. Afraid of being seen as "soft on crime," legislators in twenty states have abolished discretionary parole altogether or for certain categories of crimes. In other states, although it exists in theory (and law), parole is all but impossible to obtain in practice. In 1977 about 72 percent of people released from prison were released on parole. By 2010 parolees made up only 19 percent of those released.[18] Those numbers are lower for people serving life sentences. Between 2006 and 2015 the Maryland Parole Commission approved parole for around seventy of the twenty-one hundred eligible lifers—3 percent.[19] Even after reforms designed to ensure that more lifers in California were released, almost 70 percent of those who appeared before the parole board were denied in 2015.[20]

Most states require those seeking parole to serve a minimum number of years or percentage of their sentence before meeting with the parole board. In states with "truth-in-sentencing" laws, people generally do not become parole eligible until they have served 85 percent of their sentences.[21] Geriatric and medical parole can also provide pathways to release for those who qualify. But grants of parole based on age or infirmity are used sparingly, particularly in cases where the person has been convicted of a crime involving violence. For one incarcerated woman in Maryland, for example, diagnoses of stage-four metastatic breast cancer, Parkinsonism, and paranoid schizophrenia, debilitating weakness from chemotherapy, being confined to a wheelchair, being unable to care for herself, and the threat of the COVID-19 pandemic were not sufficient to persuade the Maryland Parole Commission to release her on medical parole.

Parole is a political process. Parole board members are generally political appointees with varying degrees of relevant experience. Few parole boards have specific criteria for membership (California is an exception). Often parole boards draw members from "law and order" backgrounds, like policing, prosecution, and corrections, who may be cautious about releasing those convicted of crimes and skeptical about their rehabilitation. Parole boards are typically risk-averse, recognizing that the decision to release people from prison, particularly if they reoffend, can have serious political consequences. Robert Dennison, the chair of the New York Parole Board under Governor George Pataki, said that while Pataki never directly pressured him, he understood that Pataki did not want those convicted of violent crimes to be released. Moreover, Dennison said, "if you were sponsored by a particular state senator and you made a decision he didn't like, it is conceivable that the next time you are up to be reappointed, he may not push your name to the governor."[22]

Parole boards are often given (by statute or regulation) a list of factors to consider. A national survey of parole board chairs found that the nature and severity of the crime are the two most important factors in considering parole; the testimony and demeanor of the person seeking parole were toward the bottom of the list.[23] Parole hearings frequently begin by focusing on the crime, sometimes asking people to provide a minute-by-minute account of events that occurred years, even decades, previously. That kind of recall can be impossible for criminalized survivors, who may have blocked traumatic memories of those events. Those incarcerated for violent crimes are often denied parole based on the nature of the crime, notwithstanding their accomplishments while incarcerated. Sometimes a person is denied because the parole board believes they have not yet done enough time to merit consideration, despite a person's growth while incarcerated or mitigating circumstances. The crime is the one thing that an incarcerated person can never change. If the nature of the crime is the basis for denial, social work professor Kathy Boudin observed, "there is nothing the individual can do to make a difference in the outcome of her parole hearing."[24]

People seeking parole are expected not only to recount the crime but to provide insight into why they committed the crime and to reassure the parole board that they have been transformed by their incarceration. As Jennifer Shaffer of the California Board of Parole Hearings explained: "If you don't understand the factors that led you to do what you did before, how would anybody know that you're not going to do it again?"[25] Violating prison rules suggests that a person has not truly reformed. Educational and other programming can provide evidence of transformation, but only if the person appears to have internalized the lessons and can articulate what they have learned to the parole board's satisfaction.

Parole boards want to see that people feel remorse for their actions. But "proving" remorse can be tricky. Incarcerated people are often prohibited from contacting victims or victims' families, which makes a direct expression of remorse impossible. Parole board members may be skeptical of the genuineness of a person's expression of remorse or believe that the person is saying what they think the parole board wants to hear—"the duplicitous marks of a hardened criminal."[26] Breaking institutional rules can be used to show lack of remorse. So can attempting to persuade the parole board that a person has changed: "Anyone who believes in their capacity for change cannot be truly remorseful."[27] There is no evidence that either insight or remorse is connected to decreased recidivism. "I think it just makes everyone in the room feel better," law professor Heidi Rummel said.[28]

In many states prosecutors have the opportunity (and in some states, the responsibility) to weigh in on requests for parole. Some prosecutors make campaign promises to attend every parole hearing to ensure that people convicted of violent offenses serve their full sentences. Others have a blanket policy of opposing parole, requiring attorneys to draft letters immediately after trial recommending denial of parole for hearings that will not happen until well into the future. The prosecutor in Kelly Savage-Rodriguez's case opposed her parole. Savage-Rodriguez observed that, for the prosecutor, "none of the current work or change in my life over the last 23 years of incarceration should be considered.... My age at the time of the crime should also not be taken into consideration. Nor the prior abuse history."[29] Prosecutors see themselves as the voice of victims and use parole hearings as an opportunity to remind board members of the nature of the crime and the toll that crime took on the victims. But prosecutorial interference in parole decisions is deeply problematic, law professor R. Michael Cassidy has argued. Prosecutors' knowledge of these cases often ends at the point when the person is convicted. With no new evidence and a stake in maintaining a tough-on-crime image, prosecutors frequently use inflammatory and irrelevant information to justify denials of parole.[30] The parole board can be swayed by these presentations, changing a decision to grant to a denial based on a prosecutor's opposition.

Parole boards may also hear from victims at parole hearings. Many states have adopted laws granting victims the right to be heard at parole hearings and requiring the parole board to consider victims' statements. People seeking parole may not be permitted to address victims (leading victims to conclude that the person lacks remorse or does not want to apologize), question victims, or respond directly to anything a victim has said. For victims who are still grieving or angry, the parole hearing can be an opportunity to focus their pain and anguish on the person who caused that harm. Some victims are willing to do almost anything to ensure a parole denial, including providing the parole board with false or misleading information about the person seeking parole. Not surprisingly, the grant rate for parole is significantly higher when victims do not attend hearings. Between 2007 and 2010 the California Board granted parole in 13.8 percent of cases where the victim was not present, but in only 5 percent of cases where the victim attended.[31]

Parole boards are required to conduct risk assessments of people seeking release in many states. Risk assessment tools attempt to predict the likelihood of recidivism based on past behavior. Risk assessments give the parole process the veneer of scientific certainty. But risk assessment can be problematic. The tools that parole boards use are not always reliable and the reliability of the tool can vary depending upon the person administering it. Risk assessments often overpredict future risk of dangerousness, especially for women and Black people. Risk assessment tools that rely on factors like age at first arrest or number of arrests fail to correct for the racism that leads Black people to be arrested at younger ages and more times than others. People seeking parole are often denied access to their risk assessments and therefore have no ability to challenge the results or correct information that may have affected the outcome.[32] And the risk assessment process takes time. In Maryland those serving life sentences can wait years for a risk assessment after an initial parole hearing. Between 2004 and 2019 eleven people died in Maryland prisons while waiting for their risk assessments.[33]

Because parole boards have tremendous discretion in deciding whether to grant or deny parole and very little oversight of their decisions, it can be difficult to know why they have decided what they have decided. Former New York parole board member Carole Shapiro explained that "for some, the offense is it, no matter what. For some, it's the victim impact [statement]. Everyone has their own values and draws different lines in the sand."[34] As antiparole activist Bret Vincour has said: "We have no idea how to determine what criteria they're using to make parole decisions. It's a crap shoot. You just don't know."[35]

How parole hearings are conducted varies from state to state. In most states parole board members do not meet personally with those seeking parole. In two states those seeking parole are not permitted to be present for hearings. In some states the hearing is conducted by video. In others, staff members meet with those seeking parole and submit reports to parole board members, who vote without hearing directly from the person seeking parole. Hearings range from minutes to hours but are frequently quite short, averaging three to twenty minutes per person.[36] Parole board members approach their work with varying levels of interest, professionalism, and preparation. In Missouri, for example, parole board members played a game with staffers during parole hearings, seeing if they could get people seeking parole to repeat a "word of the day" unrelated to their cases and earning points when the person repeated the word.[37]

Former Ohio parole board member Shirley Smith described how the sheer number of cases left parole board members with a tight hearing schedule and little time to familiarize themselves with individual cases. "You have to face parole board members that seemingly are rude, because they're eating, they're not paying attention, they don't look up, and sometimes they don't ask questions." Smith noted that parole board members voted in cases despite missing the hearings, making it difficult for them to assess the person's readiness for release. Smith also observed that parole board members were "harsher and stricter with people of color. . . . I think they treat them like they're dogs sometimes."[38] Kate described her experience before the New York parole board: "I had one Commissioner that was sleeping. The rest of my Parole Board was teleconferenced, which I think is so impersonal. I waited two years for this 2 ½ minutes, and you can't even come before me? This is my life."[39] The parole board's indifference can be read as a signal that they have made up their minds before the hearing begins, leaving those seeking parole feeling that the hearing is futile.

Parole board members can be dismissive, even abusive. An incarcerated woman recalled one parole board member, a former police officer, who

> talks to the women worse than any verbal abuser I ever heard. He says horrible things to them about how bad they are and usually reduces them to tears. Then he says they are "too emotionally unstable to be paroled!" If they stand up for themselves, they have "an attitude that he can't parole." If they refuse to react to his cruel proddings, they are "too cold and unfeeling." No way to win!![40]

These problems might be mitigated if people seeking parole were entitled to have someone represent them during parole hearings. But there is no constitutional right to counsel during a parole hearing. At least two states prohibit those seeking parole from being represented by attorneys. Other states limit counsel's participation to the submission of written materials pre-hearing. Barring or limiting representation at parole often means that the parole board does not have a full understanding of the facts of a case or the context within which a case arises.

In cases involving intimate partner violence, for example, simply seeing that a person harmed their partner does not provide the parole board with a picture of the history of their relationship and the reasons why that person might have acted to defend themself. Relying only on transcripts (particularly when a person took a plea or when the relevant details weren't fully explored at trial) deprives the parole board of information it needs to assess the risk that release poses. Lawyers also help parole boards understand the changes that people have undergone during their incarceration, amassing documents and testimony about the person's work history, educational attainments, and programming, the person's support in the community, and the observations of those best placed to see a person's growth—correctional officers and others with long-term relationships with the person.

Without lawyers, incarcerated people may not be permitted to view their parole files, leaving them without knowledge of what is in those files and making it impossible to correct incomplete or inaccurate information. During hearings, lawyers could help those seeking parole tell their stories and answer questions that they may not understand. For example, in a parole hearing in Maryland, a commissioner asked a criminalized survivor why the prosecutor charged her with second-degree murder rather than manslaughter. The woman had no idea why the prosecutor had made that choice and did not understand the distinction between the two. Flustered, she was unable to concentrate on other questions the board asked because she was focused on her inability to address that issue—something a lawyer could have handled easily.

For those who are permitted to appear in person, law professor Hadar Aviram has written, a parole hearing "is a performative space in which inmates are expected to conform to a meticulously choreographed set of expectations."[41] Those seeking parole must tell a story of remorse and redemption, and they must tell that story the right way, to explain their past actions without trying to excuse them and assure the parole board that nothing similar will happen again. Taking responsibility, Boudin has observed, is the difference between saying "The gun went off" and "I shot the gun"—only one of those stories is acceptable to a parole board.[42] To perform well, a person seeking parole must be able to verbalize their thoughts and emotions, appear reflective, and do so in a "socially legitimate form"—all things that incarcerated people might otherwise avoid doing in prison out of self-protection.[43]

Raising experiences of victimization in parole hearings makes the performance much more complicated. Although some state laws specifically provide for the consideration of domestic violence in parole proceedings, parole boards are very clear that there is only one victim in these hearings, and that person is not the person seeking parole. Some parole boards are unwilling to consider the impact of gender-based violence on a person's crime, especially if that evidence is not part of the official record. "Credible" evidence of gender-based violence—hospital records, police records, court documents—is not always available and difficult for incarcerated people to obtain. Raising the history of victimization can undermine remorse—how can a person seeking parole truly be remorseful if they are still claiming to be a victim?

Presenting information about their previous victimization requires people seeking parole to strike a delicate balance. People who have experienced gender-based violence that is linked to their crime must persuade the parole board that although that violence does not excuse their actions (it is too late to argue self-defense in a parole hearing), it does help to explain why they did what they did, and more important, why they are unlikely to do it again.[44] How they perceive that information, former parole board member Frederic Reamer has written, can determine whether the parole board reacts "punitively and judgmentally or with a deep, forgiving appreciation of the toxic circumstances that led to their conduct."[45]

If the person seeking parole chooses to talk about their victimization, they must conform to expectations and stereotypes of victims of gender-based violence. Few states require that parole board members have the kind of experience with or training in gender-based violence that might overcome those stereotypes. That lack of knowledge is clear to those who go up for parole. Angie, for example, described her past trauma and was denied parole. She believes the denial was linked to the way she presented herself during her hearing. "I think had I went in there with that victim mentality it probably would have been better with the last parole board, people, I think. Because I think that I was too confident. I think that my self-confidence and my self-esteem hurt me in that parole board hearing 'cause I'm not the same person I was then. So they see this person and they're probably like . . . I don't see it."[46] Presenting as a victim is even more complicated for women of color because of the ways that femininity and victimization are raced: "When you go before the [parole] board, you have to dress and act like you're white."[47]

Appearing before the parole board is a nerve-wracking experience. People seeking parole, particularly those serving long sentences, rely on hope of release to sustain them. Boudin, incarcerated in New York for more than twenty years, described what hope feels like: "For a brief moment, you had dreamed of being outside of prison wearing your blue jeans and a black shirt—the forbidden colors of blue and black, walking down the street and into a restaurant."[48] Being denied parole crushes those dreams. "Mentally we try to grasp the concept that our lives are in 5 people's hands (the parole board) that don't know us at all . . . letting them get their hopes up when it's a parole hearing time, then denying the lifer 5 or 8 more years, that feels like mental abuse."[49]

Some people choose not to engage with the parole system at all or, after repeated denials, resolve not to go up for parole again. "The idea that the answer may be no is significantly worse than knowing the answer is no. People just don't wanna hope."[50] When people who have completed every program available to them, have flawless institutional records and external support, and are able to demonstrate insight and remorse are nonetheless denied, they are left to wonder what would be good enough, particularly when the parole board is not required to produce a written decision or refuses to provide any additional instruction on what they should do differently. As Jane Dorotik wrote while incarcerated at the California Institution for Women:

LA has been in front of the parole board five times. Commissioners acknowledge her "low-risk" psychological evaluation; they applaud all her rehabilitation and her non-existent serious disciplinary record after 30 years. In her most recent hearing, after being told she was being denied yet again, she said to the commissioners, "I don't know what you want me to do, or say. I truly don't." The commissioners had written in her denial recommendations, "Stay write-up free, participate in self-help groups." Those are the same boiler plate recommendations they make 90 percent of the time . . . all of which LA has done and will continue to do.

In five years (her next opportunity for freedom), she will be 70 years old. I can guarantee you she will now have approximately 40 self-help, educational and vocational completions in her file. I am confident she will still have no serious disciplinary infractions. What I don't know is if she will finally measure up in their eyes, or if she will be one of the other statistics— died before being found suitable for parole.[51]

While in theory the right to appeal a parole decision exists in many states, in practice there is little meaningful review of parole boards. In states like New York and California, people seeking parole can appeal denials to state courts. But the standard for upholding parole board decisions is typically quite low. In California the court must find only that there is "some evidence" supporting the decision; the nature of the crime is enough to justify a denial.[52] In New York parole board decisions can be overturned if they are "arbitrary and capricious" or demonstrate a "showing of irrationality bordering on impropriety." In the unlikely event that the court makes such a finding, cases are sent back to the parole board for rehearing, but the result is unlikely to change.[53] In about 20 percent of states there is no review of parole decisions at all.[54]

For all of these reasons, Niki Rossakis's experience is the exception, not the norm. Rossakis was convicted of second-degree murder in 1993 for shooting her husband, who physically and sexually abused her throughout their marriage. After one rape resulted in pregnancy, Rossakis had an abortion. While Rossakis was healing from the abortion and under doctor's advice not to have sex for six weeks, her husband digitally raped her and threatened to vaginally rape her. The next morning, her husband again reached toward Rossakis's vagina; when Rossakis pushed him away, he said, "I will get you later bitch." Rossakis took his gun from the nightstand and shot him. Rossakis was sentenced to twenty-three years to life, later reduced to fifteen to life. During her first twenty years of incarceration, Rossakis obtained two college degrees, completed significant programming, and worked steadily. Her risk evaluation showed a low likelihood of future violence. Nonetheless, she was denied parole three times. At her third hearing, Rossakis said,

> I did the worst thing someone could do, and I killed . . . Gary, and I'm very, very sorry for that. . . . When I first started my bid, I saw myself as the victim. Today I know that Gary is the victim. I no longer harp on the abuse just to justify what I did to my husband. I was wrong. I should have just gotten up and left. I should have made more of an attempt to reach out and talk to people. I didn't do that. . . . I made a horrible decision, and I'm sorry.[55]

The parole board found that granting Rossakis parole "was incompatible with the welfare of society" and that Rossakis "lacked remorse . . . she continued to blame decedent for his death and continued to identify as an abuse victim despite the jury's guilty verdict."[56]

In New York courts can review parole decisions, and the seriousness of the crime is not a sufficient basis to deny parole. Rossakis appealed the denial of parole. The New York Supreme Court Appellate Division found that the board's denial of Rossakis's application for parole was in fact irrational bordering on impropriety and therefore arbitrary and capricious. The court noted that "apologizing for the shooting while steadfastly maintaining that she was an abuse victim does not indicate a lack of remorse for her actions" and that despite the victim's family's statements that Rossakis was dangerous, a risk assessment proved otherwise. The court ordered that Rossakis have a new parole hearing staffed only by parole board members who had not participated in her earlier hearings.[57] Rossakis was released on parole in 2017.

By her third hearing, Niki Rossakis may have understood that the parole board would not see her as a victim and would use her description of her husband's violence to justify her continued incarceration. She retracted any claim to victimization she had made in earlier hearings and expressed unqualified remorse. But having once declared herself a victim seemed to make it impossible for the parole board to hear that remorse. Focused only on the nature of the crime and their assessment of Rossakis as unrepentant, the parole board likely would have continued to deny her parole but for the court's intercession.

CLEMENCY

Clemency is "the last hope" for some criminalized survivors seeking release.[58] Clemency allows the executive (the president or state governors) to reduce a prison sentence, restore rights that would otherwise be denied as a result of a criminal conviction, eliminate fines and other penalties, forgive violations of the law altogether, and stop an execution.[59] But political concerns, particularly the need to appear tough on crime, have meant that clemency is used sparingly at best, even in cases that would seem to merit the combination of justice and mercy that clemency provides.

For decades, antiviolence activists have organized to seek clemency for criminalized survivors. The emergence of battered woman syndrome (BWS) as an explanation for why some women killed their abusive partners motivated the first wave of this work. In some states courts were unwilling to admit evidence of BWS, finding it irrelevant and not well accepted enough in the scientific community to justify admission. In others, courts and legislatures were willing to consider BWS, but women convicted prior to the admissibility of that evidence did not benefit from these changes. Either way, the failure to consider such evidence prevented judges and juries from understanding the context within which people harmed their partners, resulting in unjust sentences. Advocates turned to state executives, asking them to use the clemency power to right these wrongs.

The mass clemency movement for criminalized survivors of intimate partner violence first emerged in Ohio, where courts were hostile to evidence of BWS. LIFE (Looking Inward for Excellence), a support group for women serving life sentences, began thinking about clemency as a vehicle for release of survivors of domestic violence. The group met with Dagmar Celeste, the wife of Ohio governor Richard Celeste, and Celeste aide Linda Ammons, who worked with them to develop a clemency process. LIFE members applied for clemency and encouraged other incarcerated women to do so, helping them "overcome denial about their abuse, understand that they had been abused, remember incidents of battering, and recall where documentation of their experiences might be found."[60] Calling the women's cases "genuine tragedies," in December 1990 Governor Celeste granted clemency to twenty-five women (in ten cases, despite negative recommendations from the parole board) and sent thirty-four cases back to the parole board.[61] Although the response to the clemencies was largely positive, prosecutors and some in the media decried the decision, arguing that "Celeste effectively declared open season on husbands in his state."[62]

Motivated by LIFE's work, members of Convicted Women Against Abuse at the California Institution for Women wrote to Governor Pete Wilson, asking him to commute their sentences.[63] Thirty-four women, with the assistance of lawyers and advocates, drafted and filed petitions for clemency. In 1993, Wilson released one woman and reduced another's sentence. He later commuted two additional sentences, leading to one woman's release and another's sentence reduction.[64] In 1993 and 1994, Governor William Weld of Massachusetts commuted the sentences of six of the "Framingham Eight"—the eight women serving time in Massachusetts state prison for killing their partners. Debra Reid, a Black lesbian, was one of the two women denied clemency by Weld. Recognizing that they would have to overcome the prejudices of the panel hearing the clemency claims, author Carmen Maria Machado wrote,

> Debra's lawyers did their best to leverage the committee's inherent assumptions and prejudices by painting her as "the woman" in the relationship: she cooked, she cleaned, she cared for the children. The attorneys believed, rightly, that Debra needed to fit the traditional domestic abuse narrative that people understood: the abused needed to be a "feminine" figure—meek, straight, white—and the abuser a masculine one. That Debra was black didn't help her case; it worked against the stereotype.[65]

The clemency board denied Reid release, finding that she and her partner had been involved in "a mutual battering relationship . . . even thought it had never come up during the hearing."[66] Reid was paroled in 1994. Governors in several other states granted multiple requests for clemency as well. Between 1990 and 2000 at least sixty-nine women subjected to abuse were granted clemency by state governors.[67] The governors who granted clemencies were motivated by their belief that the women suffered from

BWS, the women's inability to introduce evidence of battering at trial, and their concerns for justice and mercy.[68]

The clemency process varies substantially from state to state. In some places recommendations about clemency are made by the parole board, raising questions about the likelihood of success in cases where the parole board has already denied parole to the person seeking clemency. Changing the makeup of the parole board can change clemency decisions in individual cases. Arkansas's parole board recommended clemency for Willie Mae Harris five times before April 2019. Those recommendations documented Harris's victimization at the hands of her husband, whom she shot in self-defense, as well as her family ties and her work as a reading tutor in prison. But in April 2019 only two of the seven members of the Arkansas parole board voted to rehear her case, finding that Harris's application was "without merit" and that her life sentence was "not excessive." Harris, seventy-two years old and blind, was finally granted parole in May 2020, after Governor Asa Hutchinson expressed support for her release.[69]

In other states the process is different depending on a person's criminal history. In California clemency petitions are sent directly to the governor unless the person has a prior felony conviction, in which case the Board of Parole Hearings and the Supreme Court of California both have input. Some states hold hearings on clemency petitions. Others are decided in what is essentially a "black box." Incarcerated people ordinarily have no right to representation, to present additional information, or to address claims made by prosecutors and others at clemency hearings. For people serving life without parole sentences, clemency is the first step in a longer process: having the governor convert a life without parole sentence to a life with parole—or even better, a term of years sentence—allows the person to seek parole but does not guarantee that parole will be granted.

Clemency is the only option available to Angel Stewart. Stewart was nineteen years old when she, her one-year-old son, Shane, and her friend, Angel Chamberlain, arranged to get a ride from Steven Bradley in June 1994. Bradley took the girls and the baby to the home of Garland Shaffer, telling them they would leave in the morning. Instead, the next day the girls found that they were locked in the house. They attempted to leave through a window but found Shaffer watching them. Shaffer held Stewart at gunpoint and told the girls they could not leave. Over the next week

Shaffer and Bradley tortured the girls. Shaffer threatened that he would hurt Shane if Stewart disobeyed him. When out in public, the sixty-eight-year-old Shaffer and the thirty-two-year-old Bradley forced the girls to act as if they were dating the much older men. After Shaffer learned that two elderly neighbors had raised concerns about the girls' safety, Shaffer and Bradley kidnapped the older women and brought them to Shaffer's house. Shaffer forced Bradley, Stewart, and Chamberlain to beat the women and told Stewart to strangle one of the women with an extension cord. Shaffer ultimately killed one of the women in Iowa and the other in Missouri. Shaffer repeatedly threatened to kill them all if they did not participate in or told anyone about the crime.

Police ultimately found Shaffer, Bradley, Chamberlain, Stewart, and Shane hiding at a motel in Iowa. Stewart, whose I.Q. is between 65 and 70, was initially unable to describe what had happened to police. Soon after they were taken into custody, however, Stewart begged officers not to send her back to Shaffer, telling them, "He's going to kill me. I mean that."[70] Stewart described how Shaffer had held a gun to Shane's head and threatened to kill him if she did not obey. Charged with murder and kidnapping in both Iowa and Missouri and facing a death sentence in Missouri, Stewart pled guilty and was sentenced to life without parole in Iowa (the same sentence Shaffer and Bradley received) and to life with the possibility of parole in Missouri. In 2018, Stewart was granted parole in Missouri. But because she has a life-without-parole sentence in Iowa, Stewart remains incarcerated, unless and until Iowa's governor grants her petition for clemency. The officer who originally arrested her hopes that she is released. "I think she deserves a second chance.... I don't think she's going to be a menace on society."[71]

Clemency was crucial for Assia Serrano as well. Serrano, an undocumented immigrant from Panama, was twenty-two when, under the influence of a much older abusive intimate partner, she was convicted of robbing and murdering an elderly woman. During her fifteen years of incarceration, Serrano received a bachelor's degree and worked as a translator, caregiver, and teacher. Serrano was resentenced under the DVSJA and released from prison in May 2021. But because Serrano was undocumented, she was immediately reincarcerated by US Immigration and Customs Enforcement. A pardon would have prevented her from being separated from her two children and returned to the country where she has not lived since she was fifteen.[72] Instead, a few weeks after her release, Serrano was deported to Panama.

Clemency can alleviate the collateral consequences of conviction, like having to register as a sex offender. Hope Zeferjohn was fourteen the first time Anthony Long raped her. Long later sold her to other men and sold videos of them having sex. Zeferjohn felt trapped in the relationship, addicted to the drugs Long furnished and afraid of Long's threats. Long used Zeferjohn's Facebook page to connect with other girls to sell. When Long was arrested, Zeferjohn testified against him. But at seventeen Zeferjohn was also prosecuted as an adult for sex trafficking. Prosecutors argued that if she had initially been a victim, by the end she was a "willing participant."[73] Under the threat of a long prison sentence, Zeferjohn pled guilty and was sentenced to six years in prison. As a result of that plea, she must register as a sex offender for life upon release. Seeking relief from that condition (and release from prison), Zeferjohn has twice asked Kansas governors for clemency. Prosecutor Mike Kagay opposed the request, saying that prosecutors could not corroborate Zeferjohn's claim that she had been victimized and that "clemency for Zefferjohn [sic] would unfairly absolve her of responsibility for the harm that she caused these victims."[74] The Kansas Prisoner Review Board recommended that the governor deny Zeferjohn's petition for clemency.[75]

Clemency is also available on the federal level. The federal clemency process requires those seeking commutations or pardons to complete an application that asks about the underlying crime and the reasons a person believes they should receive a sentence commutation or pardon. Pardon applications require additional information, including a listing of every residence and place of employment since release from prison, questions about debts, liens, and other financial obligations, charitable and community activities, and information about substance abuse and mental health issues. Applications for clemency either go through seven levels of review at the US Department of Justice before they reach the president or, if a person has access, are submitted directly to the president.

As of 2021, around fifteen thousand clemency petitions were pending with the Department of Justice. Among those petitions, approximately fifteen were filed by the Human Trafficking Clemency Initiative (HTCI), a consortium of law school clinics and legal services providers representing survivors of human trafficking convicted of crimes related to that trafficking. Most of those seeking commutation or pardon through HTCI were sold for sex at least once, some multiple times. Some had been sold with or attempted to protect another victim and were later charged with trafficking that victim. Some were barely more than eighteen years old when charged. And some, like Desalashia Williams, were sold by intimate partners who physically, emotionally, and sexually abused them. Their petitions have been pending for years, with no relief in sight.

A few states have created laws specifically designed to extend clemency to criminalized survivors of gender-based violence. California's clemency statute includes "evidence of intimate partner battering and its effects" as a potential ground for clemency. The statute also precludes the parole board (which sends recommendations about clemency to the governor) from finding that a person lacks insight into the crime because they have presented evidence of intimate partner violence.[76] In 2020, Texas created a special process for criminalized survivors of human trafficking and intimate partner violence to seek clemency after Governor Greg Abbott vetoed a bill that would have established a panel to review clemency applications submitted by criminalized survivors.[77]

Significant obstacles face those seeking clemency. Clemency is a discretionary process. Governors can create whatever guidelines they want, or none at all. Decisions about clemency are not reviewable and people seeking clemency are not entitled to explanations of those decisions. Applicants for clemency almost never meet with the governor personally, leaving those seeking clemency feeling as though the decision-maker knows nothing about them. Clemency is a political process. Fear of being perceived as soft on crime prevents governors from granting clemency, particularly to those convicted of violent crimes. As longtime Michigan clemency advocate Carol Jacobsen has noted, clemency may only be a viable option at the end of a governor's final term, when they are no longer worried about re-election. In Pennsylvania the governor cannot grant clemency without a unanimous recommendation from the Board of Pardons, which includes Pennsylvania's attorney general and lieutenant governor—both elected officials. Asked for input, prosecutors frequently oppose grants of clemency; so do parole boards and other bodies tasked with making recommendations.

Clemency is also a gendered process, during which criminalized survivors are frequently revictimized. In Michigan, for example, those seeking clemency are interrogated by prosecutors during hearings. The questioning can last up to eight hours without recess. As Jacobsen and sociologist Lora Bex Lempert have written: "Its form is accusatory rather than receptive, antagonistic rather than impartial, dogmatic rather than flexible, with a cumulative effect of bullying and bias." The prosecutor interrupts, challenges, and belittles the people seeking clemency, as these examples illustrate:

> You were the 21-year-old topless dancer who had, so to speak, been around the block a few times.

> So we've established so far that you were not a virgin when you got married and in fact you were carrying another man's child.

> You know, one of the things that struck me [was] what a meaningless life you seemed to be living.

These hearings juxtapose the power of the state against the "dangerous" female, casting doubt on her credibility while simultaneously emphasizing her failure to comport with gendered norms. "It would be difficult to imagine a socially sanctioned, public venue where a female petitioner or her supporters would be afforded less personal and social power than at a commutation hearing."[78]

Criminalized survivors take a risk when they raise their own victimization in the clemency process. While that victimization is essential to understanding their crimes, it can also be perceived as attempting to excuse their actions, undermining their claims of remorse and exposing them to criticism from others in the process. Moreover, if information about the abuse was not offered at trial, was contested at trial, or is not in official records (like presentence investigation reports), it is often dismissed as untrue.

Delores Kapuscinski was repeatedly raped and emotionally abused by her husband during their seventeen years of marriage. In 1987, Kapuscinski shot and killed her husband. Kapuscinski said she acted because of the abuse. Prosecutors argued that she killed her husband to collect his life insurance. Kapuscinski was convicted of murder and sentenced to life in prison. At a clemency hearing after thirty-one years in prison, Michigan parole board member Anthony E. O. King accused Kapuscinski of inventing a history of abuse to justify her actions. "You're now redefining your life experiences based upon the knowledge that you've acquired about domestic violence and abuse as a very serious social problem in this country. And if you're trying to force that onto your life, retrospectively, it can be problematic."[79] Kapuscinski's clemency petition was denied.

Susan Farrell's husband Terry sexually assaulted her so many times that she had to have surgery to repair vaginal and bowel prolapses. He punched her, grabbed her, and slapped her. In 1989, Susan's son Robert Baker Jr. beat Terry to death with a sledgehammer during an argument, then told his mother that he would tell police she conspired with him to kill her husband if she did not lie to police about his guilt. Baker testified at trial that his mother killed Terry to collect his life insurance. Baker was sentenced to thirty to sixty months in prison. Susan was sentenced to life without parole. In 2018 she sought commutation. Prosecutor Jessica Cooper responded,

> Inmate Farrell's convictions arose from her direct and significant participation in the planning and brutal murder of her husband. Her desire was to end...her boring and unsatisfying marriage in a manner that would ensure that she received a financial windfall from her soon-to-be late husband's estate. Allowing inmate Farrell to re-create her past in an attempt to present herself as the victim in this case does a disservice to those genuinely battered women. Inmate Farrell is not a victim. She is a ruthless and calculating murderer.[80]

Susan Farrell was denied clemency. She died in prison of COVID-19 in 2020. She was seventy-four.

Downplaying or renouncing prior claims of victimization may be the key to obtaining clemency. In 2018, Oklahoma's Pardon and Parole Board refused to recommend commutation for Tondalo Hall, who by then had spent more than a decade in prison for failing to protect her children from Robert Braxton's abuse. In 2019, however, the board reversed its decision and recommended to Governor Kevin Stitt that he commute Hall's sentence. Prosecutor David Prater supported the commutation request but made it clear that he disagreed with assertions that the initial prosecution had been unjust or the sentence unduly harsh. Prater wrote,

> I believe it most important to consider Ms. Hall's own words to explain how and why she received the sentence she did from Judge Elliott. Her honest, reflective words contained in a letter of apology sent to Judge Elliott, cut through the dishonest narrative that has swirled around this case in the last several years. In a letter received by Judge Elliott on March 17, 2009, Ms. Hall wrote: "I need to apologize for my actions and for my attitude. I have had time to sit back and understand that it is better to tell the truth than to tell a lie. Lying led me to prison. I do take full responsibility that I should have paid more attention to my children and when I did see something happen, I should have separated my children and myself from my abuser." I believe that really says what needs to be said about this case.[81]

Hall's willingness to take responsibility for her boyfriend's conduct and to largely (but not completely) abandon her explanation of why she could not leave Braxton changed Prater's position on the appropriateness of continuing to punish her. Tondalo Hall's sentence was commuted in November 2019.

ISSUES ON RELEASE

Resentencing, parole, and clemency can seem like the end of the process for criminalized survivors: the triumphant release from prison as the final frame of the movie. In real life, though, reentry raises a whole new set of issues for criminalized survivors. Just being in the world can be difficult for formerly incarcerated people, especially when they have been in prison for long periods of time. Formerly incarcerated people have to learn or relearn the basics, which may have changed significantly during their time in prison: how to ride a bus, how to eat in a restaurant, how to socialize. As Boudin wrote: "Even using an umbrella after years of using garbage bags requires an effort. Umbrellas are not allowed in prison, people use plastic garbage bags in the rain, so it becomes a challenge to actually know when to close one when going into a subway. Other difficulties include using a subway metro card instead of a token; choosing an appropriate pair of shoes; and using a cell phone."[82]

Having the resources to buy a pair of shoes or a cell phone, to say nothing of paying rent, is another substantial challenge. Many incarcerated women were living below the poverty line when they were first incarcerated.[83] Release doesn't change that economic reality. The median income for formerly incarcerated people in their first year after reentry is $6,248.[84] In one study of women on parole the average income for women who were employed ranged from less than $10,000 to $22,000; 68 percent had incomes of $10,000 or less. Employers were reluctant to hire those convicted of violent crimes. One woman recalled feeling confident about her ability to land a job until asked what crime she had committed. "The next day I received a job rejection letter from her saying that it would be devastating for her to work with a murderer."[85] Trans people face significant obstacles to employment without criminal convictions; with them, finding legal work is almost impossible. Nonetheless, formerly incarcerated people must cover their basic human needs as well as any supervision fees, fines, or other financial penalties associated with their convictions. Some people turn to work in the underground economy when other work can't be found, making them vulnerable to recriminalization.

Having stable housing is often a precondition for release.[86] But affordable housing for formerly incarcerated people is scarce. They cannot live in certain types of public housing and landlords may be reluctant to rent to those with criminal records. Shelters may not be an option, either. For instance,

> Elizabeth describes how she needed to line up outside one of the local homeless shelters by 3:00 in the afternoon. At 4:00 the shelter would announce how many beds were available that night. Because the number varied, Elizabeth could not know in advance whether a particular shelter would work out for her on any given night. By the time she would find out that there was no available bed at the first shelter she tried, it would be too late to get into another shelter.[87]

Without a permanent place to stay, Elizabeth was forced to find space for her belongings, which she could not take with her to job interviews or to see apartments. For trans women these obstacles are compounded by the unwillingness of some women's shelters to admit them at all.

Lack of housing makes women vulnerable to rearrest. In their study of formerly incarcerated women in Massachusetts, sociologists Susan Sered and Maureen Norton-Hawk found that "quite a few women have been arrested for littering, loitering, public intoxication, or soliciting sex-acts that they would not have been arrested for if they had housing."[88] Left with few, if any, options, some formerly incarcerated survivors return to violent relationships, trading housing for physical and emotional safety.[89]

Ideally services are available to assist those leaving prison, though, as Cyntoia Brown-Long has written, it is ironic that people have to go to prison to access them. "The whole gym was filled with Tennessee nonprofits offering reentry resources . . . places these ladies could turn to when they got release. *Ain't it kinda sad no one gets the word out about these places before we get locked up?* I thought. That's when we really could use a fair like this."[90] But resources can be scarce, particularly for formerly incarcerated women. In Maryland, for example, there has not been a community-based prerelease facility for women, providing job training, housing referrals, and access to other services, in more than a decade. Although legislation passed in 2020 will create a new facility, it is not expected to open before June 2023. And criminalized survivors, marked as perpetrators, may not be able to access community gender-based violence resources because of their convictions.[91]

Being on parole poses an additional set of challenges. People on parole are required to follow a strict set of rules. Parole conditions can include regularly reporting to parole officers, refraining from drug and alcohol use, submitting to drug testing, working or seeking employment, not associating with other formerly incarcerated people, not possessing a firearm, and reporting changes of residence or employment. Those on parole may be required to pay fees to cover the costs of supervision. In addition, there may be special conditions based specifically on the crime for which the person was convicted. For those convicted of trafficking, that may mean not possessing a cell phone or using social media and waiving privacy rights to all electronic communications, including personal documents on a computer.[92] And then there are conditions that are so subjective as to be meaningless: "abandon evil associates and ways," for instance.[93]

Kelly Savage-Rodriguez was paroled after twenty-three years of incarceration. At her first meeting with her parole officer, she received a document with eight pages of requirements. She had to remain in transitional housing for a year. She could not travel without her parole officer's approval. She was required to complete anger management and parenting classes. She could not spend time with children under seven years old unsupervised and needed her parole officer's permission to date anyone with physical custody of a child under seven. She could not associate with her son's immediate family members—which she understood to mean her daughter and her siblings—and she could not have a picture of her son Justin or any of his belongings, even though she had kept pictures of him in prison (these restrictions were later eased by her parole officer). Savage-Rodriguez was also subject to the rules of the transitional house, which included giving her ATM card to program staff, not leaving the house without a pass, and not talking to people outside the program unless she had a pass or other authorization.[94] "Most of us could not live under the rules of parole," Brian Fischer, the former commissioner of the New York State Department of Corrections and Community Supervision explained, "because there are too many of them."[95]

Electronic monitoring as a condition of parole is becoming more common. Wearing devices that track a user's whereabouts, those being monitored are often closely confined to home and work and need permission from their parole officers to go anywhere else. People being monitored communicate with their parole officers through call centers. Reaching call centers can be frustrating; people on parole report missing work, job interviews, and medical appointments because the call center failed to respond. The rules of electronic monitoring are not always clear to those on parole. And electronic monitoring can make people vulnerable to gender-based violence. As Monica Cosby of the Illinois Women's Justice Initiative reported, "I know several women who have been in bad relationships and have been threatened with having their boxes thrown out the window or removed and getting taken back to prison because they would not consent to have sex with a partner or landlord."[96]

Parole was meant to be an opportunity to reintegrate into the community with professionals—parole officers—facilitating that transition. But over time the role of the parole officer has shifted from a hybrid of support and public safety to a focus on control and risk management. People on parole experience it as a "form of surveillance rather than a reintegrative process."[97] Violations of parole conditions can have serious consequences. In 2016 more than sixty thousand people returned to prison not because they committed a new crime, but because of violations of the conditions of their parole.[98] Being on parole means constantly worrying that you will be sent back to prison. Formerly incarcerated survivors describe the utter panic they feel when they cannot reach their parole officers to clear an outing or make an appointment. One survivor described her paralyzing fear of crossing the street when she was first released, convinced that she would be picked up for jaywalking and returned to prison.

For some criminalized survivors, parole or clemency comes too late. After eight years in prison, Teresa described herself as "not the same little girl that went away.... I'm all messed up now."[99] Mildred Strickland was seventy-five years old before Pennsylvania governor Frank Wolf granted her clemency in February 2021. Strickland was serving a life sentence for stabbing her boyfriend, Frank Sweeney, in 1985. Sweeney slapped, beat, hit, and stabbed Strickland for six years. One day, Strickland left their home and went to a friend's house to escape the abuse. Sweeney found her and grabbed her, hit her, and "tortured" her with a paring knife. Strickland's "mind went blank." Sweeney was found dead in the street. Like many criminalized survivors, Strickland missed the childhoods of her own children—and of her twenty grandchildren.[100]

For Deborah Jennings, clemency literally came at the last minute. On May 13, 1999, Michael Jennings killed Thomas Beyers in Eagle Creek Park in Findlay, Illinois. Beyers was in Eagle Creek Park because Deborah had asked Beyers to meet her there. Married in 1993, Michael began to physically abuse Deborah soon after, escalating quickly from pushing and shoving to severe beating. He tied her up and threw metal darts at her back—more than once. He set booby traps in the house. He beat her with a club. He locked her in the closet for a week with a gallon of water and a loaf of bread. He broke her nose and her ribs. He raped her and held her down while other men raped her.

Beyers and Deborah Jennings were close friends. Beyers was afraid for Deborah and tried to help her leave her marriage. But Michael had threatened to kill his wife if she left, and she was sure that he would. Beyers and Deborah eventually had an affair. When Michael became aware that Deborah and Beyers had become close, he told Deborah to bring Beyers to the park, where he said he was going to kill Beyers. Michael threatened to sexually assault Deborah's disabled daughter and kill Deborah and her children if she did not comply. Deborah did not believe that Michael would kill Beyers, and she was very, very afraid of Michael. She brought Beyers to the park, where Michael pinned Beyers to the ground. Michael then ordered Deborah to hit Beyers with a rock. Fearing for her life and her children's lives if she refused, she did so. Michael continued to hold Beyers down. Beyers died of suffocation.

Deborah Jennings pled guilty to first-degree murder and testified against her husband. But Michael Jennings told a very different story at his murder trial, testifying that he had found Beyers and his wife having sex in the park and he had killed Beyers in a rage. He was convicted of second-degree murder and sentenced to fifteen years. He was released from prison around 2009. Deborah Jennings was sentenced to twenty-five years in prison. In June 2018 she became seriously ill, vomiting, losing weight, and experiencing significant pain. Deborah asked to see medical staff on numerous occasions and was told that she had either gastroesophageal reflux or a cold and that it would "work its way out." In November 2018 she was admitted to the infirmary, where she was again told that she had a cold. In December 2018 and January 2019 she was taken to the hospital three times. A PET scan and biopsies finally revealed that stage-four lung cancer had metastasized to her liver. Doctors gave her six months to live.

In March 2019, Deborah Jennings petitioned for clemency based on her medical condition, her history of abuse, her involuntary participation in the crime, and her strong institutional record. By that time she had served almost twenty years of her twenty-five-year sentence. Her attorneys, Rachel White-Domain and Margaret Byrne, noted that the trial judge had not intended to impose a life sentence on her, telling her that she would be released in her "senior years."[101] Deborah Jennings was released from prison on May 7, 2019. She died within two months of her release.

As Terrell Carter, Rachel López, and Kempis Songster have written, "To live a life without hope is to live a life with the kind of emptiness that can only be found in a grave."[102] Resentencing, parole, and clemency give criminalized survivors hope—but they also assume the legitimacy of a system that revictimizes survivors of gender-based violence. These remedies accept as given that intervention by the criminal legal system is appropriate and inevitable. But it is possible to imagine a world in which survivors are never forced into the criminal legal system at all. Abolition feminism can help us see that future.

6   Abolition Feminism

The criminal legal system routinely punishes imperfect victims of gender-based violence. That punishment begins when victims are children, continues when victims seek protection from the state or are compelled to participate in prosecution, and is at its apex when victims become defendants in criminal cases. Victims are detained, arrested, prosecuted, sentenced, and incarcerated. They are placed on sex offender registries and live under draconian conditions of parole. Criminalization was intended to benefit victims of gender-based violence, to keep them safe and ensure that those who harmed them were held accountable. Instead, the criminal legal system has done immeasurable damage to those it was meant to protect.

For some, the answer to this problem is reform: to fix the parts of the system that are harming victims of violence while leaving the apparatus of state punishment intact. But reforms cannot and will not prevent the punishment of survivors of gender-based violence. Abolition feminism is the only politics and practice that can do that work.

THE LIMITS OF REFORM
Fixing the Juvenile System

Advocates for girls and TGNC (transgender and gender-nonconforming) youth have suggested several reforms to mitigate or avoid the harms of criminalization. Gender-informed programming, for example, is frequently cited as a fix for the problems in the juvenile system. The 1992 federal Juvenile Justice and Delinquency Prevention Act provided funding for states to improve their responses to girls. The Office of Juvenile Justice and Delinquency Prevention has led several initiatives exploring gender-responsive programming for girls. But a 2008 review of gender-responsive programs for girls found that few had been properly evaluated and none were effective.[1] Similarly, in 2001, Connecticut legislators required juvenile agencies to implement gender-specific services. Seven years after that mandate, the Connecticut Office of the Child Advocate declared that "girls in Connecticut are in serious trouble," documenting the system's failure to adequately serve incarcerated girls.[2]

Some jurisdictions have tried "Girls' Courts," "an alternative track for female offenders within the juvenile justice court that recognize that young women enter the system with unique and gender-specific traits." Such courts sometimes provide programming including "parenting classes, yoga, community service, and therapy."[3] These courts raise several concerns. Such courts might expand the involvement of the juvenile system in girls' lives, increase the number of girls in detention, keep girls under the supervision of the courts for longer than necessary, and decrease community-based resources for girls by siting services in courts.[4]

Reformers sometimes use the term "diversion" to describe schemes that are essentially "criminalization lite." In New York, for example, children engaging in commercial sexual activity are referred to the child welfare system for services. But if children come back before the court because they fail to comply with services or engage in commercial sexual activity again, the court can adjudicate them delinquent.[5] In Florida, rather than arrest girls for domestic violence, police can issue civil citations and place them in domestic violence respite programs. If the girls successfully complete services, the domestic violence charges are dropped. Florida legislators also approved a law creating "secure safe houses" for victims of trafficking where victims could be held for up to ten months. As a retired juvenile judge observed, however, "the term 'secure safe house' may sound comforting and reassuring to adults. . . . But to a traumatized child who has spent a lot of time on the streets and in juvenile detention, it's a jail."[6] In some states girls can be released from detention, placed on house arrest, and required to wear electronic monitors. But house arrest presupposes a secure and stable place to live, electronic monitoring is invasive and expensive, and one study found that most released girls were rearrested while being monitored.[7]

Diversion programs are not keeping girls out of the juvenile system. In Florida, for example, 75 percent of the girls who were arrested for domestic violence from June 2018 to May 2019 were not diverted out of the criminal legal system using civil citations or some other alternative. Some 256 girls who could have gone to respite programs were placed in secure detention, more than half of the time because of the lack of space in respite programs.[8] Diversion also raises concerns about who receives the benefit of such decisions. As law professor Priscilla Ocen has noted, discretionary decisions like whether to divert girls and TGNC youth away from prosecution are "driven more by the characteristics of the child or the biases of the law enforcement official than the conduct of the child or the elements of the offense" and often disadvantage Black youth.[9]

As of 2017, thirty-five states had passed safe harbor laws intended to prevent trafficked minors from being prosecuted for crimes related to their own trafficking, including but not always limited to prostitution.[10] The research is mixed as to the effectiveness of these laws. Early research found that in many states safe harbor laws did not generally result in fewer arrests of juveniles; a later study found that safe harbor laws did decrease the number of juveniles arrested for prostitution.[11] Although some judges believed that safe harbor laws changed judicial attitudes about prostitution cases involving juveniles, others expressed concern that the laws provided the illusion of effort with little real change and, while acknowledging that the juveniles were victims, suggested they would still hold those victims in secure detention to prevent them from running away or to secure their testimony in their traffickers' prosecutions.[12] The existence of safe harbor laws did not change law enforcement's treatment of juveniles engaged in commercial sexual activity or the interactions of those youth with law enforcement.[13]

Courts have declined to apply safe harbor laws to crimes related to a juvenile's commercial sexual exploitation. Alexis Martin, introduced in chapter 2, asked the juvenile court to find that she was a victim of trafficking and apply Ohio's safe harbor law in her case, which could have paused the criminal proceeding while she complied with a court order regarding services. Prosecutors argued that Martin was not a victim of trafficking but a "manipulator" who exploited her relationship with Angelo Kerney to facilitate his murder. Despite the court's finding that Martin had been trafficked repeatedly, her case was transferred to adult court. Martin was sentenced to twenty-one years to life for Kerney's murder. On appeal, the Ohio Supreme Court found that Martin's offenses were not closely enough related to her trafficking to warrant overturning the conviction.[14] Prosecutor Rick Raley told the Ohio Parole Board that "the Safe Harbor law is not 'well, just say you have a pimp and you get out of any sort of criminal responsibility.'" Martin's sentence was commuted in April 2020. She will be on parole until at least 2034, a condition she referred to as a "mental prison." Martin is required to wear a GPS monitoring device and may be placed on a violent offender registry.[15]

Relief is potentially available after a minor's conviction. Pending federal legislation would allow judges to impose lighter sentences on trafficked minors convicted of violent offenses against their traffickers, a bill inspired by the case of Sara Kruzan, who was sentenced to life without parole after killing her trafficker when she was sixteen.[16] All but six states have vacatur laws, which allow judges to set aside previously obtained convictions and provide relief to those convicted of crimes related to their own trafficking. New York courts have vacated the prostitution-related convictions of trafficked minors who were prosecuted as adults in several cases.[17] But most state laws fail to provide easily accessible, timely, comprehensive, and confidential relief.[18] Moreover, vacatur laws only become operative after victims of trafficking have already been prosecuted, convicted, and in some cases, incarcerated. While eliminating a criminal history has clear and tangible benefits, by the time a victim seeks vacatur, much damage has already been done.

Reforming the Adult System

Reforms at the front end of the criminal legal system are designed to bring fewer victims of gender-based violence into that system. Court-based diversion programs, like the Human Trafficking Intervention Courts (HTICs) in New York City, empower judges to order victims of trafficking

into services including drug treatment, education, shelter, and job training. But even in cities with diversion programs, trafficking victims are
being incarcerated. In response, some "progressive" prosecutors, like Eric
Gonzalez in Brooklyn and Marilyn Mosby in Baltimore, have pledged not
to prosecute prostitution cases. As Gonzalez has explained, "The current
way of handling sex workers is dangerous. It drives them underground, it
doesn't keep us safe, and it's not really getting to the issue of trafficking."
Gonzalez has recognized that his decision not to prosecute might undermine the work of the HTICs. But, Gonzalez has argued, "to arrest a sex
worker . . . and prosecute in the name of giving them assistance just isn't
right. Forcing people through the criminal justice system is not a way to
get them help."[19]

Adding or amending defenses is another popular reform. At least thirty
states allow victims of trafficking to use their victimization as an affirmative defense to crimes they were forced to commit by their traffickers.
The crimes to which those laws apply vary considerably. In some states
trafficking is an affirmative defense to prostitution and prostitution-
related charges, but not to more serious crimes. At the back end of the
system, reformers have tackled sentencing, arguing for legislation like
the DVSJA and other provisions enabling judges to reexamine sentences
imposed years ago. Similarly, some prosecutors have created sentencing
review units to reconsider long sentences in old cases. As noted in chapter 5, those reforms have had some success in freeing or decreasing the
sentences of criminalized survivors. States are also considering legislation
that would cap sentences for particular crimes, which could benefit criminalized survivors.

Reformers are working to improve prison conditions. The latest version of VAWA includes the Ramona Brant Improvement of Conditions for
Women in Federal Custody Act. The act requires that incarcerated people
with children be housed in facilities as close to their children as possible.
The Bureau of Prisons is tasked with determining whether transgender
people should be placed in male or female prisons on a case-by-case
basis. The act forbids placing pregnant or postpartum people in segregation, restricts opposite-sex strip searches and bathroom monitoring, and
requires that correctional officers receive trauma-informed training. The
act guarantees that all incarcerated people receive "adequate" health care

and hygienic products at no charge. Correctional officers are precluded from examining a person "for the sole purpose of determining the prisoner's genital status or sex." The act pilots a program allowing incarcerated women who give birth while in prison to live with their children for as long as thirty months and requires the development of a gender-responsive reentry model.[20]

The development of gender-responsive (usually meaning responsive to the needs of women), trauma-informed programming has long been a priority for reformers. Although some correctional officials have pushed for equity in the conditions of imprisonment in men's and women's institutions, others have argued that incarcerated women should be treated differently, in large part because of their histories of trauma. As a correctional officer explained to sociologist Jill McCorkel, "In the short time I'm here, I know we can't treat them like regular inmates, like men.... In some ways, it's like these girls are more fucked up than men and less fucked up than men, you know? There's a whole lot going on—a lot of abuse and bad stuff—but they can't really be thought of as dangerous." Others in the prison shared this perspective: "We're talking about women who've suffered years of abuse, from the time they were little girls. Most of them are in trouble because of abusive men, you think they just went out and pulled off some carjacking on their own?" Another staff member concluded, "You can't 'get tough' with them. I mean, you can, but that's not going to fix anything in terms of whether they reoffend when they get out of here. In fact, if you do... more of them is gonna end up back in here. Why? 'Cause they were abused before they got in here and they committed crimes."[21]

In theory, gender-responsive programs foster "safety, respect, and dignity," using "policies, practices and programs that are relational."[22] Gender-responsive institutions are designed to recognize and address the specific challenges faced by incarcerated women: mental health, substance abuse, gender-based violence, poverty. Gender-responsive programs aspire to transform carceral settings into empowering spaces where treatment is the norm—a "nurturing prison."[23] What that means in practice varies significantly: configuring prison spaces to look more like dormitories than cells, allowing incarcerated people to have jewelry or makeup, building nurseries in prisons, or providing gender-specific vocational programming, including cosmetology, culinary, and sewing programs.

Safety, trustworthiness, choice, collaboration, and empowerment are the principles undergirding trauma-informed correctional institutions. Those principles are meant to be manifested through trauma-informed practice, infused in the physical layout of the prison, the language used by correctional officers and others in the prison, the prison's procedures, the treatment provided to those who have experienced trauma, and the general environment of the facility. Trauma-informed programs say they use these principles to inform their intake and other processes, interpersonal interactions with incarcerated people, programming, and disciplinary procedures. In a trauma-informed facility, for example, correctional officials should move quietly and respectfully interact with incarcerated people rather than yelling and refer to incarcerated people by name rather than number. Physical contact is supposed to be explained before being used.[24]

Preventing sexual abuse by law enforcement is another priority for reformers. Although most states continue to allow police officers to have sex with people they have detained so long as the sexual activity is consensual (leading to credibility contests between officers and the people they detain), there is a growing movement to make all such sexual activity illegal. The Prison Rape Elimination Act (PREA), enacted in 2003, prohibits correctional officers from engaging in sexual behavior with or sexually harassing incarcerated people, limits cross-gender searches and supervision in certain circumstances (like showering), and requires prisons to have procedures for handling sexual abuse complaints and preventing retaliation. PREA's focus is process, not outcomes. Compliance with PREA's provisions is not mandated and the consequences of violating PREA are minimal. And several states—including California, Connecticut, Massachusetts, New Jersey, and Rhode Island—now place transgender people in prisons consistent with their gender identity, a change meant to protect them from emotional, physical, and sexual abuse (but which did not prevent Rae Rollins from being beaten at Edna Mahan).[25]

Reformers have pushed for restrictions on the use of solitary confinement. The ACLU has argued that solitary confinement should only be used "in exceptional cases as a last resort," never for longer than fifteen days, and never on those who are particularly vulnerable, including pregnant and postpartum people, people with medical or mental health issues,

children, and people over age fifty-five.[26] New York recently passed the
Humane Alternatives to Long-Term Solitary Confinement Act, which
largely follows those guidelines. Rather than housing transgender people
in solitary confinement, some reformers have suggested creating trans-
only or LGB/TGNC units or facilities. In the Los Angeles County Jail, for
example, people were admitted to the K6G unit if they could convince
deputies of their knowledge of "gay subcultural terminology" and the
neighborhood where white gay men in Los Angeles congregated. Once
admitted to the unit, people were given different colored uniforms to identify them.[27]

The clemency process could also be reformed. Parole boards could
include members with experience beyond law enforcement and corrections. Risk assessments could be validated and available to those seeking
parole. People seeking parole could have the right to present their cases at
hearings where they are represented by counsel. Parole decisions could be
reviewable. Victim statements could be limited to concerns about future
risk, rather than rehashing the crime itself. Prosecutors could be excluded
from the parole process altogether. Supporters of incarcerated people
could be allowed to speak at parole hearings. The conditions of parole
could be less onerous, and terms could be shorter. Parole could meet the
treatment needs of those released into the community, and terms could
be reduced for compliance with the conditions of parole.[28] The federal
clemency process could be streamlined and could incorporate the input
of people outside the Department of Justice.[29] And in preparation for
release, prisons could make gender-specific reentry services available.

THE PITFALLS OF REFORM

These reforms may be well-intentioned, and many respond to real problems in the criminal legal system. But because they largely accept the
intervention of the criminal legal system as a given, they have the potential
to do serious harm and to preempt the kind of change needed to prevent
survivors from being criminalized in the first place. Prostitution diversion
programs, for example, rely on police to make arrests to bring victims of
trafficking (and others) into the system. Prosecutors decide who is eli-

gible for diversion into the program and what services they must accept. These programs use incarceration as both a carrot (the incentive to enter the program) and a stick (for those who do not complete the program or, in some cases, because the court believes incarceration will keep them safer). Describing such interventions as victim-centered doesn't change their essence. "Progressive" prosecutors are still prosecutors, and, as Survived & Punished New York has argued, even when progressive prosecutors claim to "support survivors," "we know that it will be poor people of color, including survivors fighting for their literal survival, who will be warehoused in cages rife with sexual and physical violence."[30]

Gender-responsive and trauma-informed prisons are still prisons. As Amber Rose Howard, statewide coordinator for Californians United for a Responsible Budget, has explained, "It's ridiculous to think that 'gender-responsive' facilities are somehow better, or to think that women are going to be in a setting where they can somehow grow or be cared for and nurtured. My experience [of] being in jail is that it is completely abusive."[31] Reforming these systems does not undo the damage they cause, both while people are incarcerated and after they are released. Upon leaving prison, criminalized survivors have to completely rebuild their lives—find housing and jobs, repair relationships with children and families—"in a society that does not easily forgive convicted felons."[32] Decreasing the collateral consequences of conviction can make some of this easier, but the stigma of incarceration and negative public perception of formerly incarcerated people remains, even if those convictions are vacated.

Reforms that involve making and changing laws will not, on their own, transform how the criminal system sees and treats survivors of gender-based violence. The legal rules may change, but the system actors remain the same. Changing laws will not uproot the stereotypes and misconceptions people hold about gender-based violence. To the extent that reforms require the exercise of discretion, those reforms will always be problematic. Primary aggressor provisions, meant to mitigate the harms of mandatory arrest laws, allow police to use discretion in ways that continue to ensnare criminalized survivors in the legal system. Pledges not to prosecute certain crimes (like prostitution) rely entirely on the priorities of the individual in the prosecutor's office and that person's willingness to withstand pressure to prosecute.

Such pledges do not preclude police from continuing to arrest for those crimes. Pledges not to prosecute certain individuals (like criminalized survivors) are meaningful only to the extent that prosecutors and survivors see these cases the same way. In the 2021 election several of the candidates for Manhattan district attorney pledged that they would not prosecute survivors of gender-based violence who act to protect themselves. But district attorneys often disagree with survivors about whether they are in fact survivors. In Tracy McCarter's case, for example, the Manhattan District Attorney's Office has denied that McCarter is a survivor, describing her as jealous and abusive. Prosecutors withheld information about James Murray's violence toward McCarter from the grand jury because they do not believe McCarter's story that Murray was violent on the evening of his death; therefore, they contend, "any prior history of violence toward the defendant or otherwise is irrelevant."[33] Despite a 2020 tweet in which he claimed to "#StandWithTracy," and his contention that "prosecuting a domestic violence survivor who acted in self-defense is unjust," as of 2022, Manhattan district attorney Alvin Bragg (elected in November 2021) has yet to drop the charges against Tracy McCarter.[34]

In the prison system reforms rely on administrators to institute and fund and staff to embrace them. While the federal Bureau of Prisons gives lip service to the idea of trauma-informed prisons, a September 2018 report documented the Bureau of Prisons' failure to adequately resource the trauma treatment program and provide training to executive staff, who are tasked with making policy decisions.[35] Similarly, the Department of Justice has used its discretion to certify a pool of PREA auditors made up largely of former correctional officials who have issued glowing reports on prisons that incarcerated people and their advocates describe quite differently.

Resentencing and clemency rely on exercises of discretionary power as well. In some states, like Maryland, asking the court to vacate a trafficking survivor's conviction requires the assent of the prosecutor. Under the DVSJA, prosecutors can oppose resentencing requests. Judges decide whether the abuse is substantial enough and sufficiently tied to the crime that led to incarceration, whether the sentence was unduly harsh, and whether a person is a threat to public safety. Discretion is built into these choices. In clemency, discretion is vested in the executive: the governor or the president. Many executives have chosen to use that power sparingly at best. In Michigan, for example, only five women convicted of first-degree murder and sentenced to life in prison have been granted clemency in the past thirty years. Over his ten years in office, former New York governor Andrew Cuomo granted commutations to just four criminalized survivors—despite the COVID-19 pandemic. For survivors with "bad facts"—histories of substance abuse, fighting back, being unfaithful in relationships, being angry, jealous, or "less than perfect ladies"—the likelihood of having a sentence commuted plunges.[36]

Discretion enables police, prosecutors, courts, and executives to rely on stereotypes to dismiss the victimization claims of imperfect victims. Discretion allows law enforcement to blame victims who do not turn to the criminal legal system for assistance. Discretion creates space for judgments that the failure to leave or call police or assist with prosecution means that a victim's story of violence is not credible. Discretion can mask implicit bias and outright racism in how police, prosecutorial, and executive power is exercised. Discretion is why Nikki Addimando was initially sentenced to nineteen years to life and why she was resentenced to seven-and-a-half years. Discretion enabled prosecutors to bring cases against Rudeara Bailey and Tanisha Williams despite their coerced participation in crimes and their willingness to help law enforcement find the people responsible for those crimes. Discretion is what kept Eraina Pretty in prison for forty-two years. But the response to historical critiques of discretion—that police and prosecutors failed to use their power to criminalize gender-based violence—has been problematic as well. Mandatory arrest laws, which led to huge increases in the number of women and girls coming into the criminal legal system, were an answer to unfettered police discretion. Mandatory sentencing laws, which led to Dixie Shanahan's original fifty-year sentence, were meant to curb judicial discretion. Both of these "corrections" have had disastrous consequences for criminalized survivors.

Reform often focuses on the individual: diverting a person into a program, vacating or commuting a sentence, punishing a correctional officer for sexual abuse, fixing the deficiencies in a particular prison. This focus on the individual fails to address the structural conditions that bring criminalized survivors into the system. "Violence," law professor Deborah Weissman has argued, "is a function of poverty, inequality, and the quotidian experiences and conditions wrought by systemic degradation."[37] Without confronting these structural issues, survivors of violence will continue to come into the criminal legal system, and they will continue to be punished by that system.

By leaving the basic structure of the criminal punishment system intact, reform legitimates that system and stymies more radical change. As law professor Paul Butler has argued in the context of policing, "'successful' reform efforts substantially improve community perceptions about the police without substantially improving police practices. The improved perceptions remove the impetus for the kinds of change that would actually benefit the community."[38] Similarly, as Survived & Punished New York explains, the DVSJA "does not say that punishing survivors is illegitimate; it does not say that survival is an absolute defense to criminalization.... By sending the message that domestic violence as a cause of criminalized conduct justifies only *less* punishment—and not something else altogether, like providing resources, and emotional or psychological support— the DVSJA implicitly validates the criminal punishment system."[39] The appellate court's ruling in Nikki Addimando's case underscores this point: the problem was not that Addimando was punished at all, but that she was punished more harshly than the court believed appropriate. There is a cruelty in having a court declare that it believes that a person has been horribly abused and that the abuse is connected to the actions for which the person is being punished—and then punish that person nonetheless.

Gender-responsive programming justifies continued incarceration of survivors under the guise of nurture and treatment, bolstering the role of the criminal legal system in providing much needed services that could be available in more appropriate and less harmful settings. Allowing mothers who give birth while incarcerated to spend a year with their newborn children, as Minnesota recently did, makes the system seem responsive and caring. But such laws only mean that mother and child are incarcerated (in prison or in "community-based prison alternatives") together for a year. If the mother's sentence is longer than a year, the pain and trauma of that separation are delayed, not avoided.

Reform expands the reach of the criminal legal system. As community organizer Woods Ervin has noted, "the prison-industrial complex—both

prisons, policing, surveillance—they feed off of reform. With each itera-
tion, they've gotten bigger, more deeply entrenched into our communities,
and more powerful."[40] Early reforms like mandatory arrest and no-drop
prosecution significantly increased the resources dedicated to criminalization and the number of survivors ensnared by the criminal legal system,
both as victims and as defendants. People resentenced under the DVSJA
are being ordered to serve long periods of postincarceration supervision.
Judges fail to see supervision as punishment; prosecutors argue for it to
provide services and to ensure that people do not reoffend. What neither
appreciates is that supervision extends the reach of the criminal legal system into the lives of those who are resentenced and increases their vulnerability to rearrest for technical violations.

Criminologist Jennifer Musto has argued that the growth of anti-
trafficking efforts in the United States has "stretched the bounds of the
carceral state in new gendered and punitive-protective dimensions."[41]
Reforms focus time, resources, and attention on the criminal legal system.
Massachusetts estimates that to replace MCI-Framingham, the oldest
women's prison in the country, will cost $50 million, in addition to the
$162,000 it costs to incarcerate one woman for one year.[42] Investing in
new prisons increases dependence on the carceral system and makes the
development of alternatives more difficult—money spent on prisons is not
put into communities or services. Reforms are used to justify doubling
down on incarceration.

As Angela Y. Davis has argued, prison reform has often led to the creation of "bigger, and what are considered 'better,' prisons."[43] Proposals to
create gender-responsive prisons and separate prisons for transgender
people—what Critical Resistance's Rose Braz has referred to as "boutique
prisons"—follow this pattern.[44] A proposal to build a gender-responsive
prison in California, for example, would have meant creating the capacity
to cage an additional forty-five hundred people.[45] Prison construction, in
turn, feeds increased criminalization—once prisons are built, they must
be filled. And, as law professor Kate Levine has observed, "if we make
prisons pretty enough, people may believe that they're something other
than cages."[46]

Reforms express confidence that the criminal legal system is working—that it is creating safety, preventing violence, holding people

accountable—and that it needs only a few tweaks. But there is no evidence that the criminalization of gender-based violence is doing that work. Policing, prosecution, and incarceration do not prevent crime and are particularly ineffective in preventing the kinds of survival-based actions taken by victims of violence.[47] Fear and violence do not prevent violence. As organizer and educator Mariame Kaba has written, "a safe world is not one in which the police keep Black and other marginalized people in check through threats of arrest, incarceration, violence and death."[48] What the criminal system does efficiently and effectively is deploy violence to exert control—criminalization is "violence work."[49] The criminal system's violence shores up powerful economic and social interests and marginalizes communities of color, particularly poor Black communities. Reform efforts are "doomed," Butler has argued, because "they are trying to fix a system that is not actually broken."[50] As organizer Nadja Eisenberg-Guyot has explained, "the dehumanization and violence is the point."[51]

Preventing the punishment of survivors of gender-based violence requires that we radically reconsider our response to harms. Abolition, and specifically abolition feminism, can help us get there.

ABOLITION

Abolition imagines a world where the solution to social problems, including violence, is not police, punishment, and prison. Although sometimes referred to as prison abolition, closing prisons is only one plank of the abolitionist platform. Abolition also requires moving away from a mindset that equates punishment with justice and abandoning the tools the state uses to exercise punitive control (police, electronic surveillance, probation, parole) and those that substitute for prisons (child welfare systems, mental health facilities, civil commitment)—what journalists Maya Schenwar and Victoria Law have called "prison by any other name."[52]

Abolition contemplates the dismantling of broader structural factors—racism, heteropatriarchy, transphobia, capitalism—that contribute to oppression both within and outside of carceral systems.[53] Rather than continuing to tinker with the existing system, abolition challenges us to envision a different world entirely, a world where, Kaba has explained, "we have everything we need: food, shelter, education, health, art, beauty, clean water, and more things that are foundational to our personal and community safety."[54] Most abolitionists see abolition as a process—both a goal to reach and a politics to guide our work today.

Abolition is necessarily about building. Without giving people access to the things that they need not only to survive but to thrive, abolition is impossible. That building is not just individual—it must be structural as well, investing in health, education, and safety, creating new and resilient institutions that deliver justice without relying on state violence. As Ervin has noted, abolition is not always linear: "One shorthand we use at Critical Resistance is 'dismantle, change, build.'... They have to be happening simultaneously because they're happening in relationship with each other, and the processes inform each other so that what you are able to build is actually in direct relationship to the community that is building it."[55] Abolition, then, is not an event but a process, where the development of alternatives to the carceral system eventually eliminates any justification for maintaining that system, what Critical Resistance has called "shrink[ing] the system into non-existence."[56] Abolition requires that we change as well. "Our imagination of what a different world can be is limited," Kaba has written. "We are deeply entangled in the very systems we are organizing to change.... We have all so thoroughly internalized these logics of oppression that if oppression were to end tomorrow, we would be likely to reproduce previous structures."[57]

In an abolitionist world, law professor Allegra McLeod has observed, justice "involves at once exposing the violence, hypocrisy, and dissembling entrenched in existing legal practices, while attempting to achieve peace, make amends, and distribute resources more equitably."[58] Justice is achieved not through punishment, but by severing the relationship between harm and carceral punishment and enacting policies and practices that ensure equitable distribution of resources, repair relationships, and transform the conditions that enable harms to occur. Law can be used to create structures that enable justice to flourish, just as law now facilitates punishment and undergirds punitive institutions. Abolition requires a leap of faith. It asks us to reject the carceral system without being ready to plunk an alternative down in its place. "But," Kaba has warned, "there

will never be a day when the skies open up and the angels sing, 'Abolition!' " Rather,

> the conditions in which abolitionist approaches flourish won't magically
> appear. They must be fought for and nurtured and defended. For those con-
> ditions to exist, we need to put in the steady work of eliminating the use
> of surveillance, policing, sentencing, and imprisonment. For those condi-
> tions to exist, we need to practice operating without using those systems and
> institutions. For those conditions to exist, we must create them.[59]

ABOLITION FEMINISM

Abolition feminism is, quite simply, "feminism that opposes, rather than
legitimates, oppressive state systems."[60] As Kaba frequently says, "Prison is
not feminist." Abolition feminists understand the violence inherent in the
carceral system and share the abolitionist commitment to rejecting punitive structures and building institutions that will facilitate safety, health,
and well-being.

The abolitionist movement has deep ties to the movement to end
gender-based violence. Several prominent abolitionists, including Kaba
and Beth Richie, began their work in the antiviolence movement. It was
through that work that they came to appreciate the damage done by
the antiviolence movement's collusion with the state in building repres-
sive systems to police and punish gender-based violence. They saw that
intervention by the criminal legal system did not prevent harm or change
society's perception of gender-based violence. State intervention managed
violence but did not end it.[61] They questioned how systems that regularly
did violence to women and queer and trans people, particularly Black
people, could be expected to keep victims of gender-based violence safe.
They recognized the state as a serial perpetrator of gender-based violence,
through policing, imprisonment, the child welfare system, and the drug
treatment system.

Abolition feminists reframed the work to end gender violence, Richie
has written, as "work against the patriarchal carceral state, and the archi-
tecture of racism and related forms of oppression upon which that patriarchal carceral state is built."[62] They agreed with abolitionist and geography

professor Ruth Wilson Gilmore that "where life is precious, life is precious," which meant looking for solutions to gender-based violence that valued those who were harmed and those who did harm, held those who did harm accountable, and incorporated community responses to harm that affirmed those values.[63] For Richie and others it is impossible to be an antiviolence feminist without also being an abolition feminist.[64]

Abolition feminism demands that we end the criminalization of survival, that we no longer arrest, prosecute, convict, or cage victims of gender-based violence. While the goal is to restructure society, abolition feminism recognizes that we will have to dismantle, change, and build as we go. As Angela Y. Davis, Gina Dent, Erica R. Meiners, and Richie write: "Holding on to this both/and, we can and do support our collective immediate and everyday needs for safety, support, and resources while simultaneously working to dismantle carceral systems.... Campaigns to close jails and prisons can move forward as we continue to teach classes inside prisons and as we support restorative justice processes and organize around parole hearings."[65]

Defunding the structures that drive criminalization—police, prosecutors, criminal courts, prisons, probation, parole—and dedicating that funding to services, programs, and people to prevent harm and ensure that all human needs are met is the core abolitionist demand. As Critical Resistance noted, the real work of abolition is done not in prisons but in battles over federal, state, and local budgets.[66] As of 2017, the United States spent approximately $100 billion on policing and $80 billion on incarceration.[67] Government funding is a zero-sum game; over time the "public safety" budgets of most cities have grown, while money for social services is increasingly scarce. Dollars that are dedicated to police and prisons are not spent on housing, education, youth programs, health care, mental health services, transportation, cash assistance for survivors of violence, economic development, community centers and green spaces, and noncarceral crisis responses.

Shifting funding also shifts power—away from the carceral state, toward the communities who distribute those funds. Taking money away from police, prosecutors, and prisons—money that is often given to them in the name of survivors—means not arresting, coercing participation in prosecution, prosecuting, or incarcerating survivors (as victims or defendants). Putting those funds into the community would prevent the violence that ultimately leads survivors to become entrapped in the criminal system and increase the options available to those experiencing gender-based violence. Criminalized survivors have much to gain in a defunded world.

Until full defunding happens and the criminal system is dismantled, abolition feminism instructs us to pursue "nonreformist reforms" and to use whatever tools are available to free criminalized survivors. "Reformist reforms" tinker around the edges of the criminal legal system without challenging its legitimacy. Nonreformist reforms move society closer to abolition and do not make it more difficult to dismantle oppressive systems and create replacements. Nonreformist reforms shrink the criminal legal system, free people from cages, and diminish the state's capacity for violence. Decreasing budgets for carceral systems, ending cash bail, disarming the police, and creating community-based interventions are all examples of nonreformist reforms.[68]

It can sometimes be difficult to distinguish reformist from nonreformist reforms. The DVSJA is a case in point. While the law makes it possible to free some criminalized survivors, Survived & Punished New York has argued that the DVSJA is a reformist reform: it accepts the legitimacy of the criminal legal system by providing for shorter sentences rather than no punishment; it vests discretion to determine who should qualify for relief in judges and prosecutors, which increases their power; it creates a pathway to relief for a narrow category of people; and its passage "serves as a 'mission accomplished' moment" that will make it more difficult to make change in the future."[69] Nonetheless, a pragmatic abolition feminist argument can be made for using such laws to free as many people as possible, even if we would not have advocated for those laws in the form that they emerged from the legislative process. Ultimately the abolition feminist position should be to free people today using imperfect, even problematic, laws, while simultaneously working in the short term to address their shortcomings and expand their reach and in the long term to dismantle the criminal legal system altogether.

Abolition feminists should oppose new criminal laws that purport to make society safer while increasing the reach of the carceral state. Both in the United States and internationally, for example, many in the antiviolence movement are advocating for criminalizing coercive control. "Coercive control" refers to a constellation of behaviors used to restrain a person's liberty and autonomy. Proponents of coercive control laws argue that the criminal law does not presently reach many forms of coercively controlling behavior, including isolation, surveillance, and emotional and economic abuse. They contend that enacting laws criminalizing coercive control would enable the criminal legal system to respond to patterns of abuse rather than isolated incidents and increase community awareness of coercive control. But criminalizing coercive control would also increase the reach of the criminal legal system, and just as previous reforms, like mandatory arrest, have been used against survivors of violence, coercive control laws are likely to be misused as well, particularly against people of color.[70]

An abolition feminist response to criminalized survivors also requires the repeal of existing laws that bring survivors into the criminal legal system. For example, exempting girls and TGNC youth from prosecution for domestic violence and prostitution would prevent their criminalization. Five states have set a minimum age for enforcing laws on domestic violence. The Texas Supreme Court has clarified that those younger than fourteen cannot be held criminally liable for prostitution.[71] Five other states have passed legislation setting a minimum age for prostitution prosecution.[72] Decriminalizing sex work for everyone would prevent victims of trafficking from being arrested for prostitution and related crimes, like loitering (referred to in New York as the "Walking While Trans Ban"— "a targeted Stop & Frisk program for trans folks of color in particular"[73]).

An abolition feminist response to gender-based violence would repeal mandatory arrest laws, which have been responsible for substantial numbers of women and girls, particularly Black women and girls, being charged with domestic violence. It would forbid prosecutors from seeking and judges from issuing material witness warrants to compel the testimony of victims of violence. Some prosecutors have pledged not to seek material witness warrants. But others continue the practice, and the most recent version of VAWA legitimates seeking material witness warrants by requiring only that prosecutors' offices develop policies on and train their staff about their use.

Abolition feminism supports meaningful pretrial reform. Courts make decisions in every criminal case about whether to hold people pending trial or allow them to return to the community, sometimes on their own recognizance, sometimes only if they can post cash bail or pay for electronic monitoring. Bail was meant to ensure that people would return to court; the failure to return would mean forfeiting a substantial monetary sum. But in the context of gender-based violence, pretrial incarceration has become the norm. Particularly for those accused of intimate partner violence, judges assume that release is dangerous and either deny bail or set bail at ridiculously high levels. Although several states are considering or have implemented bail reform, many exclude crimes that victims of violence are frequently charged with, including domestic violence, from those reforms.[74]

Moreover, several states are using electronic monitoring as an alternative to pretrial detention in domestic violence cases, which, while it enables people to avoid lengthy stays in jail pending trial, needlessly increases the reach of the carceral state into their day-to-day lives. Pretrial reforms that abolish cash bail without carve-outs for certain kinds of crimes and which don't substitute e-carceration for decarceration are abolition feminist reforms.[75] Until such reforms happen, abolition feminists should partner with organizations like the National Bail Out, which coordinates the Black Mama's Bail Out, a yearly effort to post cash bail for Black women and femmes around Mother's Day, to free criminalized survivors pending trial.

Survivor defense work is another component of an abolition feminist strategy. Such defense work goes back to the early days of the feminist antiviolence movement. Advocates formed committees to support women accused of killing their partners; antiviolence and racial justice activists joined together to protest outside of Joan Little's trial. Survivor defense committees are how Marissa Alexander, Bresha Meadows, Nikki Addimando, and other criminalized survivors have become known to the public. Defense campaigns tell the stories of individual survivors both to raise awareness of the individual's plight and to educate the public about how the criminal legal system stereotypes and punishes survivors, particularly people of color, low-income people, and LGB and TGNC people. Defense campaigns can include letter writing, financial support, and visits to the incarcerated person, fundraising to support the incarcerated person, public art, rallies and other organizing events, social media outreach, recruiting lawyers, court watching, pressuring prosecutors to drop charges, and showing community support for an accused survivor through letters and testimony.[76]

Repealing laws that disproportionately punish criminalized survivors, like felony murder and mandatory minimum sentence statutes, should be on the abolition feminist agenda. While many countries have long since abandoned felony murder (and some never had it at all), most states in the United States continue to extend liability for a death that occurs during the commission of another felony to anyone involved in that incident. Felony murder "is a convenient tool for prosecutors that makes it much easier to yield convictions, since they do not have to prove the mental intent required for murder."[77] A handful of states have either abolished or restricted the application of the felony murder doctrine in recent years. Repealing felony murder laws would significantly decrease the number of criminalized survivors incarcerated for murder. A California study found that 72 percent of women serving life sentences for murder were not the killers; in almost 66 percent of cases, the woman's partner was the actual killer, and many of those partners had been abusive.[78] California repealed its felony murder law in 2019 and made the law retroactive, meaning that people convicted before 2019 under the felony murder law can ask to have their sentences decreased pursuant to the new law. States should also repeal their failure-to-protect laws given how those laws are used to punish criminalized survivors for the actions of their abusive partners.

States should roll back mandatory minimum sentence laws of the kind that left Judge Charles Smith with no option but to sentence Dixie Shanahan to fifty years' incarceration for defending herself and her unborn daughter. Mandatory minimums disproportionately affect Black women. In Oregon, for example, Black women were three times as likely as white women to be indicted for crimes carrying mandatory minimums.[79] Although some states have moved to eliminate mandatory minimums, that movement has largely been restricted to "nonviolent" offenses. As with bail reform, such changes would exclude many crimes for which survivors are convicted.

Clemency is a cornerstone of abolition feminist organizing. "Some might suggest that it is a mistake to focus on freeing individuals when all prisons need to be dismantled," Kaba has argued. "But this argument renders the people who are currently in prison invisible, and thus disposable, while we are organizing toward an abolitionist future."[80] Clemency campaigns prevent people from disappearing into prisons. Parole boards and governors have the power to grant clemency to criminalized survivors but have used it sparingly. As of 2020, Survived & Punished California estimated that there were at least 150 applications for commutation pending before Governor Gavin Newsome that involved victims of intimate partner violence, including Tomiekia Johnson, a former California highway patrol officer whose husband was shot and killed after he assaulted Johnson and they struggled over a gun.[81] Other governors have been similarly restrained. Abolition feminists should demand that they use that power.

Abolition feminists concerned about criminalized survivors should join movements to decrease the collateral consequences of conviction. In 2019 forty-three states and the District of Columbia removed a variety of penalties associated with convictions, including restoring the right to vote, serve on juries, and hold public office. States also expanded the reach of expungement and shielding statutes (which allow people to remove some criminal charges from public records), limited the use of criminal records in occupational licensure, employment, and housing, and eliminated driver's license penalties unrelated to driving.[82] But obstacles remain. The process of applying for these remedies can be complicated, costly, and time intensive. Streamlined systems for accessing benefits, petitioning for restoration of rights, and eliminating convictions from the public record are essential. Abolition feminists should advocate for ending the registration of and removal of the onerous conditions placed on people convicted of sex offenses upon release. And abolition feminists should work to develop abolitionist reentry services—services that engage formerly incarcerated people in their design and delivery, understand and are attentive to the structural factors undergirding mass incarceration and how those structural factors continue to make life difficult for formerly incarcerated people after their release, are community-based, and are not entangled with carceral systems.[83]

Closing jails and prisons is an abolitionist goal. Inez Bourdeaux, a criminalized survivor and "nurse-turned-community organizer," was incarcerated in Saint Louis's notorious Workhouse. Bourdeaux described the conditions in the Workhouse: "the infestation of rats and roaches, the black mold growing on the walls, toilets that don't flush and showers that don't work, water that smells and tastes funny." After her release she channeled her anger into "trying to destroy the systems that destroyed me," including shutting down the Workhouse. In 2021 the Saint Louis Board of Aldermen voted unanimously to close the Workhouse.[84] But plans to close facilities often involve opening "newer, better" ones. New York City wants to close Rikers Island—"the most modern and 'humane' jail complex of its own era"—and replace it with (among other facilities) one or two new gender-responsive jails where mothers and children can be caged together.[85]

Organizing led by directly impacted people can stop the construction of new jails and prisons. In Travis County, Texas, county commissioners were close to paying $4.3 million for a new women's jail. But organizers like Annette Price, a formerly incarcerated woman and the director of Grass-roots Leadership in Texas, argued that the money could be spent differently, "invested in re-entry programs, mental health and behavioral health, as well as substance abuse, housing, job training, shelters for domestic violence and programs that could help support a safe community."[86] After hearing from more than one hundred formerly incarcerated women and advocates, county commissioners voted to table the project for a year.[87]

In California people incarcerated in women's prisons banded together to protest plans to build gender-responsive prisons, understanding that constructing new prisons would only expand the state's capacity to cage people without changing the day-to-day conditions of their lives. Recognizing that the facilities in which people are currently held are abusive at best and inhumane at worst, abolition feminists should resist the construction of new facilities and focus their efforts on helping criminalized survivors get free. Abolition feminists should champion the construction of projects like Home Free, a housing complex in San Francisco designed specifically for criminalized survivors leaving prison, that can provide the stability and autonomy that people leaving prison frequently find elusive.

Preventing gender-based violence and offering alternatives to police, prosecution, and prison when harm occurs are also essential. Preventing violence starts by making sure everyone has what they need to live: housing, employment with a living wage, physical and mental health care, safe quality childcare, transportation. Offering alternatives to the carceral system means identifying and supporting noncarceral first responders and developing accountability processes that take harm seriously without relying on the carceral system. Transformative justice provides a theoretical framework for these efforts. Transformative justice, Kaba has explained,

> is a community process developed by antiviolence activists of color, in particular, who wanted to create responses to violence that do what the criminal punishment systems fail to do: build support and more safety for the person harmed, figure out how the broader context was set up for this harm to happen, and how that context can be changed so that this harm is less likely to happen again.[88]

Transformative justice recognizes the stake that each community member should have in creating and maintaining a peaceful community and builds on community experiences and strengths to create processes and institutions to support that work. Transformative justice is hard work. It requires much more from the community than deferring to the carceral state to punish. But the returns on that investment of time, effort, and other resources can be huge: prevention of violence through transforming the conditions that create violence, meaningful active accountability rather than passive punishment, people engaged in communities instead of caged in prisons.

Only abolition feminism can prevent the continued caging of criminalized survivors. But abolition feminists cannot be focused solely on survivors. Exceptionalism—asking that one group's needs be privileged over others—confers benefits on some groups while abandoning others. As Gilmore has written, arguing that one group of people (like criminalized survivors) "don't belong" in the carceral system "establishes as a hard fact that some people *should* be in cages.... And it does so by distinguishing degrees of innocence such that there are people, inevitably, who will become permanently not innocent, no matter what they say or do."[89] There are no deserving and undeserving incarcerated people—almost everyone is an imperfect victim in one way or another.[90]

Angela Y. Davis has long argued that those who work to end gender-based violence should be "on the front line of abolitionist struggle."[91] Abolition is a big ask, particularly for an antiviolence movement founded on the belief that only carceral punishment would save lives and hold those who did harm accountable. There will be—there already have been—consequences for those in the antiviolence movement who question the role of policing and prosecution. Embrace, a community-based antiviolence program in rural Wisconsin, lost significant funding after posting Black Lives Matter signs at its offices; local law enforcement led the charge to defund the organization. Several state domestic violence coalitions faced similar backlash for signing on to a statement calling for diversion of funds from the criminal legal system into communities.

Working toward abolition will take a sustained effort over a long period of time, and change may be hard to see in the short term. But preventing criminalized survivors (and others) from being harmed by the criminal legal system justifies the work. The only way to ensure that criminalized survivors are no longer punished by the criminal legal system is to eliminate that system. People created the carceral system. We can dismantle it and build something healing and liberatory in its place.

Notes

CHAPTER 1. THE CRIMINALIZATION OF SURVIVAL

1. Jeltsen, "Bresha Meadows Thought."

2. Jeltsen, "Bresha Meadows Thought."

3. I have chosen to use "victim" and "survivor" interchangeably in this book, although I recognize that others distinguish between those terms.

4. Because I believe that it produces very little by way of justice, I refer to the system that others call the "criminal justice system" as the "criminal legal system." My thanks to Joanne Belknap, who also refers to it as the "criminal processing system," for this construction. See Erez and Belknap, "In Their Own Words."

5. The United Nations defines "trafficking" as "the recruitment, transportation, transfer, harboring, or receipt of persons by improper means (such as force, abduction, fraud, or coercion) for an improper purpose including forced labor or sexual exploitation." National Institute of Justice, "Overview of Human Trafficking." "Sex trafficking" refers to forced or coerced sexual labor, including prostitution, dancing or stripping, and webcam work. Because the term is so broad, its use can be misleading—every trafficking case is not the worst version of a trafficking case, as is true for some of the survivors convicted of trafficking that I represent. In this book I have tried wherever possible and whenever I had the relevant information to describe the actual conduct that was criminalized rather

than using the blanket term "trafficking" to avoid that perception. My thanks to Kate Mogulescu for this insight.

6. Brown, "Missouri v. Celia, a Slave"; Kaba, *We Do This*; McLaurin, *Celia, a Slave*.

7. Wallace, "Lena Baker."

8. Haley, *No Mercy Here*, 190 (explaining that between 1909 and 1936 in Georgia, most women who sought clemency and claimed self-defense were Black).

9. *People v. Lucas*, 324 P.2d 933, 934 (Cal. Ct. App. 1958).

10. "Prosecution Sums Up," 1.

11. *People v. Lucas*, 324 P.2d at 934.

12. Ramsey, *Houses of Pain*.

13. *It Aint' Me Babe* as quoted in Jacquet, *Injustices of Rape*, 79.

14. The details of Little's case are recounted in Jacquet, *Injustices of Rape*, 129.

15. Greene, "'She Ain't No Rosa Parks,'" 428; Galloway as quoted in Jacquet, *Injustices of Rape*, 118.

16. Jacquet, *Injustices of Rape*, 124–25.

17. Kaba, *We Do This*, 114; Thuma, "Joan Little," 21.

18. Chenier as quoted in Jacquet, *Injustices of Rape*, 131.

19. Wallace, "Inez Garcia," 11.

20. Garcia as quoted in Thuma, *All Our Trials*, 35.

21. Thuma, *All Our Trials*, 35.

22. "Inez Garcia Acquitted."

23. Mahoney, "Misunderstanding Judy Norman," 682–86, 690–97.

24. Mahoney, "Misunderstanding Judy Norman," 671, 676.

25. Leonard as quoted in "Battered Wife Gets Six."

26. Schechter, *Women and Male Violence*, 173.

27. Mahoney, "Misunderstanding Judy Norman," 671, 676.

28. Thuma, *All Our Trials*, 107.

29. Jones, *Women Who Kill*, 292.

30. Brown-Long and Mauger, *Free Cyntoia*, 163.

31. Melamed, "Philly Woman Killed the Boyfriend."

32. Thuma, *All Our Trials*, 106.

33. Ramsey, *Houses of Pain*.

34. Bernstein, "Militarized Humanitarianism," 48.

35. Kim, "Carceral Creep," 256.

36. Goodmark, *Decriminalizing Domestic Violence*.

37. Comack, *Women in Trouble*, 153 (quoting sociologist Laureen Snider).

38. Shepard and Pence, "An Introduction," 7.

39. Thuma, *All Our Trials*, 32.

40. Goodmark, *Troubled Marriage*, 63–64.

41. Dunn, *Courting Disaster*, 83.

42. Dunn, *Courting Disaster*, 10.

43. Nancarrow, *Unintended Consequences*, viii.

44. Dunn, *Courting Disaster*, 95–97.

45. Rajan and McCloskey, "Victims of Intimate Partner Violence," 36.

46. On sex workers, see Ritchie, *Invisible No More*, 192. On lesbians, see Machado, *In the Dream House*, 137. On trans people, see Goodmark, "Transgender People."

47. James, *Resisting State Violence*, 144; Richie, *Arrested Justice*, 7, 15–16; Ritchie, *Invisible No More*, 197.

48. Joshi, e-mail with the author.

49. Rajan and McCloskey, "Victims of Intimate Partner Violence," 36.

50. Comack, *Women in Trouble*, 19.

51. Jacquet, *Injustices of Rape*, 130.

52. Miller, *Victims as Offenders*, 3, 11.

53. Dasgupta, "Framework for Understanding," 1365.

54. Chesney-Lind, "Patriarchy, Crime, and Justice," 18.

55. Kunzweiler as quoted in Stillman, "America's Other Family-Separation Crisis."

56. Dasgupta, "Framework for Understanding," 1365; Hamberger and Potente, "Counseling Heterosexual Women Arrested for Domestic Violence"; Miller and Becker, "Are We Comparing Apples and Oranges?"

57. Gruber, *Feminist War on Crime*, 88.

58. Straus, "Thirty Years of Denying the Evidence."

59. Scarduzio et al., "'Maybe She Was Provoked.'"

60. Rajan and McCloskey, "Victims of Intimate Partner Violence," 35.

61. Durfee, "Situational Ambiguity and Gendered Patterns of Arrest," 75; Schwartz, Steffensmeier, and Feldmeyer, "Assessing Trends in Women's Violence."

62. Sawyer and Wagner, "Mass Incarceration."

63. Kajstura, "Women's Mass Incarceration."

64. Sawyer, *Gender Divide*.

65. Chesney-Lind, "Patriarchy, Crime, and Justice," 6, 17.

66. Western, *Homeward*, 139.

67. Owen, Wells, and Pollock, *In Search of Safety*, 21.

68. Sentencing Project, *Incarcerated Women and Girls*.

69. Kajstura, "Women's Mass Incarceration."

70. Levine and Meiners, *Feminist and the Sex Offender*, 61.

71. National Center for Transgender Equality, *LGBTQ People behind Bars*, 5.

72. Levine and Meiners, *Feminist and the Sex Offender*, 61.

73. Dichter, *Women's Experiences of Abuse*.

74. Richie, "Abolition Feminism."

75. Harris as cited in van der Leun, "'No Choice but to Do It.'"

76. Dichter, *Women's Experiences of Abuse*, 2–3.

77. Owen, Wells, and Pollock, *In Search of Safety*, 27.

78. DeHart, "Pathways to Prison," 1378.

79. Owen, "Women and Imprisonment in the United States," 90.

80. James et al., *Report of the 2015 U.S. Transgender Survey*.

81. The vast majority of the research on criminalized survivors focuses on the experiences of women. This book, however, uses a broader definition of criminalized survivor. I use the terms "victim" or "criminalized survivor" whenever possible but use specifically gendered language whenever that language more accurately describes either the person, the research, or the context being discussed.

82. Survived & Punished New York, "Vision & Purpose," 3.

83. Oregon Justice Resource Center, *Herstory Oregon Survey*.

84. van der Leun, "'No Choice but to Do It.'"

85. Kraft-Stolar et al., *From Protection to Punishment*.

86. Memorandum Opinion and Order, *Moore v. City of Chicago*, No. 1:12-cv-00238 (N.D. Ill. 2014), https://www.washingtonpost.com/news/volokh-conspiracy/wp-content/uploads/sites/14/2014/05/MoorevCityofChicago.pdf?itid=lk_inline_manual_1; Ritchie, *Invisible No More*, 188–89.

87. Londberg, "Mom Thrown in Jail."

88. Sharp, *Mean Lives*, 12.

89. Daly, "Women's Pathways to Felony Court."

90. Comack, *Women in Trouble*, 23; Owen, Wells, and Pollock, *In Search of Safety*, 34, 40; Sharp, *Mean Lives*, 21.

91. Lawston and Meiners, "Ending Our Expertise," 7 (emphasis in original).

92. Richie, *Compelled to Crime*.

93. Richie, *Compelled to Crime*, 4.

94. Larance and Miller, "In Her Own Words."

95. Dasgupta, "Framework for Understanding ," 1372–78; Larance and Rousson, "Facilitating Change"; Melton and Belknap, "He Hits, She Hits," 339–44; Owen, Wells, and Pollock, *In Search of Safety*, 94–97; Weston, Marshall, and Coker, "Women's Motives."

96. Nancarrow, *Unintended Consequences*, 142, 152; West, "'Sorry, We Have to Take You In,'" 103.

97. Potter, *Battle Cries*, 34, 66.

98. Quoted in Comack, *Women in Trouble*, 77.

99. Quoted in Comack, *Women in Trouble*, 98–99.

100. Richie, *Compelled to Crime*, 115.

101. Becker and McCorkel, "Gender of Criminal Opportunity," 99–100, 103; DeHart, "Pathways to Prison," 1366.

102. van der Leun, "'No Choice but to Do It.'"

103. Sharp, *Mean Lives*, 63.

104. Brant, "Ramona Brant."

105. James, "Ending the Incarceration of Women and Girls."

106. Quoted in Richie, *Compelled to Crime*, 127–28.

107. Richie, *Compelled to Crime*, 113.

108. Selma as quoted in Richie, *Compelled to Crime*, 114.

109. Moe, "Blurring the Boundaries," 116.

110. Richie, *Compelled to Crime*, 106.

111. INCITE! Women of Color Against Violence and Critical Resistance, "Statement on Gender Violence."

112. Bierria et al., *#SurvivedandPunished*.

113. Syedullah, "Hearts We Beat."

114. Bierria et al., *Free Marissa Now*.

115. Bierria et al., *Free Marissa Now*.

116. Survived & Punished New York, *No Good Prosecutors Now or Ever*, 6.

117. Note that the abolition feminism discussed here is distinct from—and at odds with—the use of the term "abolition" in the context of trafficking. Davis, Dent, Meiners, and Richie, *Abolition. Feminism. Now.*, 60.

118. Sered and Norton-Hawk, *Can't Catch a Break*; Goodwin, *Policing the Womb*; Schenwar and Law, *Prison by Any Other Name*.

119. Simon, *Governing through Crime*.

120. Kelley, "Permanent War."

121. Wang, "Cyntoia Brown."

122. Comack, *Women in Trouble*, 126 (emphasis in original).

CHAPTER 2. YOUTH

1. Sherman, "Justice for Girls," 1586.

2. Chesney-Lind, "Are Girls Closing the Gender Gap," 19.

3. Feld, "Violent Girls or Relabeled Status Offenders?," 249.

4. Sherman and Balck, *Gender Injustice*, 5–6.

5. Ehrmann, Hyland, and Puzzanchera, *Girls in the Juvenile Justice System*, 6.

6. Ehrmann, Hyland, and Puzzanchera, *Girls in the Juvenile Justice System*, 18.

7. Jones, "Visualizing the Unequal Treatment of LGBTQ People."

8. Chesney-Lind, "Girls and Violence," 1.

9. Scelfo, "Bad Girls Go Wild"; Williams, "Where Sugar and Spice Meet Bricks and Bats."

10. Poulin, "Female Delinquents," 541–75, 557; Chesney-Lind, "Girls and Violence," 4.

11. American Bar Association and National Bar Association, "Justice by Gender," 79–80, 97; Heipt, "Girl's Court," 808–9.

12. Sangoi and Goshin, "Women and Girls' Experiences," 148.

13. Acoca, "Investing in Girls," 5.

14. Foy, Ritchie, and Conway, "Trauma Exposure, Posttraumatic Stress, and

Comorbidities"; Le, "Gender-specific Treatment," 26–27; Miller, "Punishing the Broken and Invisible," 35; Simkins et al., "School to Prison Pipeline for Girls," 60–61; Simkins and Katz, "Criminalizing Abused Girls," 1483–84.

15. Annie E. Casey Foundation, *Making Detention Reform Work for Girls*, 8; Saar et al., *Sexual Abuse to Prison Pipeline*, 7.

16. Annie E. Casey Foundation, *Making Detention Reform Work for Girls*, 8; Foy, Ritchie, and Conway, "Trauma Exposure, Posttraumatic Stress, and Comorbidities"; Saar et al., *Sexual Abuse to Prison Pipeline*, 7; Simkins et al., "School to Prison Pipeline," 61; Simkins and Katz, "Criminalizing Abused Girls," 1483–84.

17. McClellan, *Our Girls, Our Future*, 7.

18. Sentencing Project, *Women and Girls Serving Life Sentences*, 2; Simkins et al., "School to Prison Pipeline for Girls," 61.

19. Foy, Ritchie, and Conway, "Trauma Exposure, Posttraumatic Stress, and Comorbidities"; Miller, "Punishing the Broken and Invisible," 33.

20. Quoted in Gaarder, Rodriguez, and Zatz, "Criers, Liars, and Manipulators," 557–58.

21. Craig et al., "Frequencies and Patterns."

22. Davis, *Fighting for Hope*; Chesney-Lind, "Are Girls Closing the Gender Gap," 22.

23. Goldman, "Throwaway Kids."

24. Brown, "Little Girl Lost," 472–73.

25. Goodmark, "Impact of Prosecutorial Misconduct," 657.

26. Goldman, "Throwaway Kids."

27. Voy as quoted in Brown, "Little Girl Lost," 497–98.

28. Goldman, "Throwaway Kids."

29. Musto, *Control and Protect*, 105.

30. Musto, *Control and Protect*, 107.

31. Musto, *Control and Protect*, 107.

32. Chabria, "This Sex Trafficking Victim Is Behind Bars."

33. Quoted in Walters, "An 11-year-old Reported Being Raped Twice."

34. Linnane, "Maricella's Last Breath."

35. Godsoe, "Contempt, Status," 1099.

36. Sentencing Project, *Incarcerated Women and Girls*, 5.

37. Flores, *Caught Up*, 9.

38. Wood as quoted in Schaffner, "Female Juvenile Delinquency," 14.

39. Hawes and Flores, "Does Abuse Lead to Incarceration for Girls?"

40. Taylor-Thompson, "Girl Talk," 1146.

41. Arthur and Waugh, "Status Offenses," 555.

42. Chesney-Lind, "Criminalizing Victimization," 84.

43. Sherman, "Justice for Girls," 1594.

44. Annie E. Casey Foundation, *Making Detention Reform Work for Girls*, 11.

45. Sherman and Balck, *Gender Injustice*, 17.

46. Strom et al., "Policing Juveniles," 444.

47. Sherman, *Unintended Consequences*, 5–7.

48. Acoca, "Investing in Girls," 7–8.

49. Sherman, *Unintended Consequences*, 7.

50. Fedders, "More Young Women in the Juvenile Justice System," 104.

51. Quoted in Hawes and Flores, "Does Abuse Lead to Incarceration for Girls?"

52. Quoted in Gaarder, Rodriguez, and Zatz, "Criers, Liars, and Manipulators," 565–66.

53. Sherman, *Unintended Consequences*, 7.

54. Basile et al., "Interpersonal Violence Victimization among High School Students," 30–32.

55. Oudekerk and Repucci, "Romantic Relationships Matter," 53.

56. Miller, *Getting Played*, 174–75.

57. Molidor, Tolman, and Kober, "Gender and Contextual Factors"; Miller, *Getting Played*, 176–77.

58. Durfee, "Arresting Girls for Dating Violence."

59. Contrera, "Sex-trafficked Kids Are Crime Victims."

60. Sherman, "Justice for Girls," 1606.

61. Freeman and Hamilton, *Count of Homeless Youth*.

62. National Survivor Network, *National Survivor Network Members Survey*.

63. Chapin, "She Was Sex Trafficked."

64. Ocen, "(E)racing Childhood," 1589.

65. Godsoe, "Punishment as Protection," 1323.

66. Peterson, "Criminalization of Children."

67. Quoted in Musto, *Control and Protect*, 86–87.

68. Musto, *Control and Protect*, 101–2.

69. Godsoe, "Punishment as Protection," 1364.

70. Weiss, "Children Paid for Sex Acts."

71. Brown-Long and Mauger, *Free Cyntoia*, xvi.

72. Benkarski, "Cyntoia Brown Steps into Freedom."

73. Quoted in Cho and Cornett, "Cyntoia Brown-Long to Lester Holt."

74. Brown-Long and Mauger, *Free Cyntoia*, 93, 113.

75. Chabria, "This Sex Trafficking Victim Is behind Bars."

76. Quoted in Chapin, "She Says Her Best Friend Sold Her."

77. Girls for Gender Equity, *School Girls Deserve*, 7.

78. Crenshaw, Ocen, and Nanda, *Black Girls Matter*, 35.

79. Miller, *Getting Played*, 102–3.

80. Girls for Gender Equity, *School Girls Deserve*, 12; Miller, *Getting Played*, 111.

81. Belknap, Holsinger, and Dunn, "Understanding Incarcerated Girls," 394.

82. Crenshaw, Ocen, and Nanda, *Black Girls Matter*, 10.

83. Sherman, "Justice for Girls," 1617.

84. Birckhead, "'Youngest Profession,'" 1059; Brown, "Little Girl Lost," 2; Chesney-Lind and Shelden, *Girls, Delinquency, and Juvenile Justice*, 171; Fedders, "More Young Women in the Juvenile Justice System," 108; Gaarder, Rodriguez, and Zatz, "Criers, Liars, and Manipulators," 566; Godsoe, "Contempt, Status," 1110; Rhor, "Pushed Out and Punished"; Sherman, "Justice for Girls," 1599; Sherman, *Unintended Consequences*, 3.

85. Fahy, "Safe Harbor"; Simkins et al., "School to Prison Pipeline for Girls," 57; Walters, "An 11-year-old Reported Being Raped Twice."

86. Linnane, "Maricella's Last Breath"; Musto, *Control and Protect*, 43.

87. McClellan, *Our Girls, Our Future*, 8.

88. McClellan, *Our Girls, Our Future*, 27.

89. Gies et al., *Safe Harbor Laws, Phase 1*, 4.

90. Musto, *Control and Protect*, 4.

91. Sullivan, "Raised by the Courts," 37, 39.

92. Simkins and Katz, "Criminalizing Abused Girls," 1491, 1493.

93. Stoddard, "Report: Multiple Leadership, System Failures."

94. Hunt and Moodie-Mills, *Unfair Criminalization*.

95. Davis, "Fighting for Hope," 138.

96. Quoted in Jeltsen, "Bresha Meadows Thought."

97. White, "Path to Healing."

98. Acoca, "Investing in Girls," 6; Saar et al., *Sexual Abuse to Prison Pipeline*, 4.

99. Linnane, "Maricella's Last Breath."

100. Murphy, "Solitary Confinement of Girls," 701–2.

101. Davis, "Fighting for Hope," 148.

102. Davis, "Fighting for Hope," 42; Saar et al., *Sexual Abuse to Prison Pipeline*, 14–15.

103. Quoted in Davis, "Fighting for Hope," 1.

104. Miller, "Punishing the Broken and Invisible," 43–44; Sinon, "Failing Girls," 73.

105. Nellis, *Lives of Juvenile Lifers*, 19.

106. Nanda, "Blind Discretion," 1529.

107. Taylor-Thompson, "Girl Talk," 1138.

108. Brief of Defendant in Support of Expert Testimony, *State of Washington v. Maryanne Marie Atkins* (Cause No. 16-1-01935-4 SEA).

109. Brief of Defendant in Support of Expert Testimony, *State of Washington v. Maryanne Marie Atkins* (Cause No. 16-1-01935-4 SEA).

110. Leslie Briner, one of the experts prepared to testify for Maryanne Atkins, recalls that the judge found the expert testimony on Atkins's history of trauma irrelevant because Atkins was charged with felony murder and because the prosecution had evidence that the felony in question (robbery) was premeditated. Briner, email to author.

111. Clawson and Grace, *Finding a Path*, 2; Halter, "Factors That Influence."

112. Contrera, "State of Ohio."

113. Brown-Long and Mauger, *Free Cyntoia*, 185.

114. Flores, *Caught Up*, 103–4.

115. James, *Resisting State Violence*, 141.

116. Vansickle and Li, "Police Hurt Thousands of Teens."

117. Ocen, "(E)racing Childhood," 1597.

118. Ehrmann, Hyland, and Puzzanchera, *Girls in the Juvenile Justice System*, 8, 13.

119. Sherman and Balck, *Gender Injustice*, 14.

120. McClellan, *Our Girls, Our Future*, 2.

121. Durfee, "Arresting Girls for Dating Violence," 69; Ocen, "(E)racing Childhood," 1591.

122. Rhor, "Pushed Out and Punished."

123. Brown-Long and Mauger, *Free Cyntoia*, 1256; Kempf-Leonard and Sample, "Disparity Based on Sex," 107; Moore and Padavic, "Racial and Ethnic Disparities," 280.

124. McClellan, *Our Girls, Our Future*, 2–3.

125. National Council on Crime and Delinquency, and Delores Barr Weaver Policy Center, *Girls in Secure Juvenile Detention*, 5.

126. Melendrez and Young Women's Freedom Center, *Centering the Lives*, 17

127. Ocen, "(E)racing Childhood," 1591.

128. Sherman and Balck, *Gender Injustice*, 14.

129. Davis, "Fighting for Hope," 18 (summarizing research).

130. Melendrez and Young Women's Freedom Center, *Centering the Lives*, 42.

131. Epstein, Blake, and González, *Girlhood Interrupted*, 1, 5–6; Morris, *Pushout*, 59; Nanda, "Blind Discretion," 1531; Ocen, "(E)racing Childhood," 1593–94.

132. Epstein, Blake, and González, *Girlhood Interrupted*, 1.

133. Epstein, Blake, and González, *Girlhood Interrupted*, 8.

134. Sherman and Balck, *Gender Injustice*, 11.

135. Flores, *Caught Up*, 114.

CHAPTER 3. ARREST AND PROSECUTION

1. First Amended Complaint, *Simone E. Phoenix v. Day One et al.*, US District Court for the District of Rhode Island (2020) (C.A. No. 20-cv-152-WES-PAS).

2. McMenemy, "Wife Files Abuse Complaint"; McMenemy, "Police Affidavit Details"; McMenemy, "Fired Dover Cop Seeks Access."

3. Jones, "Visualizing the Unequal Treatment of LGBTQ People."

4. Roberts, "Arrests as Guilt," 987–1028, 989, 997–98.

5. Logan and Valente, *Who Will Help Me?*

6. Farrell et al., "Prosecution of State-Level Human Trafficking," 48.

7. National Survivor Network, "National Survivor Network Members Survey."

8. Backus, "Women of Color Overrepresented."

9. Burk, "ABA Summit Keynote."

10. Solutions Not Punishment Collaborative, *"Most Dangerous Thing,"* 11.

11. Logan and Valente, *Who Will Help Me?*

12. Finn and Bettis, "Punitive Action."

13. Yost as quoted in Moore, "8 Women Rescued."

14. Seattle Police Department, "In our experience."

15. Wu and Yelderman, *Prosecution at Any Cost?*

16. Farrell et al., *Identifying Challenges*, 122.

17. Farrell et al., "Failing Victims?"

18. Global Health Justice Partnership of the Yale Law School, Yale School of Public Health, and the Sex Workers Project of the Urban Justice Center, *Diversion from Justice*, 33, 55.

19. Kempdaoo, "Modern-Day White (Wo)Man's Burden," 13.

20. Quoted in Flaherty, "Is the State of Alaska."

21. Williams as quoted in Ritchie, *Invisible No More*, 183.

22. Goodmark, "Hands Up at Home," 1186.

23. Global Health Justice Partnership of the Yale Law School and the Sex Workers Project of the Urban Justice Center, *Un-Meetable Promises*, 44.

24. Burns, "People in Alaska's Sex Trade," 8.

25. Torres and Paz, *Denied Help!*, 22.

26. Best Practices Policy Project, Desiree Alliance, and Sex Workers Outreach Project—NYC, *Human Rights Violations of Sex Workers*, 7; Ditmore, *Use of Raids*, 44.

27. Finn and Bettis, "Punitive Action."

28. Balgamwalla, "Trafficking Rescue Initiatives," 210.

29. Farrell et al., *Identifying Challenges*, 116–17.

30. Hua, "Telling Stories of Trafficking," 204.

31. Goodmark, "When Is a Battered Woman Not a Battered Woman?"; Segrave, Wilson, and Fitz-Gibbon, "Policing Intimate Partner Violence."

32. Miller, *Victims as Offenders*, 28; Richie, *Arrested Justice*, 15–16.

33. Richie, *Arrested Justice*, 24; Richie, *Compelled to Crime*, 119.

34. Galvan and Bazargan, *Interactions of Latina Transgender Women*, 8.

35. Ritchie, *Invisible No More*, 197; Goodmark, "Transgender People," 76.

36. Finn and Bettis, "Punitive Action."

37. Chesney-Lind, "Patriarchy, Crime, and Justice"; Rajan and McCloskey, "Victims of Intimate Partner Violence," 36; West, "'Sorry, We Have to Take You In.'"

38. Miller, *Victims as Offenders*, 79.

39. Hill, *See What You Made Me Do*, 220.

40. Potter, *Battle Cries*, 180.

41. Hirschel, McCormack, and Buzawa, "10-Year Study of the Impact."

42. Muftić, Bouffard, and Bouffard, "An Exploratory Study"; West, "'Sorry, We Have to Take You In.'"

43. Finn and Bettis, "Punitive Action."

44. Frye, Haviland, and Rajah, "Dual Arrest."

45. Goodmark, "When Is a Battered Woman Not a Battered Woman?"; Ritchie, *Invisible No More*, 192, 197.

46. Rajan and McCloskey, "Victims of Intimate Partner Violence," 37–38.

47. Finn and Bettis, "Punitive Action," 279.

48. Rajan and McCloskey, "Victims of Intimate Partner Violence," 34.

49. Connecticut Coalition Against Domestic Violence, "New Dominant Aggressor Law."

50. Finn and Bettis, "Punitive Action," 283.

51. King County Coalition Against Domestic Violence, *Victim-Defendants*, at 30–31.

52. Grace, "'They Just Don't Care.'"

53. No To Violence, "Predominant Aggressor Identification," 8.

54. Ditmore, *Use of Raids*, 8; Farrell et al., "Failing Victims?"

55. Farrell et al., *Identifying Challenges*, 125.

56. Ditmore, *Use of Raids*.

57. Quoted in Ditmore, *Use of Raids*, 8.

58. Farrell et al., *Identifying Challenges*, 87.

59. Details from Miller and Armstrong, "An Unbelievable Story of Rape."

60. Bernard, "KU Student Who Reported Rape."

61. Details from Shugerman, "A Kansas Law School Student Reported a Rape."

62. Hill, *See What You Made Me Do*, 301; Ritchie, *Invisible No More*, 191; Segrave and Carlton, "Women, Trauma, Criminalisation and Imprisonment," 292.

63. Bowen, "They Went to an Emergency Room for Help."

64. Bowen, "They Went to an Emergency Room for Help."

65. Quoted in Dichter, "'They Arrested Me—And I Was the Victim,'" 90.

66. Quotes in Ditmore, *Use of Raids*, 8.

67. Richie, *Arrested Justice*, 190.

68. Boyd, e-mail to author.

69. Kraft-Stolar et al., *From Protection to Punishment*, 3.

70. Ditmore, *Use of Raids*, 41.

71. Swavola, Riley, and Subramanian, *Overlooked*, 29.

72. West, "'Sorry, We Have to Take You In,'" 99.

73. Solutions Not Punishment Collaborative, *"The Most Dangerous Thing,"* 14.

74. Quoted in Ditmore, *Use of Raids*, 16.

75. Swavola, Riley, and Subramanian, *Overlooked*, 19.

76. Roberts, "Arrests as Guilt," 997–98, 1019.

77. Grant, "Human Trafficking Courts."

78. Davis, "Prosecution of Black Men," 178–79.

79. Davis, "Prosecution of Black Men," 178–79.

80. CREW, *Race to Justice*, 6.

81. O'Neill, "Understanding Federal Prosecutorial Declinations," 1439.

82. Gruber, Cohen, and Mogulescu, "Penal Welfare," 1337.

83. Quoted in McCray, "Jailing the Victim."

84. Miller and Meloy, "Women's Use of Force."

85. Farrell et al., *Identifying Challenges*, 130.

86. Gruber, Cohen, and Mogulescu, "Penal Welfare," 44–46.

87. Law, "Abuse Excuse."

88. Ferraro, *Neither Angels nor Demons*.

89. Follingstad et al., "Decisions to Prosecute"; Farrell et al., *Identifying Challenges*, 125.

90. Yaroshefsky, "State of Washington," 16.

91. Yaroshefsky, "State of Washington," 22.

92. Becker, "Passions of Battered Women"; Ferraro, *Neither Angels nor Demons*; Tarrant, Tolmie, and Giudice, *Transforming Legal Understandings*.

93. Newman, "Barred from Her Own Home."

94. Criscione, "Native American Says."

95. Law, "Maddesyn George Killed Her Alleged Rapist."

96. Deer, "Bystander No More?"

97. US Sentencing Memorandum, *United States v. Maddesyn Danielle George*, Case No. 2:20-CR-00153-RMP-1 (E.D. Washington, October 13, 2021).

98. Defendant's Response to Government's Sentencing Memorandum, *United States v. Maddesyn Danielle George*, Case No. 2:20-CR-00153-RMP-1 (E.D. Washington, October 26, 2021).

99. Deer, "Bystander No More?"

100. Ross, *Inventing the Savage*, 52.

101. "Defense Committee Statement on Sentencing."

102. Lyon, Hughes, and Thomas, "People v. Juanita Thomas," 36.

103. Quoted in O'Hagan, "In Baltimore, a Victim."

104. Miles, "System's Response," 2.

105. Farrell et al., "Prosecution of State-level Human Trafficking," 8.

106. Aloe, "Domestic Violence: Orleans County."

107. Gunter, "Why Are Crime Victims Being Jailed."

108. Michaels, "Courts Are Jailing Victims."

109. Daranciang, "Assault Victim Arrested"; McCray, "Jailing the Victim."

110. Clark quoted in Morabito, "Advocates Horrified."

111. Oliver quoted in Morabito, "Advocates Horrified."

112. Clark quoted in Morabito, "Advocates Horrified."

113. Maloney quoted in Barber, "Prosecutor Orders Arrest."

114. Boston quoted in Fleischer, "Innocent Victim Speaks Out."

115. Belgard quoted in Frey, "Abuse Victims Can Sit."

116. Cannizzaro quoted in Hatch, "District Attorney Defends Jailing"; Gunter, "Why Are Crime Victims."

117. Cannizzaro quoted in Maldonado, "Prosecutor Tried to Jail Victim."

118. Chrastil, "DA's Office Refused."

119. Complaint and Jury Demand at 33–34, *Singleton v. Cannizzaro*, No. 2:17-CV-10721 (E.D. Louisiana, October 17, 2017).

120. Stillman, "Why Are Prosecutors Putting Innocent Witnesses."

121. Complaint and Jury Demand, *Singleton v. Cannizzaro*, 2.

122. Complaint and Jury Demand, *Singleton v. Cannizzaro* 2, 33–34.

123. Mitchell quoted in Stillman, "Why Are Prosecutors Putting Innocent Witnesses."

124. Complaint and Jury Demand, *Singleton v. Cannizzaro*, 3, 5, 37.

125. Complaint and Jury Demand, *Singleton v. Cannizzaro*, 29–30.

126. Anderson quoted in Michaels, "Courts Are Jailing Victims."

127. Hesson quoted in Levin, "'Traumatized Every Day.'"

128. Woolington, "Ex-prison Guard Guilty."

129. "Oregon Prison Guard Freed."

130. Wu and Yelderman, "Prosecution at Any Cost?," 24.

131. *Imbler v. Pachtman*, 424 U.S. 409, 427 (1976); *Flagler v. Trainor*, 663 F.3d 543, 547 (2011).

132. *Adams v. Hanson*, 656 F.3d 397, 400, 406 (2011).

133. *Adams v. Hanson*, 656 F.3d 397 (2011).

134. Memorandum Opinion and Order, *Jane Doe v. Harris County, Texas et al.* (2017) (Civil Action No. H-16-2133).

135. Kelly quoted in Byars, "Boulder DA Discusses Recent Decision."

136. Morabito, "DOJ Helping."

137. McCray, "Jailing the Victim"; Sledge, "Two More Settlements Reached."

138. S.B. 291, Session 85(R) (Texas 2017).

139. Guida et al., "Sex Work and the Law," 514.

140. American Bar Association, "Criminal Justice Standards: Prosecution Function §3-4.3."

141. Davis, "Prosecution of Black Men," 182.

142. CREW, *Race to Justice*, 6.

143. Global Health Justice Partnership of the Yale Law School, Yale School of Public Health, and the Sex Workers Project of the Urban Justice Center, *Diversion from Justice*, 30.

144. Sheehy, Stubbs, and Tolmie, "Battered Women Charged with Homicide."

145. Romain and Freiburger, "Chivalry Revisited."

146. Demleitner, "State Prosecutors at the Center," 4.

147. Roberts, "Arrests as Guilt,"1025.

148. Gruber, Cohen, and Mogulescu, "Penal Welfare," 26–27.

149. Gruber, Cohen, and Mogulescu, "Penal Welfare," 39–40.

150. Paul, "Murder Case Exposes Bail System's Flaws."

151. Gill, "Prosecutors Ignored Evidence"; Law, "After Six Months on Rikers."

152. Law, "Punished for Survival."

153. Howard, *Unusually Cruel*, 29.

154. Alkon, "Hard Bargaining in Plea Bargaining."

155. Fontier et al., *New York State Trial Penalty*; Van Cleve, *Crook County*, 84, 173.

156. King County Coalition Against Domestic Violence, *Victim-Defendants*, 20; Sheehy, Stubbs, and Tolmie, "Defences to Homicide," 469.

157. Kiner, "How the Marissa Alexander Plea Deal"; Powers, "Angela Corey's Overzealous Prosecution"; Sanders, "Florida Woman."

158. Bierria and Lenz, "Battering Court Syndrome," 98.

159. Quoted in Jacobs, "Requiring Battered Women Die," 579.

160. Bierria and Lenz, "Battering Court Syndrome," 98.

161. Brico, "State Laws Can Punish Parents."

162. Quoted in Alfonsi, "Failure to Protect."

163. Alfonsi, "Failure to Protect"; Petition for Writ of Habeas Corpus, *Tondalo Hall v. Debbie Aldridge*, CV-17-67 (District Court of Pottawatomi County, Oklahoma, June 22, 2017).

164. Quoted in Pishko, "Serving Life for Surviving Abuse."

165. Law, "Abuse Excuse."

166. Quoted in Bierria and Lenz, "Battering Court Syndrome," 99–100.

167. Lempert, *Women Doing Life*, 13.

168. Howard, *Unusually Cruel*, 47.

169. Mallick and Chatfield, "California Accomplices to a Felony."

170. Smith, "Landmark California Law."

171. Albrecht, "Data Transparency."

172. Trial transcript, *State of Maryland v. Rudeara Bailey*, No. 5749 Criminal (Circuit Court for Dorchester County, 1989).

173. Brant, "Ramona Brant."

174. Branigin, "In Lisa Montgomery."

175. Shared Hope International, *Responding to Sex Trafficking* , 48–49.

176. Volk is quoted in McDermott, "States Working to Toughen Laws."

177. McMahon, "Homicide, Self-defence."

178. Schechter, *Women and Male Violence*, 172.

179. Yaroshefsky, "State of Washington," 15.

180. Jacobsen, Mizga, and D'Orio, "Battered Women, Homicide Convictions."

181. Maguigan, "Battered Women and Self-Defense"; Nourse, "Self-Defense and Subjectivity"; Tolmie et al., "Social Entrapment."

182. Jones, *Women Who Kill*, 316.

183. Shakur, "Women in Prison."

184. Shakur, "Women in Prison."

185. Ewing, "Psychological Self-defense."

186. Walker, *Battered Woman Syndrome.*

187. Faigman, "Battered Woman Syndrome and Self-Defense."

188. Gondolf and Fisher, *Battered Women as Survivors.*

189. Allard, "Rethinking the Battered Woman Syndrome."

190. National Institute of Justice and National Institute of Mental Health, *Validity and Use of Evidence.*

191. Osthoff and Maguigan, "Explaining without Pathologizing"; Dressler and Maguigan, "Battered Women, Self-Defense."

192. Tarrant, Tolmie, and Giudice, *Transforming Legal Understandings*, 8.

193. Fischer, *Domestic Violence Expert Witnesses*, 20.

194. Paulhus quoted in Becker, "Passions of Battered Women," 45.

195. Dewey et al., *Outlaw Women*, 135.

196. Franks, "Real Men Advance," 1123.

197. Flock, "Brittany Smith Loses"; Flock, "How Far Can Abused Women Go."

198. Flock, "Brittany Smith Loses"; Flock, "How Far Can Abused Women Go."

199. Thornton, "Alabama Woman Who Killed."

200. Quoted in Brydum and Kellaway, "This Black Trans Man."

201. Sullivan quoted in Patterson and Mayfield, "Break the Cycle."

202. Dye and Aday, *Women Lifers*, 62.

203. Quotes from van der Leun, "'No Choice but to Do It.'"

204. van der Leun, "'No Choice but to Do It.'"

205. Trial transcript at 46, *People of the State of Michigan v. Patrick Allen Martin*, No. 10-034316-FC-1 (Michigan Court of Appeals, February 4, 2011)

206. Dewey et al., *Outlaw Women*, 93.

207. Richie, *Compelled to Crime*, 149.

208. Kiefer, "State of Arizona."

209. Kiefer, "State of Arizona."

210. Arizona's Family Digital News Staff, "Jodi Arias' Prosecutor."

211. Lyon, Hughes, and Thomas, "People v. Juanita Thomas."

CHAPTER 4. PUNISHMENT AND SENTENCING

1. Goodmark, "Punishment of Dixie Shanahan."

2. Feeley, *Process Is the Punishment.*

3. Herman, "Justice from the Victim's Perspective," 574.

4. Burke and Gray News Staff, "80-Year-Old Woman Sentenced."

5. Busch, *Finding Their Voices*, 66.

6. Harding, "Do Prisons Make Us Safer?"

7. Goodmark, *Decriminalizing Domestic Violence.*

8. Quoted in Jones, *Women Who Kill*, 315.

9. WarBonnett et al., "Women in Prison Tell It Like It Is," 9.

10. Carvalho and Chamberlen, "Why Punishment Pleases," 217.

11. Yepsen, "Let Shanahan Case Run Course," 3.

12. Van Cleve, *Crook County*, 51–53.

13. Dewey et al., *Outlaw Women*, 28–29.

14. Alfonsi, "Failure to Protect."

15. *State of Oklahoma v. Tondalo Rochelle Hall*, No. CF-2004-7403 (District Court In and For Oklahoma County, December 20, 2006).

16. *State of Oklahoma v. Tondalo Rochelle Hall.*

17. Slipke, "Mother Imprisoned."

18. Alaska Statute Annotated § 12.55.155(d)(16) (2020); Indiana Code § 35-38-1-7.1(b)(11) (2018).

19. Angiolillo, "Seeking Truth, Preserving Rights," 256.

20. Garber quoted in Carpizo, "Domestic Violence Victim Sentenced."

21. Block, *Crimes and Punishments*, xiv.

22. Auerhahn, "Adjudication Outcomes."

23. Schneider, *Battered Women Doing Time*, 20.

24. Jacobsen, Mizga, and D'Orio, "Battered Women, Homicide Convictions."

25. Whittier, *Frenemies*, 124.

26. Block, *Crimes and Punishments*, 104.

27. Sheehy, "Battered Women and Mandatory Minimum Sentences."

28. Sentencing transcript, *State v. Shanahan*, No. FECR006475 (Iowa District Court Shelby County 2004).

29. Transcript of sentencing, *United States v. Ashley Nicole Barnett*, No. 6:14-cr-96-Orl-22GJK (Middle District Florida December 18, 2014).

30. Kraft-Stolar et al., *From Protection to Punishment*, 11–12.

31. New York Penal Law § 60.12.

32. Law, "New York Law"; Snyder, "When Can a Woman"; van der Leun, "Evidence against Her."

33. Law, "New York Law"; Snyder, "When Can a Woman"; van der Leun, "Evidence against Her."

34. Nelson and Patillo, dir., *And So I Stayed.*

35. Details quoted in van der Leun, "Evidence against Her."

36. van der Leun, "Evidence against Her."

37. van der Leun, "Evidence against Her."

38. Decision and Order, *People v. Nicole Addimando*, Ind. No. 74/2018, February 2020.

39. Sentencing transcript, *People v. Nicole Addimando*, CC# 68319675H, February 11, 2020.

40. Sentencing transcript, *People v. Nicole Addimando*, CC# 68319675H, February 11, 2020.

41. Law, "New York Lawmakers Fear Court."

42. Opinion and order, *People v. Nicole Addimando*, 197 A.D.3d 106 (New York 2021).

43. Randall, "Nicole Addimando's Sentence Reduced."

44. Quoted in Law, "New York Law."

45. Bernstein and McElwee, "Poll: Oregon Voters Demand."

46. Sivin, "Oregon's Fight."

47. Howard, *Unusually Cruel*, 45, 49.

48. Nellis, *No End in Sight*, 8.

49. Nellis, *In the Extreme*, 11.

50. Lempert, *Women Doing Life*, 15, 48.

51. Cupe quoted in American Friends Service Committee, *From Her Mouth*, 13.

52. Leonard, *Convicted Survivors* (cited in Sentencing Project, *Women and Girls Serving Life Sentences*).

53. Dye and Aday, *Women Lifers*, 5.

54. Jacobsen, Mizga, and D'Orio, "Battered Women, Homicide Convictions," 40.

55. Dye and Aday, *Women Lifers*, 58.

56. Alice Project, *Women on Death Row*.

57. Jeltsen, "Tortured Life"; Schreyer, "Prisoner of War Story."

58. Subramanian and Shames, *Sentencing and Prison Practices*, 10.

59. Sentencing Project, *Incarcerated Women and Girls*.

60. Meyer et al., "Incarceration Rates and Traits."

61. Howard, *Unusually Cruel*, 62.

62. Petersilia, *When Prisoners Come Home*, 5.

63. Zaitzow, "Pastel Fascism," 39.

64. American Friends Service Committee, *From Her Mouth*, 13.

65. Lempert, *Women Doing Life*, 60.

66. Witherspoon, "My Story," 237.

67. Dye and Aday, *Women Lifers*, 74, 134–44.

68. Davis and Shaylor, "Race, Gender, and the Prison Industrial Complex," 7.

69. Dye and Aday, *Women Lifers*, 109.

70. Cosby quoted in Davis et al., *Abolition. Feminism. Now.*, 112.

71. Quoted in WarBonnett et al., "Women in Prison Tell It Like It Is," 11.

72. Crabapple, "Project Rose Is Arresting Sex Workers."

73. Dorotik, "Summertime Woes in Prison," 1–2; Harris, "Untitled," 28–31.

74. Harris, "Untitled," 28.

75. Owen, Wells, and Pollock, *In Search of Safety*, 47.

76. Owen, Wells, and Pollock, *In Search of Safety*, 64.

77. Dye and Aday, *Women Lifers*, 114–15.

78. Roache quoted in Jacobsen, *For Dear Life*, 106.

79. Roache quoted in Jacobsen, *For Dear Life*, 106.

80. Harris, "Untitled," 28.

81. Lempert, *Women Doing Life*, 164.

82. Lempert, *Women Doing Life*, 166.

83. *Montgomery v. Barr et al.*, No. 1:20-cv-03214 (US District Court for DC. 2020).

84. van der Leun, "Confinement and Contagion."

85. Hicks, "Women in Dallas County Jail."

86. Lempert, *Women Doing Life*, 152.

87. Gagné, *Battered Women's Justice*, 182.

88. Kruttschnitt and Gartner, "Women's Imprisonment," 32.

89. Shapiro, Pupovac, and Lydersen, "In Prison, Discipline Comes."

90. US Commission on Civil Rights, *Women in Prison*, 124.

91. Shapiro, Pupovac, and Lydersen, "In Prison, Discipline Comes."

92. Correctional Association of New York, *It Reminds Us How We Got Here*, 16.

93. Lempert, *Women Doing Life*, 111.

94. US Department of Justice, *Investigation of the Edna Mahan Correctional Facility*, 7.

95. Harris, "Untitled," 29.

96. Quoted in Owen, Wells, and Pollock, *In Search of Safety*, 143.

97. Correctional Association of New York, *It Reminds Us How We Got Here*, 15.

98. Vanderford, "Minnesota Malice," 59.

99. Brown, "Protest Planned after Brutal Attack."

100. Nelson, "Dozens Suspended at N.J. Prison."

101. Nelson, "Inmate at Troubled N.J. Prison."

102. Quoted in Tully, "31 Guards Suspended."

103. Diaz, "New Jersey Prisoners."

104. Carlton and Russell, *Resisting Carceral Violence*, 122.

105. Davis, *Abolition Democracy*, 44.

106. McCarter, "At Riker's I had to submit."

107. Lempert, *Women Doing Life*, 153.

108. Lempert, *Women Doing Life*, 153.

109. Richie, *Arrested Justice*, 52.

110. *Henry v. Hulett*, 969 F.3d 769, 775 (7th Circuit 2020).

111. *Henry v. Hulett*, 969 F.3d at 775.

112. Complaint, *Throgmorton v. Reynolds*, 3:12-cv-03087-RM-TSH (2012).

113. Benford, "Cadets Violently Strip Searched Us."

114. Quoted in Law, *Resistance behind Bars*, 66.

115. Whitehorn, introduction, vi.

116. Gagné, *Battered Women's Justice*, 178.

117. Love quoted in nemec, "No One Enters Like Them," 248.

118. Love quoted in nemec, "No One Enters Like Them," 248.

119. Jenness et al., *Violence in California Correctional Facilities*.

120. Shear, "Prison Guard Raped Me."

121. *Sconiers v. Lockhart*, 946 F.3d 1256, 1259 (11th Circuit 2020).

122. US Department of Justice, *Investigation of the Edna Mahan Correctional Facility*; US Department of Justice, *Investigation of the Lowell Correctional Institution*; US Department of Justice, *Investigation of the Julia Tutwiler Prison*.

123. Law, *Resistance behind Bars*, 74–75.

124. Ellenbogen, "Rape Is Rampant."

125. Ovalle, "She Was Raped."

126. Heintz, "Guarded Secrets."

127. Small, "#MeToo Behind Bars."

128. Beck and Johnson, *Sexual Victimization*, 5.

129. Small, "#MeToo Behind Bars."

130. Nozicka, "Therapist Sexually Abused Women."

131. Buchanan, "Impunity," 65–67.

132. US Department of Justice, *Investigation of the Edna Mahan Correctional Facility*, 8–9.

133. Kubiak et al., "Reporting Sexual Victimization during Incarceration."

134. Rantala, *Sexual Victimization Reported*.

135. Fedock et al., "Incarcerated Women's Experiences."

136. *Tangreti v. Bachmann*, 983 F.3d 609 (2d Circuit 2020).

137. Law, *Resistance behind Bars*, 66.

138. US Department of Justice, *Investigation of the Lowell Correctional Institution*, 18.

139. US Department of Justice, *Investigation of the Lowell Correctional Institution*, 22.

140. Jacobsen, *For Dear Life*, 167.

141. Law, "New Report."

142. Shear, "Prison Guard Raped Me."

143. Lempert, *Women Doing Life*, 174.

144. Quote in Owen, Wells, and Pollock, *In Search of Safety*, 165.

145. Hawes, "Incarcerated Women Are Punished."

146. Haines, "Usually in the Free World," 26.

147. This poem appears in American Friends Service Committee, *From Her Mouth*, 35.

148. ACLU, *Still Worse Than Second-Class*, 7.

149. Association of State Correctional Administrators and the Arthur Liman Public Interest Program at Yale Law School, *Aiming to Reduce Time-in-Cell*, 39.

150. US Department of Justice, *Report and Recommendations*.

151. van der Leun, "'I Hope Our Daughters.'"

152. Jacobsen, *For Dear Life*, 180.

153. US Commission on Civil Rights, *Women in Prison*, 31–37.

154. Stahl, "Shocking, Painful Trauma."

155. Humphreys et al., "Telomere Shortening."

156. Patterson, "Dose-Response of Time Served."

157. Jacobsen, *For Dear Life*, 106.

158. Davis and Shaylor, "Race, Gender, and the Prison Industrial Complex," 9; Wolf, Bloom, and Krisberg, "Incarceration of Women in California," 147.

159. Gann, "Trans Health Care," 23–24.

160. Drain, "Happy Mother's Day," 33–34.

161. Jacobsen, *For Dear Life*, 86.

162. Phillips, "What Happens in Prison," 31.

163. Ciarmamella, "These Women Received a Death Sentence."

164. van der Leun, "Death of a Survivor."

165. van der Leun, "Confinement and Contagion."

166. van der Leun, "Confinement and Contagion."

167. Sharp, *Mean Lives*, 60.

168. Howard quoted in Tereshchuk and Fong, "U.S. Jail Populations Drop."

169. Disability Rights Maryland, *Segregation and Suicide*, 14, 17.

170. DeCou, Lynch, and Cole, "Physical and Sexual Victimization Predicts Suicidality."

171. Carlton and Russell, *Resisting Carceral Violence*, 38–39.

172. Adcox, "Female Inmates at Columbia Prison."

173. Disability Rights Maryland, *Segregation and Suicide*, 6–7.

174. Sufrin et al., "Pregnancy Outcomes in U.S. Prisons."

175. Daniel, "Prisons Neglect Pregnant Women."

176. Disability Rights Maryland, *Segregation and Suicide*, 16.

177. *Doe v. Gustavus*, 294 F. Supp. 2d 1003 (Eastern District. Wisconsin 2003).

178. Aday and Farney, "Malign Neglect."

179. Chew, "Aging in Prison."

180. Complaint, *Scott v. Clarke*, No. 3:12-cv-00036 (Western District Virginia, July 24, 2012).

181. Oliver, "Five Years Later."

182. Girshick, "Out of Compliance."

183. Jones, *Women Who Kill*, 335.

184. Comack, *Women in Trouble*, 142.

185. Dye and Aday, *Women Lifers*, 63.

186. Dewey et al., *Outlaw Women*, 156.

187. Jacobsen, *For Dear Life*, 156.

188. Swavola, Riley, and Subramanian, *Overlooked*.

189. Bunney, "One Life in Prison," 30.

190. Law, *Resistance behind Bars*, 220.

191. Menjivar and Walsh, "Gender-based Violence in Central America."

192. Heffron, Serrata, and Hurtado, *Latina Immigrant Women*.

193. Alvarado et al., "Deaths in Custody."

194. Iskander, "On Detention and Skill."

195. Brief of Amici Curiae, *Menocal v. The GEO Group*, 30 F.R.D. 258 (No. 1:14-cv-02887-JKL) (District of Colorado 2017).

196. Ohta and Long, "How Should Health Professionals and Policy Makers Respond."

197. Alvarado et al., "Deaths in Custody"; Chapin, "Women Are Being Denied Cancer Treatment."

198. ACLU California, *Barriers to Reproductive Justice*.

199. Center for Reproductive Rights, *Pregnant Immigrants and Asylum Seekers*.

200. O'Toole, "19 Women Allege Medical Abuse"; Vasquez, "Exclusive: Georgia Doctor."

201. O'Leary, "Addressing the Epidemic of Sexual Assault."

202. Kriel, "ICE Guards 'Systematically' Sexually Assault Detainees"; Law, *Resistance behind Bars*, 150.

203. Law, *Resistance behind Bars*, 153.

204. ACLU California, *Barriers to Reproductive Justice*, 14; Kriel, "ICE Deported a Woman."

205. Frankel, *"Do You See How Much."*

206. Frankel, *"Do You See How Much."*

207. Heffron, Serrata, and Hurtado, *Latina Immigrant Women*, 11.

208. Heffron, Serrata, and Hurtado, *Latina Immigrant Women*, 11.

209. Adkins, Mogulescu, and White, "Labels, Supervision and Surveillance."

210. Meiners, "Awful Acts."

211. Corda, "Introduction"; Levine and Meiners, *Feminist and the Sex Offender*, 10; Logan, "Challenging the Punitiveness."

212. Schenwar and Law, *Prison by Any Other Name*, 104.

213. Levine and Meiners, *Feminist and the Sex Offender*, 11.

214. Nobles, Levenson, and Youstin, "Effectiveness of Residence Restrictions," 492.

215. Schenwar and Law, *Prison by Any Other Name*, 107.

216. Complaint, *Doe v. Miami-Dade County*, 2014 WL 539228 (Southern District Florida 2014).

217. Jennings, "L.A. Sees Parks."

218. Memorandum opinion and order, *Doe v. Marshall*, Case No. 2:15-CV-606-WKW (Middle District Alabama 2019); Brief of Amicus Curiae Michigan Attorney General Dana Nessel, *Doe v. Snyder*, Supreme Court No. 153696 (2019).

219. Rankin, "Court Strikes Down."

220. Pilkington, "'There Was a Lot of Shame.'"

221. Pilkington, "'There Was a Lot of Shame.'"

222. Moreno, "Sex Offender Sues Hospital."

223. Condon, "Sex Offender Registry."

224. Nobles, Levenson, and Youstin, "Effectiveness of Residence Restrictions," 495–96. Brief of Amicus Curiae Michigan Attorney General Dana Nessel, *Doe v. Snyder*, Supreme Court No. 153696 (2019); Pishko, "Expert: Crime Registries."

225. McLeod, "Regulating Sexual Harm," 1562.

226. Hoskins, *Beyond Punishment?*, 110.

227. Levine and Meiners, *Feminist and the Sex Offender*, 3, 51.

228. Brief of Amicus Curiae Michigan Attorney General Dana Nessel, *Doe v. Snyder*, Supreme Court No. 153696 (2019).

229. *Doe v. Marshall*, 367 F. Supp. 3d 1310 (Middle District Alabama 2019).

230. McLeod, "Regulating Sexual Harm," 1581.

231. Linden and Rockoff, *There Goes the Neighborhood?*

232. *Smith v. Doe*, 538 U.S. 84, 99 (2008).

233. Logan, "Challenging the Punitiveness."

234. 142 Congressional Record H4453 (May 7, 1996).

235. Adkins, Mogulescu, and White, "Labels, Supervision and Surveillance."

236. *People v. Snyder*, 175 A.d.3d 1331, 1333 (2019).

237. Mogulescu and Goodmark, "Surveillance and Entanglement."

238. Juvenile Law Center, "Juvenile Sex Offender Registry (SORNA)."

239. Levine and Meiners, *Feminist and the Sex Offender*, 134.

240. Pishko, "Expert: Crime Registries."

241. Ramsey, "Stereotyped Offender."

242. Larance, "Current Controversies," 320.

243. Larance and Miller, "In Her Own Words," 1539.

244. Miller and Meloy, "Women's Use of Force."

245. Larance and Rousson, "Facilitating Change."

246. Law, "Immigrants Who Defend Themselves."

247. Burton, *Becoming Ms. Burton*, 154.

248. Hoskins, *Beyond Punishment?*, 22.

249. Hoskins, *Beyond Punishment?*, 14.

250. Sharp, *Mean Lives*, 80.

251. Nelson and Patillo, dir., *And So I Stayed*.

252. Musto, *Control and Protect*, 131.

253. Jacobs and Richard, "Impact of Criminal Arrest."

254. Couloute and Kopf, "Out of Prison and Out of Work."

255. Couloute, "Nowhere to Go."

256. Jacobs and Richard, "Impact of Criminal Arrest".

257. Vergano, "Criminal Justice System Is Bad for Your Health."

258. Miller, *Halfway Home*, 99.

259. Miller, *Halfway Home*, 37.

260. Blakinger, "Does Banning People."

261. Lageson, "Purgatory of Digital Punishment."

262. Musto, *Control and Protect*, 120.

263. *United States v. Nesbeth*, 188 F. Supp. 3d 179, 180 (Eastern District New York 2016).

264. Garcia-Hallett, *"We're Being Released to a Jungle,'"* 469.

CHAPTER 5. RECONSIDERATION AND CLEMENCY

1. Florida Statutes Annotated § 921.1402 (2018).

2. Omnibus Public Safety and Justice Amendment Act of 2020, 68 D.C. Reg. 4792 (January 13, 2021).

3. S.B. 1008, 80th Leg., Regular Session (Oregon 2019).

4. Hempel, "Battered and Convicted," 32.

5. S.B. 209, 99th General Assembly (Illinois 2015) (codified at 735 Ill. Comp. Stat. 5/2-1401).

6. *People v. Patrice Smith*, Indictment No. 98-3053-001 (New York County Court, September 2, 2020).

7. Coalition for Women Prisoners, *Justice and Dignity for DV Survivors*.

8. Chabria, "Sex Trafficked and Imprisoned."

9. Sledge, "One of Louisiana's Oldest."

10. *People v. Patrice Smith*, Indictment No. 98-3053-001.

11. Flynn quoted in Horvatits, "DA Unhappy."

12. *People v. Patrice Smith*, Indictment No. 98-3053-001.

13. Rowe, "Judge Has Mercy."

14. Law, "New York Law."

15. White-Domain quoted in Law, "New York Lawmakers Fear."

16. Quoted in Nelson and Patillo, dir., *And So I Stayed*.

17. Mogulescu quoted in Kamis and Rose, "Domestic Violence Survivors Justice Act."

18. Howard, *Unusually Cruel*, 114.

19. Lomax and Kumar, *Still Blocking the Exit*, 7.

20. Shammas, "Perils of Parole Hearings."

21. Barry et al., "Policies and Polling," 4.

22. Dennison quoted in Lee, "Convicted of Murder."

23. Ruhland et al., *Continuing Leverage*.

24. Boudin, "Hope, Illusion and Imagination," 568.

25. Shaffer quoted in Slater, "Can You Talk."

26. Shammas, "Perils of Parole Hearings," 3.

27. Aviram, *Yesterday's Monsters*, 170.

28. Rummel quoted in Slater, "Can You Talk."

29. Quoted in Survived & Punished, "It's breathtaking to connect."

30. Cassidy, "Undue Influence."

31. Weisberg, Mukamal, and Segall, *Life in Limbo*, 20.

32. Geraghty and Woodhams, "Predictive Validity"; Hamilton, "Sexist Algo-

rithm"; Rhine, Petersilia, and Reitz, "Improving Parole Release"; Robinson-Oost, "Evaluation as the Proper Function."

33. Marimow, "Prisoners Need This Exam."

34. Shapiro quoted in Gonnerman, "Prepping for Parole."

35. Vincour quoted in Bischoff, "Ohio Parole Board Member Quits."

36. Louis, "Remember What Parole Is For"; Rhine, Petersilia, and Reitz, "Improving Parole Release," 99.

37. Schwartzapfel, "Want to Shrink the Prison Population?."

38. Smith quoted in Pelzer, "Ohio Parole Board."

39. Kate quoted in Kraft-Stolar et al., *From Protection to Punishment*, 9.

40. Quoted in West-Smith, Pogrebin, and Poole, "Denial of Parole," 7–8.

41. Aviram, *Yesterday's Monsters*, 9.

42. Boudin, "Hope, Illusion and Imagination," 573.

43. Shammas, "Perils of Parole Hearings," 10.

44. Kraft-Stolar et al., *From Protection to Punishment*, 19.

45. Reamer, *On the Parole Board*, 37.

46. Angie quoted in Schneider, *Battered Women Doing Time*, 84.

47. Thuma, *All Our Trials*, 113.

48. Boudin, "Hope, Illusion and Imagination," 570.

49. Dye and Aday, *Women Lifers*, 177.

50. Lempert, *Women Doing Life*, 141.

51. Dorotik, "Lifer's Lifelong Search," 18–19.

52. Weisberg, Mukamal, and Segall, *Life in Limbo*, 9.

53. Kraft-Stolar et al., *From Protection to Punishment*, 19.

54. Ruhland et al., *Continuing Leverage*.

55. *Rossakis v. New York State Board of Parole*, 41 N.Y.S.3d 490, 493 (App. Div. 2016).

56. *Rossakis v. New York State Board of Parole*, 41 N.Y.S.3d at 493.

57. *Rossakis v. New York State Board of Parole*, 41 N.Y.S.3d at 495–96.

58. Jacobsen and Lempert, "Institutional Disparities."

59. Ammons, "Why Do You Do."

60. Law, *Resistance behind Bars*, 25–26.

61. Gagné, *Battered Women's Justice*.

62. Rooney, "Celeste Declares Open Season," 11A.

63. Law, *Resistance behind Bars*, 26.

64. Hempel, "Battered and Convicted," 27.

65. Machado, *In the Dream House*, 137.

66. Machado, *In the Dream House*, 138.

67. Ammons, "Why Do You Do," 550.

68. Ammons, "Why Do You Do, "557.

69. Gill, "Arkansas Grants Parole"; Gill, "Life Sentence in Arkansas."

70. Lussenhop, "After Years in Prison."

71. Lussenhop, "After Years in Prison"; Wicentowski, "Angel Stewart Won Parole."

72. Survived & Punished, "Action Toolkit to Free Assia."

73. Lowe, "Prison Board Says."

74. Lowe, "Prison Board Says."

75. Holt and McCormick, "Hope for Hope"; Lowe, "Prison Board Says."

76. California Penal Code § 4801 (2018).

77. Méndez, "Gov. Abbott Establishes Clemency Application."

78. Jacobsen and Lempert, "Institutional Disparities," 284.

79. King quoted in Shamus, "5 Michigan Women Lifers Want Clemency."

80. Cooper quoted in Shamus, "5 Michigan Women Lifers Want Clemency."

81. Letter from David Prater to Oklahoma Pardon and Parole Board (March 8, 2019).

82. Boudin, "Hope, Illusion and Imagination," 579.

83. Sharp, *Mean Lives*, 73.

84. Western, *Homeward*, 83.

85. Johnson, "Economic Impediments," 374.

86. Petersilia, *When Prisoners Come Home*, 120.

87. Sered and Norton-Hawk, "Beyond Recidivism and Desistance," 181–82.

88. Sered and Norton-Hawk, "Beyond Recidivism and Desistance," 181.

89. Sharp, *Mean Lives*, 99.

90. Brown-Long and Mauger, *Free Cyntoia*, 241.

91. Cross, "Reentering Survivors," 109.

92. Mogulescu and Goodmark, "Surveillance and Entanglement."

93. Glazer, "Why It Might Be."

94. Ocen, "Awakening."

95. Fischer quoted in Glazer, "Why It Might Be Time to Rethink."

96. Cosby quoted in Gaines, "Why Even Illinois' Department of Corrections."

97. Opsal, "'It's Their World,'" 192.

98. Kaeble, *Probation and Parole*.

99. Teresa quoted in Schneider, *Battered Women Doing Time*, 89.

100. Melamed, "Pa. Board of Pardons Recommends Clemency"; Zuckerman and Cucinella, "Read These Stories."

101. Emergency Petition for Executive Clemency for Deborah Jennings.

102. Carter, López, and Songster, "Redeeming Justice," 328.

CHAPTER 6. ABOLITION FEMINISM

1. Watson and Edelman, "Improving the Juvenile Justice System," 220–24.

2. Office of the Child Advocate, *From Trauma to Tragedy*, 9–10.

3. Heipt, "Girl's Court," 834–37.

4. Sherman and Balck, *Gender Injustice*, 10.

5. Birckhead, "'Youngest Profession,'" 1111.

6. Menzel, "Sex Trafficking Bill."

7. Flores, *Caught Up*, 48–49.

8. Lydia and Glesmann, *Addressing Barriers*.

9. Ocen, "(E)racing Childhood," 1625.

10. Gies et al., *Safe Harbor Laws, Phase I*, 17–19.

11. Gies et al., *Safe Harbor Laws, Phase I*, 10; Gies et al., *Safe Harbor Laws, Phase 2*, 24.

12. Sprang et al., "Impact of Safe Harbor Legislation," 820–24.

13. Fahy, "Safe Harbor," 154; Gies et al., *Safe Harbor Laws, Phase I*, 10.

14. *Ohio v. Martin*, 116 N.E.3d 127 (Ohio 2018); Brief of the Human Trafficking Pro Bono Legal Center as Amicus Curiae in Support of Appellant Martin Martin, 116 N.E.3d 127 (Ohio 2018) (No. 2016-1891).

15. Contrera, "State of Ohio."

16. Kruzan, "Congress Needs to Pass Sara's Law."

17. See, e.g., *People v. C.C.*, 7 N.Y.S.3d 244 (Criminal Court 2014); *People v. L.G.*, 972 N.Y.S.2d 418 (Criminal Court 2013); *People v. Doe*, 935 N.Y.S.2d 481 (Sup. Court 2011).

18. Marsh et al., "State Report Cards."

19. Gonzalez quoted in Steadman, "More Than 1,000 Open Prostitution Cases."

20. Violence Against Women Reauthorization Act of 2021, H.R. 1620, 117th Congress, Title XI (2021), https://www.congress.gov/bill/117th-congress/house-bill/1620/text#toc-H7CAB2F7D6C8D430BACCE2346F4351B03.

21. McCorkel, *Breaking Women*, 37–38.

22. Lawston and Meiners, "Ending Our Expertise," 8.

23. Tereshchuk and Fong, "U.S. Jail Populations Drop."

24. Kubiak, Conington, and Hillier, *Trauma-Informed Corrections*, 92.

25. Diaz, "New Jersey Prisoners."

26. ACLU, *Still Worse Than Second-Class*, 17.

27. Spade, "Only Way to End Racialized Gender Violence," 184.

28. Dye and Aday, *Women Lifers*, 208; Rhine, Petersilia, and Reitz, "Improving Parole Release"; Wolf, Bloom, and Krisberg, "Incarceration of Women."

29. Barkow, Holden, and Osler, "Clemency Process Is Broken."

30. Survived & Punished NY, *No Good Prosecutors Now or Ever*, 4.

31. Howard quoted in Kang-Brown and Lu, "America's Growing Gender Jail Gap."

32. Gagné, *Battered Women's Justice*, 170.

33. Gill, "Prosecutors Ignored Evidence."

34. Bragg, "I #StandWithTracy."

35. US Department of Justice, *Review of the Federal Bureau of Prisons' Management*.

36. Becker, "Passions of Battered Women," 20.

37. Weissman, "Gender Violence."

38. Butler, "System Is Working," 1425.

39. Survived & Punished New York, *Preserving Punishment Power*, 12.

40. Ervin quoted in Paiella, "How Would Prison Abolition."

41. Musto, *Control and Protect*, 14.

42. Stone et al., *Women, Incarceration, and Violent Crime.*

43. Davis and Rodriguez, "Challenge of Prison Abolition," 217.

44. Braz quoted in Samuels and Stein, "Perspectives on Critical Resistance," 7.

45. Bassichis, Lee, and Spade, "Building an Abolitionist Trans and Queer Movement," 31–32.

46. Levine quoted in Miller et al., "Changing the Way," 449.

47. Bayley, *Police for the Future*, 3; McLeod, "Prison Abolition," 1201.

48. Kaba, "Yes, We Mean Literally."

49. Seigel, *Violence Work.*

50. Butler, "System Is Working," 1425.

51. Eisenberg-Guyot quoted in Dwamena, "Closing Rikers."

52. Schenwar and Law, *Prison by Any Other Name.*

53. Davis et al., *Abolition. Feminism. Now.*, 65.

54. Kaba, *We Do This*, 2.

55. Paiella, "How Would Prison Abolition."

56. Critical Resistance, "What Is Abolition?"

57. Kaba, *We Do This*, 4.

58. McLeod, "Envisioning Abolition Democracy," 1615.

59. Kaba, *We Do This*, 137.

60. Phipps, *Me, Not You*, 163.

61. Russo, *Feminist Accountability*, 86.

62. Richie, "Keynote: Reimagining the Movement," 262.

63. Kushner, "Is Prison Necessary?"

64. Richie, "Abolition Feminism."

65. Davis et al., *Abolition. Feminism. Now.*, 5.

66. Lee, "Prickly Coalitions," 109, 111.

67. Hamaji et al., *Freedom to Thrive*, 3.

68. Kaba, *We Do This*, 13, 96.

69. Survived & Punished New York, *Preserving Punishment Power*, 12–15.

70. Walklate and Fitz-Gibbon, "Why Criminalize Coercive Control?"

71. In re: B.W., 313 S.W.3d 818 (Texas 2010).

72. Birckhead, "'Youngest Profession,'" 1067–68.

73. Survived & Punished New York, *Preserving Punishment Power*, 27.

74. Weissman, "Gender Violence."

75. Arnett, "From Decarceration to E-Carceration."

76. Bierria et al., *#SurvivedandPunished.*

77. Howard, *Unusually Cruel*, 47.

78. Bazelon, "Anissa Jordan Took Part."

79. Officer, McAlister, and Tallan, "Updated Measure 11 Indictments," 4.

80. Kaba, *We Do This*, 110.

81. Levin, "'Governor, Let Me See My Kids before I Die.'"

82. Love and Schlussel, *Pathways to Reintegration*.

83. Bell, "Abolition: A New Paradigm," 45–49.

84. Bordeaux, "Radicalized at the Workhouse."

85. Survived & Punished New York, *Preserving Punishment Power*, 9.

86. Price quoted in Weber and Quijano, "Activists Call on Travis County."

87. Fisher, "Commissioners Court."

88. Kaba, *We Do This*, 59.

89. Gilmore, "Abolition Geography," 234.

90. Bassichis, Lee, and Spade, "Building an Abolitionist Trans and Queer Movement," 39.

91. Davis, *Freedom Is a Constant Struggle*, 106.

Bibliography

ACLU California. *Barriers to Reproductive Justice While Detained.* San Francisco: ACLU California, 2020.

Acoca, Leslie. "Investing in Girls: A 21st Century Strategy." *Office of Juvenile Justice and Delinquency Prevention* 6, no. 1 (1999): 3–13.

Aday, Ronald, and Lori Farney. "Malign Neglect: Assessing Older Women's Health Care Experiences in Prison." *Journal of Bioethical Inquiry* 11, no. 3 (2014): 359–72.

Adcox, Seanna. "Female Inmates at Columbia Prison Were Punished for Seeking Help, SC Psychiatrist Reports." *Post and Courier*, October 23, 2019. https://www.postandcourier.com/politics/female-inmates-at-columbia-prison-were-punished-for-seeking-help-sc-psychiatrist-reports/article_93dfa94e-f5c2-11e9-92fc-136500b8294e.html#:~:text=Seanna%20Adcox,-Assistant%20Columbia%20bureau&text=COLUMBIA%20%E2%80%94%20Suicidal%20and%20mentally%20ill,summer%20told%20legislators%20on%20Wednesday.

Adkins, LeAnn, Kate Mogulescu, and K. B. White. "Labels, Supervision and Surveillance: Motherhood and Sex Offender Status." *Scholar & Feminist Online* 15, no. 3 (2019). http://sfonline.barnard.edu/unraveling-criminalizing-webs-building-police-free-futures/labels-supervision-surveillance-motherhood-sex-offender-status/.

Albrecht, Kat. "Data Transparency and the Disparate Impact of the Felony Murder Rule." *Duke Center for Firearms Law*, August 11, 2020. https://firear

mslaw.duke.edu/2020/08/data-transparency-the-disparate-impact-of-the-fel
ony-murder-rule/.

Alfonsi, Sharyn. "Failure to Protect: How an Oklahoma Child Abuse Law Treats
Women Differently Than Men." *CBS News*, June 7, 2020. https://www.cbsne
ws.com/news/failure-to-protect-oklahoma-child-abuse-law-60-minutes-2020
-06-07/.

The Alice Project. *Women on Death Row in the United States*. Ithaca, NY: Alice
Project, 2020.

Alkon, Cynthia. "Hard Bargaining in Plea Bargaining: When Do Prosecutors
Cross the Line?" *Nevada Law Journal* 17, no. 2 (Spring 2017): 401–28.

Allard, Sharon. "Rethinking the Battered Woman Syndrome: A Black Feminist
Perspective." *UCLA Women's Law Journal* 1 (1991): 191–207.

Aloe, Jess. "Domestic Violence: Orleans County Prosecutor Takes a Tough
Approach." *Burlington Free Press*, November 1, 2018. https://www.burlingtonf
reepress.com/story/news/2018/11/01/domestic-violence-orleans-county-prose
cutor-takes-tough-approach/997903002/.

Alvarado, Monsy, Ashley Balcerzak, Stacey Barchenger, Jon Campbell, Rafael
Carranza, Maria Clark, Alan Gomez, Daniel Gonzalez, Trevor Hughes, Rick
Jervis, Dan Keemahill, Rebecca Plevin, Jeremy Schwartz, Sarah Taddeo,
Lauren Villagran, Dennis Wagner, Elizabeth Weise, and Alissa Zhu. "Deaths
in Custody. Sexual Violence. Hunger Strikes. What We Uncovered Inside ICE
Facilities across the US." *USA Today*, December 22, 2019. https://www.usatod
ay.com/in-depth/news/nation/2019/12/19/ice-asylum-under-trump-exclusive
-look-us-immigration-detention/4381404002/.

American Bar Association. "Criminal Justice Standards: Prosecution Function
§3-4.3." 2017. https://www.americanbar.org/groups/criminal_justice/standar
ds/ProsecutionFunctionFourthEdition/ (accessed May 26, 2022).

American Bar Association and National Bar Association. "Justice by Gender: The
Lack of Appropriate Prevention, Diversion and Treatment Alternatives for
Girls in the Justice System." *William & Mary Journal of Women and the Law*
9, no. 1 (2002): 73–97.

American Civil Liberties Union (ACLU). *Still Worse Than Second-Class: Solitary
Confinement of Women in the United States*. New York: ACLU, 2019.

American Friends Service Committee. *From Her Mouth to Your Ears: A Survivor's Manual by and for Women in Prison*. Philadelphia, PA: American
Friends Service Committee, 2018.

Ammons, Linda L. "Why Do You Do the Things You Do? Clemency for Battered
Incarcerated Women, A Decade's Review." *American University Journal of
Gender* 11, no. 2 (2002–3): 533–66.

Angiolillo, Daniel D. "Seeking Truth, Preserving Rights—Battered Women's
Syndrome/Extreme Emotional Distress: Abuse Excuse or Syndrome Defense."
Pace Law Review 24, no. 1 (2003): 253–57.

The Annie E. Casey Foundation. *Making Detention Reform Work for Girls.* Baltimore, MD: Annie E. Casey Foundation, 2013.

Arizona's Family Digital News Staff. "Jodi Arias' Prosecutor Juan Martinez Has Been Disbarred." Azfamily.com, July 17, 2020. https://www.azfamily.com/news/jodi-arias-prosecutor-juan-martinez-has-been-disbarred/article_96a3babe-c874-11ea-88ff-27046c4029a4.html.

Arnett, Chaz. "From Decarceration to E-Carceration." *Cardozo Law Review* 41, no. 2 (December 2019): 641–720.

Arthur, Patricia J., and Regina Waugh. "Status Offenses and the Juvenile Justice and Delinquency Prevention Act: The Exception That Swallowed the Rule." *Seattle Journal for Social Justice* 7, no. 2 (Spring/Summer 2009): 555–76.

Association of State Correctional Administrators and the Arthur Liman Public Interest Program at Yale Law School. *Aiming to Reduce Time-in-Cell: Reports from Correctional Systems on the Numbers of Prisoners in Restricted Housing and on the Potential of Policy Changes to Bring about Reforms.* 2016.

Auerhahn, Kathleen. "Adjudication Outcomes in Intimate and Non-Intimate Homicides." *Homicide Studies* 11, no. 3 (2007): 213–30. https://doi.org/10.1177/1088767907304121.

Aviram, Hadar. *'Yesterday's Monsters: The Manson Family Cases and the Illusion of Parole.* Oakland: University of California Press, 2020.

Backus, Lisa. "Women of Color Overrepresented in CT Domestic Violence Arrests, Data Shows."

Connecticut Health I-Team, September 9, 2021. http://c-hit.org/2021/09/09/women-of-color-overrepresented-in-domestic-violence-arrests-data-show/.

Balgamwalla, Sabrina. "Trafficking Rescue Initiatives as State Violence." *Penn State Law Review* 122, no. 1 (Fall 2017): 171–216.

Barber, Alex. "Prosecutor Orders Arrest of Woman as Material Witness to Testify against Her Alleged Abuser." *Bangor Daily News,* September 20, 2013. https://bangordailynews.com/2013/09/20/news/prosecutor-orders-arrest-of-woman-as-material-witness-to-testify-against-her-alleged-abuser/.

Barkow, Rachel, Mark Holden, and Mark Osler. "The Clemency Process Is Broken. Trump Can Fix It." *The Atlantic,* January 15, 2019. https://www.theatlantic.com/ideas/archive/2019/01/the-first-step-act-isnt-enoughwe-need-clemency-reform/580300/.

Barry, Kyle C., Ben Miller, Miriam Aroni Krinsky, and Sean McElwee. "Policies and Polling on Reducing Excessive Prison Terms." The Justice Collaborative Institute and Fair and Just Prosecution, 2020.

Basile, Kathleen C., Heather B. Clayton, Sarah DeGue, John W. Gilford, Kevin J. Vagi, Nicolas A. Suarez, Marissa L. Zwald, and Richard Lowry. "Interpersonal Violence Victimization among High School Students—Youth Risk Behavior Survey, United States, 2019." *Morbidity and Mortality Weekly Report* 69, no. 1 (2020): 28–37.

Bassichis, Morgan, Alexander Lee, and Dean Spade. "Building an Abolitionist Trans and Queer Movement with Everything We've Got." In *Captive Genders: Trans Embodiment and the Prison Industrial Complex*, edited by Eric A. Stanley and Nat Smith, 21–46. Oakland, CA: AK Press, 2015.

"Battered Wife Gets Six Years for Killing Husband." *UPI*, March 6, 1987. https://www.upi.com/Archives/1987/03/06/Battered-wife-gets-six-years-for-killing-husband/1230542005200/.

Bayley, David H. *Police for the Future*. Oxford, UK: Oxford University Press, 1999.

Bazelon, Lara. "Anissa Jordan Took Part in a Robbery. She Went to Prison for Murder." *The Atlantic*, February 16, 2021. https://www.theatlantic.com/politics/archive/2021/02/what-makes-a-murderer/617819/.

Beck, Allen J., and Candace Johnson. *Sexual Victimization Reported by Former State Prisoners*. Washington, DC: US Department of Justice, 2012.

Becker, Mary. "The Passions of Battered Women: Cognitive Links between Passion, Empathy, and Power." *William & Mary Journal of Women and the Law* 8, no. 1 (Fall 2001): 1–72.

Becker, Sarah, and Jill A. McCorkel. "The Gender of Criminal Opportunity: The Impact of Male Co-Offenders on Women's Crime." *Feminist Criminology* 6, no. 2 (2011): 79–110.

Belknap, Joanne, Kristi Holsinger, and Melissa Dunn. "Understanding Incarcerated Girls: The Results of a Focus Group Study." *The Prison Journal* 77, no. 4 (December 1997): 381–404. https://doi.org/10.1177/0032855597077004003.

Bell, Marina. "Abolition: A New Paradigm for Reform." *Law & Social Inquiry* 46, no. 1 (February 2021): 32–68.

Benford, Willette. "Cadets Violently Strip Searched Us As Part of Their Training. For My Pain, I Got $325." *The Marshall Project*, May 6, 2021. https://www.themarshallproject.org/2021/05/06/cadets-violently-strip-searched-us-as-part-of-their-training-for-my-pain-i-got-a-measly-325?utm_medium=email&utm_campaign=newsletter&utm_source=opening-statement&utm_term=newsletter-20210507-2468.

Benkarski, Ashley. "Cyntoia Brown Steps into Freedom." *Tennessee Tribune*, August 9, 2019. https://tntribune.com/cyntoia-brown-steps-into-freedom/.

Bernard, Katie. "KU Student Who Reported Rape Says Lawrence Police Were Worried about Man's Law Career." *Kansas City Star*, November 5, 2019. https://www.kansascity.com/news/local/crime/article236791803.html.

Bernstein, Elizabeth. "Militarized Humanitarianism Meets Carceral Feminism: The Politics of Sex, Rights, and Freedom in Contemporary Antitrafficking Campaigns." *Signs* 36, no. 1 (2010): 45–72.

Bernstein, Molly, and Sean McElwee. "Poll: Oregon Voters Demand Reduced Prison Terms for Domestic Violence Victims." *The Appeal*, March 17, 2021.

https://theappeal.org/the-lab/polling-memos/poll-oregon-voters-demand-re
duced-prison-terms-for-domestic-violence-victims/.

Best Practices Policy Project, Desiree Alliance, and Sex Workers Outreach Project—NYC. *Human Rights Violations of Sex Workers, People in the Sex Trades,
and People Profiled as Such.* United Nations, 2014.

Bierria, Alisa, Mariame Kaba, Essence McDowell, Hyejin Shim, and Stacy Suh.
#SurvivedandPunished: Survivor Defense as Abolitionist Praxis. Love and
Protect and Survived and Punished, 2018.

Bierria, Alisa, and Colby Lenz. "Battering Court Syndrome: A Structure Critique
of 'Failure to Protect.'" In *The Politicization of Safety: Critical Perspectives on
Domestic Violence Responses,* edited by Jane K. Stover, 91–118. New York: New
York University Press, 2019.

Bierria, Alisa, Hyejin Shim, Mimi Kim, and Emi Kane. "Free Marissa Now and
Stand with Nan-Hui: A Conversation about Parallel Struggles." *Feminist Wire,*
June 30, 2015. https://thefeministwire.com/2015/06/free-marissa-and-stand
-with-nan-hui/.

Birckhead, Tamar R. "The 'Youngest Profession': Consent, Autonomy, and
Prostituted Children." *Washington University Law Review* 88, no. 5 (2011):
1055–116.

Bischoff, Laura A. "Ohio Parole Board Member Quits, Calls Agency Toxic and
Secretive." *Dayton Daily News,* January 19, 2019. https://www.daytondailyne
ws.com/news/ohio-parole-board-member-quits-calls-agency-toxic-and-secret
ive/ByJ9WXUeoJOFFhhr8dQP8M/.

Blakinger, Keri. "Does Banning People with Felonies from Dating Apps Actually
Make Anyone Safer?" *The Marshall Project,* May 20, 2021. https://www.them
arshallproject.org/2021/05/20/does-banning-people-with-felonies-from-dati
ng-apps-actually-make-anyone-safer?utm_medium=email&utm_campaign=
newsletter&utm_source=opening-statement&utm_term=newsletter-202105
20-2477.

Block, Frederic. *Crimes and Punishments: Entering the Mind of a Sentencing
Judge.* Chicago: ABA Publishing, 2019.

Bordeaux, Inez. "Radicalized at the Workhouse." *Inquest,* October 22, 2021.
https://inquest.org/radicalized-at-the-workhouse/.

Boudin, Kathy. "Hope, Illusion and Imagination: The Politics of Parole and
Reentry in the Era of Mass Incarceration." *New York University Law Review*
38, no. 4 (2014): 563–82.

Bowen, Alison. "They Went to an Emergency Room for Help after a Sexual
Assault. Instead, They Were Arrested." *Chicago Tribune,* December 10, 2019.
https://www.chicagotribune.com/lifestyles/ct-life-sexual-assault-survivors-ar
rested-emergency-rooms-20191210-sch74mzmxvdoxh2pc2xxttjik4-story.html.

Boyd, Jody. Email to author, March 27, 2020.

Bragg, Alvin (@AlvinBraggNYC). "I #StandWithTracy. Prosecuting a domestic violence survivor who acted in self-defense is unjust." Twitter, September 10, 2020. https://twitter.com/alvinbraggnyc/status/1304215413761413120?lan g=en

Branigin, Anne. "In Lisa Montgomery, Formerly Incarcerated Women See Echoes of Their Own Stories: 'She Never Had a Chance to Just Live.'" *The Lily*, January 12, 2021. https://www.thelily.com/in-lisa-montgomery-formerly-inca rcerated-women-see-echoes-of-their-own-stories-she-never-had-a-chance-to -just-live/.

Brant, Ramona. "Ramona Brant." *Nation of Second Chances*, February 16, 2018. https://www.nationofsecondchances.org/ramona-brant/.

Brico, Elizabeth. "State Laws Can Punish Parents Living in Abusive Households." *Talkpoverty*, October 25, 2019. https://talkpoverty.org/2019/10/25/failure-pr otect-child-welfare/.

Briner, Leslie. Email to author, November 8, 2021.

Brown-Long, Cyntoia, and Bethany Mauger. *Free Cyntoia: My Search for Redemption in the American Prison System*. New York: Atria, 2019.

Brown, DeNeen L. "Missouri v. Celia, a Slave: She Killed the White Master Raping Her, Then Claimed Self-Defense." *Washington Post*, June 12, 2020. https://www.washingtonpost.com/news/retropolis/wp/2017/10/19/missouri -v-celia-a-slave-she-killed-the-white-master-raping-her-then-claimed-self-de fense/.

Brown, Geneva O. "Little Girl Lost: Las Vegas Metro Police Vice Division and the Use of Material Witness Holds against Teenaged Prostitutes." *Catholic University Law Review* 57, no. 2 (Winter 2008): 471–510.

Brown, Julie K. "Protest Planned after Brutal Attack by Guards on Woman at Florida's Lowell Prison." *Miami Herald*, August 23, 2019. https://www.miami herald.com/news/state/florida/article234299092.html.

Brydum, Sunnivie, and Mitch Kellaway. "This Black Trans Man Is in Prison for Killing His Rapist." *The Advocate*, April 8, 2015. https://www.advocate.com /politics/transgender/2015/04/08/black-trans-man-prison-killing-his-rapist.

Buchanan, Kim Shayo. "Impunity: Sexual Abuse in Women's Prisons." *Harvard Civil Rights-Civil Liberties Law Review* 42, no. 1 (Winter 2007): 45–88.

Bunney, Marcia. "One Life in Prison: Perception, Reflection, and Empowerment." In *Harsh Punishment: International Experiences of Women's Imprisonment*, edited by Sandy Cook and Susanne Davies, 16–32. Boston: Northeastern University Press, 1999.

Burk, Connie. "ABA Summit Keynote." American Bar Association LGBT Domes-tic Violence Legal Issues Summit, 2008.

Burke, Maressa, and Gray News Staff. "80-Year-Old Woman Sentenced to 8 to 10 Years for Husband's Murder." *Fox19Now*, July 14, 2021. https://www.fox19.com /2021/07/15/80-year-old-woman-sentenced-8-10-years-husbands-murder/.

Burns, Tara. "People in Alaska's Sex Trade: Their Lived Experiences and Policy Recommendations." MA thesis. University of Alaska Fairbanks, 2015.

Burton, Susan. *Becoming Ms. Burton: From Prison to Recovery to Leading the Fight for Incarcerated Women.* New York: New Press, 2019.

Busch, Amy Lou. *Finding Their Voices: Listening to Battered Women Who've Killed.* Commack, NY: Kroshka Books, 1999.

Butler, Paul. "The System Is Working the Way It Is Supposed To: The Limits of Criminal Justice Reform." *Freedom Center Journal* 2019, no. 1 (2020): 75–124.

Byars, Mitchell. "Boulder DA Discusses Recent Decision to Hold Named Domestic Violence Victim in Contempt for Refusing to Testify." *Boulder Daily Camera,* June 13, 2021. https://www.dailycamera.com/2021/06/13/boulder-da-discusses-recent-decision-to-hold-named-domestic-violence-victim-in-contempt-for-refusing-to-testify/.

Carlton, Bree, and Russell Emma K. *Resisting Carceral Violence: Women´s Imprisonment and the Politics of Abolition.* New York: Palgrave Macmillan, 2019.

Carpizo, Almendra. "Domestic Violence Victim Sentenced to 4 Years after Fatally Stabbing Longtime Boyfriend." *Recordnet.com,* July 11, 2019. https://www.recordnet.com/news/20190711/domestic-violence-victim-sentenced-to-4-years-after-fatally-stabbing-longtime-boyfriend.

Carter, Terrell, Rachel López, and Kempis Songster. "Redeeming Justice." *Northwestern University Law Review* 116, no. 2 (2021): 315–82.

Carvalho, Henrique, and Anastasia Chamberlen. "Why Punishment Pleases: Punitive Feelings in a World of Hostile Solidarity." *Punishment & Society* 20, no. 2 (2017): 217–34. https://doi.org/10.1177/1462474517699814.

Cassidy, R. Michael. "Undue Influence: A Prosecutor's Role in Parole Proceedings." *Ohio State Journal of Criminal Law* 16, no. 2 (Spring 2019): 293–306.

Center for Reproductive Rights. *Pregnant Immigrants and Asylum Seekers during COVID-19.* New York: Center for Reproductive Rights, 2020.

Chabria, Anita. "Sex Trafficked and Imprisoned, California Woman Wins Freedom after Long Fight." *Los Angeles Times,* November 6, 2020. https://www.latimes.com/california/story/2020-11-06/sex-trafficked-and-imprisoned-california-woman-wins-freedom.

———. "This Sex Trafficking Victim Is Behind Bars, Suicidal. She Seeks Newsom's Clemency." *Los Angeles Times.* September 7, 2020. https://www.latimes.com/california/story/2020-09-07/sex-trafficking-victim-suicidal-newsom-clemency.

Chapin, Angelina. "She Says Her Best Friend Sold Her to a Pimp. The Court Says She's a Criminal." *HuffPost,* December 21, 2019. https://www.huffpost.com/entry/youth-sex-trafficking-violent-crimes-legal-system_n_5df7f060e4b0aeo1a1e59701.

———. "She Was Sex Trafficked at 14—Then Sentenced to 20 Years in Prison."

HuffPost, October 22, 2019. https://www.huffpost.com/entry/sex-trafficking
-teens-united-states_n_5d9f6e89e4b02c9da04692ef.

———. "Women Are Being Denied Cancer Treatment, Psychiatric Help at ICE
Detention Center." *HuffPost*, September 27, 2019. https://www.huffpost.com
/entry/immigrant-women-denied-cancer-psychiatric-care-ice-detention-cent
er_n_5d8d5880e4b0019647a5ebae.

Chesney-Lind, Meda. "Are Girls Closing the Gender Gap in Violence?" *Criminal
Justice* (Spring 2001): 19–23.

———. "Criminalizing Victimization: The Unintended Consequences of Pro-
Arrest Policies for Girls and Women." *Criminology & Public Policy* 2, no. 1
(November 2002): 81–90.

———. "Girls and Violence: Is the Gender Gap Closing?" VAWnet: The National
Online Resource Center on Violence Against Women and National Resource
Center on Domestic Violence, 2004.

———. "Patriarchy, Crime, and Justice: Feminist Criminology in an Era of Backlash." *Feminist Criminology* 1, no. 1 (January 2006): 6–26. https://doi.org/10
.1177/1557085105282893.

Chesney-Lind, Meda, and Randall G. Shelden. *Girls, Delinquency, and Juvenile
Justice*. Chichester, West Sussex, UK: John Wiley & Sons, 1998.

Chew, Cassie M. "Aging in Prison: The Forgotten Plight of Women behind Bars."
The Crime Report, August 28, 2019. https://thecrimereport.org/2019/08/28
/aging-in-prison-the-forgotten-plight-of-women-behind-bars/#:~:text=Wom
en%20Aging%20Behind%20Bars&text=A%20quarter%20of%20women%20
serving,and%20jails%20are%20awaiting%20trial.&text=About%20two%2Dt
hirds%20of%20these,receiving%20convictions%20later%20in%20life.

Cho, Michelle, and Kim Cornett. "Cyntoia Brown-Long to Lester Holt on Her
Release from Prison: 'There's Nothing Special about Me.'" *NBC News*, October
14, 2019. https://www.nbcnews.com/news/us-news/cyntoia-brown-long-lest
er-holt-her-release-prison-there-s-n1065296.

Chrastil, Nicholas. "DA's Office Refused Nearly Half of Felony Domestic Violence
Cases Last Year, Watchdog Group Finds." *The Lens*, June 2, 2020. https://thel
ensnola.org/2020/06/02/das-office-refused-nearly-half-of-felony-domestic-vi
olence-cases-last-year-watchdog-group-finds/.

Ciarmamella, C. J. "These Women Received a Death Sentence for Being Sick in
Prison." *Reason*, June 30, 2020. https://reason.com/2020/06/30/these-wom
en-received-a-death-sentence-for-being-sick/.

Citizens for Racial Equity in Washtenaw (CREW). *Race to Justice: Citizens for
Racial Equity in Washtenaw's Report on Racial Disparities in the Washtenaw
County Criminal Legal System*. Ann Arbor, MI: CREW in Washtenaw, 2020.

Clawson, Heather J., and Lisa Goldblatt Grace. *Finding a Path to Recovery: Residential Facilities for Minor Victims of Domestic Sex Trafficking*. Washington,

DC: US Department of Health and Human Services, Office of the Assistant Secretary for Planning and Evaluation, 2007.

Coalition for Women Prisoners. *Justice and Dignity for DV Survivors in the Criminal Justice System: What You Need to Know about the Domestic Violence Survivors Justice Act (S1077/A3974)*. New York: Coalition for Women Prisoners, n.d.

Comack, Elizabeth. *Women in Trouble: Connecting Women's Law Violation to Their Histories of Abuse*. New York: Columbia University Press, 1996.

Condon, Tom. "Sex Offender Registry: More Harm Than Good?" *CT Mirror*, May 21, 2018. https://ctmirror.org/2018/05/21/sex-offender-registry-harm-good/.

Congressional Record. 142 Cong. Rec. H4453 (May 7, 1996).

Connecticut Coalition Against Domestic Violence. "New Dominant Aggressor Law Positively Impacts Intimate Partner Violence Dual Arrest Rate in CT." Connecticut Coalition Against Domestic Violence, Wethersfield, CT, 2020.

Contrera, Jessica. "Sex-Trafficked Kids Are Crime Victims. In Las Vegas, They Still Go to Jail." *Washington Post*, August 26, 2021. https://www.washington post.com/dc-md-va/interactive/2021/vegas-child-sex-trafficking-victims-jai led/.

———. "The State of Ohio v. a Sex Trafficked Teenager." *Washington Post*, June 1, 2020. https://www.washingtonpost.com/dc-md-va/interactive/2021/child-sex -trafficking-alexis-martin-ohio/.

Corda, Alessandro. "Introduction: An Important Look at Foreign Policy and Practices Regarding Sex-Offense Collateral Consequences." Collateral Consequences Resource Center, November 24, 2020. https://ccresourcecenter.org /2020/11/24/sex-offense-registries-in-europe-and-around-the-world/.

Correctional Association of New York. *It Reminds Us How We Got Here: (Re)producing Abuse, Neglect, and Trauma in New York's Prisons for Women*. New York: Correctional Association of New York, 2020.

Couloute, Lucius. "Nowhere to Go: Homelessness among Formerly Incarcerated People." Prison Policy Institute, 2018. https://www.prisonpolicy.org/reports /housing.html.

Couloute, Lucius, and Daniel Kopf. "Out of Prison and Out of Work: Unemployment among Formerly Incarcerated People." Prison Policy Institute, 2018. https://www.prisonpolicy.org/reports/outofwork.html.

Crabapple, Molly. "Project Rose Is Arresting Sex Workers in Arizona to Save Their Souls." *Vice*, February 6, 2014. https://www.vice.com/en/article/av4eyb /in-arizona-project-rose-is-arresting-sex-workers-to-save-them.

Craig, Shelley L., Ashley Austin, Jill Levenson, Vivian W.Y. Leung, Andrew D. Eaton, and Sandra A. D'Souza. "Frequencies and Patterns of Adverse Childhood Events in LGBTQ+ Youth." *Child Abuse & Neglect* 107 (2020): 1–12. https://doi.org/10.1016/j.chiabu.2020.104623.

Crenshaw, Kimberlé Williams, Priscilla Ocen, and Jyoti Nanda. *Black Girls*

Matter: Pushed Out, Overpoliced and Underprotected. New York: African American Policy Forum and Center for Intersectionality and Social Policy Studies, 2015.

Critical Resistance. "What Is Abolition?" *Critical Resistance*. http://criticalresista nce.org/wp-content/uploads/2012/06/What-is-Abolition.pdf.

Cross, Courtney. "Reentering Survivors: Invisible at the Intersection of the Criminal Legal System and the Domestic Violence Movement." *Berkeley Journal of Gender, Law & Justice* 31, no. 1 (Winter 2016): 60–120.

Criscione, Wilson. "A Native American Says She Shot Her Alleged Rapist in Self-Defense. Federal Prosecutors Charged Her with Murder." *Inlander*, February 25, 2021. https://www.inlander.com/spokane/a-native-american-says-she -shot-her-alleged-rapist-in-self-defense-federal-prosecutors-charged-her -with- murder/Content?oid=21192760.

Daly, Kathleen. "Women's Pathways to Felony Court: Feminist Theories of Lawbreaking and Problems of Representation." *Southern California Review of Law and Women's Studies* 2 (1992): 11–52.

Daniel, Roxanne. "Prisons Neglect Pregnant Women in Their Healthcare Policies." Prison Policy Initiative, December 5, 2019. https://www.prisonpolicy.org /blog/2019/12/05/pregnancy/.

Daranciang, Nelson. "Assault Victim Arrested to Ensure Her Testimony." *Hawaii News*, May 12, 2011. https://www.staradvertiser.com/2011/05/12/hawaii-news /assault-victim-arrested-to-ensure-her-testimony/.

Dasgupta, Shamita Das. "A Framework for Understanding Women's Use of Nonlethal Violence in Intimate Heterosexual Relationships." *Violence Against Women* 8, no. 11 (November 2002): 1364–89. https://doi.org/10.1177/1077801 02237408.

Davis, Allison. "Fighting for Hope: The Criminalization of Trauma in Justice-Involved Girls' Lives and Stories of Resilience from a Juvenile Prison." PhD dissertation. Texas Women's University, August 2017.

Davis, Angela J. "The Prosecution of Black Men." In *Policing the Black Man: Arrest, Prosecution, and Imprisonment*, edited by Angela J. Davis, 178–208. New York: Vintage Books, 2018.

Davis, Angela Y. *Abolition Democracy: Beyond Empire, Prisons, and Torture*. New York: Seven Stories Press, 2005.

———. *Freedom Is a Constant Struggle: Ferguson, Palestine, and the Foundations of a Movement*. Chicago: Haymarket Books, 2016.

Davis, Angela Y., and Cassandra Shaylor. "Race, Gender, and the Prison Industrial Complex: California and Beyond." *Meridians* 2, no. 1 (2001): 1–25.

Davis, Angela Y., and Dylan Rodriguez. "The Challenge of Prison Abolition: A Conversation." *Social Justice* 27, no. 3 (Fall 2000): 212–18.

Davis, Angela Y, Gina Dent, Erica R. Meiners, and Beth E. Richie. *Abolition. Feminism. Now*. Chicago: Haymarket Books, 2022.

DeCou, Christopher R., Shannon M. Lynch, and Trevor T. Cole. "Physical and Sexual Victimization Predicts Suicidality among Women in Prison: Understanding Ethnic and Trauma-Specific Domains of Risk." *Current Psychology* 36 (2017): 774–80.

Deer, Sarah. "Bystander No More? Improving the Federal Response to Sexual Violence in Indian Country." *Utah Law Review* 2017, no. 4 (2017): 771–800.

"Defense Committee Statement on Sentencing." *Free Maddesyn George.* https:// www.freemaddesyn.com/sentencing (accessed November 28, 2021).

DeHart, Dana D. "Pathways to Prison: Impact of Victimization in the Lives of Incarcerated Women." *Violence Against Women* 14, no. 12 (December 2008): 1362–81. https://doi.org/10.1177/1077801208327018.

Demleitner, Nora V. "State Prosecutors at the Center of Mass Imprisonment and Criminal Justice Reform." *Federal Sentencing Reporter* 32, no. 4 (2020): 187–94. https://doi.org/10.1525/fsr.2020.32.4.187.

Dewey, Susan, Bonnie Zare, Catherine Connolly, Rhett Epler, and Rosemary Bratton. *Outlaw Women: Prison, Rural Violence, and Poverty in the American West.* New York: New York University Press, 2019.

Diaz, Jaclyn. "New Jersey Prisoners Will Be Placed Based on Gender Identity under a New Policy." *NPR*, June 29, 2021. https://www.npr.org/2021/06/29 /1011181718/new-jersey-prisoners-will-be-placed-based-on-gender-identity -under-a-new-policy.

Dichter, Melissa E. "'They Arrested Me—And I Was the Victim': Women's Experiences with Getting Arrested in the Context of Domestic Violence." *Women & Criminal Justice* 23, no. 2 (2013): 81–98. https://doi.org/10.1080/08974454 .2013.759068.

———. *Women's Experiences of Abuse as a Risk Factor for Incarceration: A Research Update.* Harrisburg, PA: National Resource Center on Domestic Violence, 2015.

Disability Rights Maryland. *Segregation and Suicide: Confinement at the Maryland Correctional Institution for Women.* Baltimore: Disability Rights Maryland, 2018.

Ditmore, Melissa. *The Use of Raids to Fight Trafficking in Persons.* New York: Sex Workers Project, 2009.

Dorotik, Jane. "Lifer's Lifelong Search for Suitability—A Sequel." *Tenacious* 43 (Winter 2020): 15–20.

———. "Summertime Woes in Prison." *Tenacious* 41 (Summer 2018): 1–2.

Drain, Victoria. "Happy Mother's Day to All Mothers Reading These Words!" *Tenacious* 39 (Spring 2017): 33–34.

Dressler, Joshua, and Holly Maguigan. "Battered Women, Self-Defense, and the Law." *Fordham Law Review Res Gestae* 79 (2011): 1–20.

Dunn, Jennifer L. *Courting Disaster: Intimate Stalking, Culture, and Criminal Justice.* New York: Transaction Publishers, 2002.

Durfee, Alesha. "Arresting Girls for Dating Violence: The Importance of Considering Intersectionality." In *The Spectrum of Women and Crime: Theories, Offending, and the Criminal Justice System*, edited by Susan F. Sharp, Susan Marcus-Medoza, Kathleen A. Cameron, and Elycia S. Daniel-Roberson. Durham, NC: Carolina Academic Press, 2016.

———. "Situational Ambiguity and Gendered Patterns of Arrest for Intimate Partner Violence." *Violence Against Women* 18, no. 1 (January 2012): 64–84. https://doi.org/10.1177/1077801212437017.

Dwamena, Anakwa. "Closing Rikers: Competing Visions for the Future of New York City's Jails." *New York Review of Books*, October 4, 2019. https://www.ny books.com/daily/2019/10/04/closing-rikers-competing-visions-for-the-future -of-new-york-citys jails/.

Dye, Meredith Huey, and Ron H. Aday. *Women Lifers: Lives before, behind, and beyond Bars*. Lanham, MD: Rowman & Littlefield, 2019.

Ehrmann, Samantha, Nina Hyland, and Charles Puzzanchera. *Girls in the Juvenile Justice System*. Laurel, MD: Office of Juvenile Justice and Delinquency Prevention, 2019.

Ellenbogen, Romy. "Rape Is Rampant at This Women's Prison. Anyone Who Complains Is Punished, Lawsuit Says." *Miami Herald*, December 4, 2019. https://www.miamiherald.com/news/special-reports/florida-prisons/article2 37797554.html.

Epstein, Rebecca, Jamilia J. Blake, and Thalia González. *Girlhood Interrupted: The Erasure of Black Girls' Childhood*. Washington, DC: Georgetown Law Center on Poverty and Inequality, 2017.

Erez, Edna, and Joanne Belknap. "In Their Own Words: Battered Women's Assessment of the Criminal Processing System's Responses." *Violence and Victims* 13, no. 3 (1998): 251–68. https://doi.org/10.1891/0886-6708.13.3.251.

Ewing, Charles Patrick. "Psychological Self-Defense: A Proposed Justification for Battered Women Who Kill." *Law and Human Behavior* 14, no. 6 (1990): 579–94. https://doi.org/10.1007/bf01044883.

Fahy, Stephanie R., "Safe Harbor of Minors Involved in Prostitution: Understanding How Criminal Justice Officials Perceive and Respond to Minors Involved in Prostitution in a State with a Safe Harbor Law." PhD dissertation. Northeastern University, 2015.

Faigman, David A. "The Battered Woman Syndrome and Self-Defense: A Legal and Empirical Dissent." *Virginia Law Review Association* 72, no. 3 (April 1986): 619–47.

Farrell, Amy, Jack McDevitt, Rebecca Pfeffer, Stephanie Fahey, Colleen Owens, Meredith Dank, and William Adams. *Identifying Challenges to Improve the Investigation and Prosecution of State and Local Human Trafficking Cases*. Washington, DC: National Institute of Justice, 2012.

Farrell, Amy, Meredith Dank, Ieke Vries, Matthew Kafafian, Andrea Hughes, and Sarah Lockwood. "Failing Victims? Challenges of the Police Response to Human Trafficking." *Criminology & Public Policy* 18, no. 3 (2019): 649–73. https://doi.org/10.1111/1745-9133.12456.

Farrell, Amy, Monica J. Delateur, Colleen Owens, and Stephanie Fahy. "The Prosecution of State-level Human Trafficking Cases in the United States." *Anti-Trafficking Review*, no. 6 (2016): 48–70. https://doi.org/10.14197/atr.20 121664.

Fedders, Barbara. "More Young Women in the Juvenile Justice System: Girls in Trouble." *Guild Practitioner* 58, no. 2 (Spring 2001): 103–11.

Fedock, Gina, Cristy Cummings, Sheryl Kubiak, Deborah Bybee, Rebecca Campbell, and Kathleen Darcy. "Incarcerated Women's Experiences of Staff-Perpetrated Rape: Racial Disparities and Justice Gaps in Institutional Responses." *Journal of Interpersonal Violence* 36 (2019): 8668–92. https://doi .org/10.1177/0886260519850531.

Feeley, Malcolm. *The Process Is the Punishment: Handling Cases in a Lower Criminal Court.* New York: Russell Sage Foundation, 1992.

Feld, Barry C. "Violent Girls or Relabeled Status Offenders?: An Alternative Interpretation of the Data." *Crime & Delinquency* 55, no. 2 (April 2009): 241–65. https://doi.org/10.1177/0011128708330629.

Ferraro, Kathleen J. *Neither Angels nor Demons: Women, Crime, and Victimization.* Boston: Northeastern University Press, 2006.

Finn, Mary A., and Pamela Bettis. "Punitive Action or Gentle Persuasion: Exploring Police Officers' Justifications for Using Dual Arrest in Domestic Violence Cases." *Violence Against Women* 12, no. 3 (March 2006): 268–87. https://doi .org/10.1177/1077801206286218.

Fischer, Karla. *Domestic Violence Expert Witnesses: Overcoming Challenges in Battered Women's Self-Defense Cases.* Philadelphia: National Clearinghouse for the Defense of Battered Women, 2016.

Fisher, Lina. "Commissioners Court Puts Women's Jail on Ice." *Austin Chronicle.* June 18, 2021. https://www.austinchronicle.com/news/2021-06-18/commissio ners-court-puts-womens-jail-on-ice/.

Flaherty, Jordan. "Is the State of Alaska Fighting Sex Trafficking or Targeting Women?" *Truthout,* November 7, 2014. https://truthout.org/articles/is-the-st ate-of-alaska-fighting-sex-trafficking-or-targeting-women/.

Fleischer, Jodie. "Innocent Victim Speaks Out about Being Jailed for 17 Days." *WSBTV.com,* May 1, 2012. https://2wsb.tv/2FNAUB9.

Flock, Elizabeth. "Brittany Smith Loses Her Stand Your Ground Hearing." *The New Yorker,* February 3, 2020. https://www.newyorker.com/news/news-desk /brittany-smith-loses-her-stand-your-ground-hearing.

———. "How Far Can Abused Women Go to Protect Themselves?" *The New Yorker,* January 13, 2020. https://www.newyorker.com/magazine/2020/01/20 /how-far-can-abused-women-go-to-protect-themselves.

Flores, Jerry. *Caught Up: Girls, Surveillance, and Wraparound Incarceration.* Berkeley: University of California Press, 2016.

Follingstad, Diane R., M. Jill Rogers, Sarah N. Welling, and F. Jill Priesmeyer. "Decisions to Prosecute Battered Women's Homicide Cases: An Exploratory Study." *Journal of Family Violence* 30, no. 7 (2015): 859–74. https://doi.org/10.1007/s10896-015-9725-7.

Fontier, Alice, Christopher W. Adams, Jennifer L. Van Ort, and Norman L. Reimer. *The New York State Trial Penalty: The Constitutional Right to Trial under Attack.* New York: National Association of Criminal Defense Lawyers and New York State Association of Criminal Defense Lawyers, 2021.

Foy, David W., Iya K. Ritchie, and Alison H. Conway. "Trauma Exposure, Post-traumatic Stress, and Comorbidities in Female Adolescent Offenders: Findings and Implications from Recent Studies." *European Journal of Psychotraumatology* 3, no. 1 (2012): 1–13. https://doi.org/10.3402/ejpt.v3i0.17247.

Frankel, Adam. *"Do You See How Much I'm Suffering Here?" Abuse against Transgender Women in US Immigration Detention.* New York: Human Rights Watch, 2016. https://www.hrw.org/report/2016/03/24/do-you-see-how-much-im-suffering-here/abuse-against-transgender-women-us#.

Franks, Mary Anne. "Real Men Advance, Real Women Retreat: Stand Your Ground, Battered Women's Syndrome, and Violence as Male Privilege." *University of Miami Law Review* 68, no. 4 (Summer 2014): 1099–1128.

Freeman, Lance, and Darrick Hamilton. *A Count of Homeless Youth in New York City: 2007.* New York: Empire State Coalition of Youth and Family Services, 2008.

Frey, Chad. "Abuse Victims Can Sit in Jail for Not Appearing in Court." *The Kansan,* April 16, 2021. https://www.thekansan.com/story/news/2021/04/16/victims-abuse-cases-can-sit-jail-not-appearing-court/6983120002/.

Frye, Victoria, Mary Haviland, and Valli Rajah. "Dual Arrest and Other Unintended Consequences of Mandatory Arrest in New York City: A Brief Report." *Journal of Family Violence* 22, no. 6 (August 2007): 397–405.

Gaarder, Emily, Nancy Rodriguez, and Marjorie S. Zatz. "Criers, Liars, and Manipulators: Probation Officers' Views of Girls." *Justice Quarterly* 21 (2004): 345–76. https://doi.org/10.1080/07418820400095901.

Gagné, Patricia. *Battered Women's Justice: The Movement for Clemency and the Politics of Self-Defense.* New York: Twayne Publishers, 1998.

Gaines, Lee V. "Why Even Illinois' Department of Corrections Wants to Fix the Way the State Does Electronic Monitor." *NPR Illinois,* February 26, 2019. https://www.nprillinois.org/post/why-even-illinois-s-department-corrections-wants-fix-way-state-does-electronic-monitor#stream/0.

Galvan, Frank H., and Moshen Bazargan. *Interactions of Latina Transgender Women with Law Enforcement.* Los Angeles: UCLA School of Law Williams Institute, 2012.

Gann, Jennifer. "Trans Health Care in Prisons." *Tenacious* 41 (Summer 2018): 23–24.

Garcia-Hallett, Janet. "'We're Being Released to a Jungle': The State of Prisoner Reentry and the Resilience of Women of Color." *The Prison Journal* 99, no. 4 (2019): 459–83. https://doi.org/10.1177/0032885519852089.

Geraghty, Kate Anya, and Jessica Woodhams. "The Predictive Validity of Risk Assessment Tools for Female Offenders: A Systematic Review." *Aggression and Violent Behavior* 21 (2015): 25–38. https://doi.org/10.1016/j.avb.2015.01.002.

Gies, Stephen, Amanda Bobnis, Marcia Cohen, and Matthew Malamud. *Safe Harbor Laws: Changing the Legal Response to Minors Involved in Commercial Sex.* Bethesda, MD: Development Services Group, 2019.

Gies, Stephen, Amanda Bobnis, Marcia Cohen, and Matthew Malamud. *Safe Harbor Laws: Changing the Legal Response to Minors Involved in Commercial Sex, Phase I. The Legal Review.* Bethesda, MD: Development Services Group, 2019.

———. *Safe Harbor Laws: Changing the Legal Response to Minors Involved in Commercial Sex, Phase 2. The Quantitative Analysis.* Bethesda, MD: Development Services Group, 2019.

Gill, Lauren. "Arkansas Grants Parole to Willie Mae Harris Three Decades after She Was Convicted for Killing Her Husband." *The Appeal*, May 20, 2020. https://theappeal.org/arkansas-grants-parole-to-willie-mae-harris-three-decades-after-she-was-convicted-for-killing-her-husband/.

———. "A Life Sentence in Arkansas. And a Lifetime of Pain." *The Appeal*, November 18, 2019. https://theappeal.org/life-sentence-arkansas-clemency/.

———. "Prosecutors Ignored Evidence of Her Estranged Husband's Abuse. She Faces 25 Years in Prison for Murder." *The Intercept*, May 24, 2021. https://theintercept.com/2021/05/24/manhattan-district-attorney-domestic-violence-tracey-mccarter/.

Gilmore, Ruth Wilson. "Abolition Geography and the Problem of Innocence." In *Futures of Black Radicalism,* edited by Gay Theresa Johnson and Alex Lubin, 225–40. New York: Verso, 2017.

Girls for Gender Equity. *The School Girls Deserve: Youth-Driven Solutions for Creating Safe, Holistic, and Affirming New York City Public Schools.* New York: Girls for Gender Equity, 2017.

Girshick, Lori. "Out of Compliance: Masculine-Identified People in Women's Prisons." In *Captive Genders: Trans Embodiment and the Prison Industrial Complex,* edited by Eric A. Stanley and Nat Smith, 215–34. Chico, CA: AK Press, 2016.

Glazer, Jessica. "Why It Might Be Time to Rethink the Rules of Parole." *FiveThirtyEight*, November 13, 2014. https://fivethirtyeight.com/features/why-it-might-be-time-to-rethink-the-rules-of-parole/.

Global Health Justice Partnership of the Yale Law School and the Sex Workers Project of the Urban Justice Center. *Un-Meetable Promises: Rhetoric and Reality in New York City's Human Trafficking Intervention.* Global Health Justice Partnership of the Yale Law School and The Sex Workers Project of the Urban Justice Center, 2018.

Global Health Justice Partnership of the Yale Law School, Yale School of Public Health, and the Sex Workers Project of the Urban Justice Center. *Diversion from Justice: A Rights-Based Analysis of Local "Prostitution Diversion Programs" and Their Impacts on People in the Sex Sector in the United States.* Global Health Justice Partnership of the Yale Law School and Yale School of Public Health and The Sex Workers Project of the Urban Justice Center, 2018.

Godsoe, Cynthia. "Contempt, Status, and the Criminalization of Non-Conforming Girls." *Cardozo Law Review* 35, no. 3 (February 2014): 1091–1116.

———. "Punishment as Protection." *Houston Law Review* 52, no. 5 (Spring 2015): 1313–84.

Goldman, Abigail. "Throwaway Kids: What to Do with Teenage Prostitutes?" *Las Vegas Sun*, March 18, 2010. https://lasvegassun.com/news/2010/mar/18/thro waway-kids-teenage-prostitutes/.

Gondolf, Edward W., and Ellen R. Fisher. *Battered Women as Survivors: An Alternative to Treating Learned Helplessness.* Lexington, MA: Lexington Books, 1990.

Gonnerman, Jennifer. "Prepping for Parole." *The New Yorker,* November 25, 2019. https://www.newyorker.com/magazine/2019/12/02/prepping-for-parole.

Goodmark, Leigh. *Decriminalizing Domestic Violence: A Balanced Policy Approach to Intimate Partner Violence.* Oakland: University of California Press, 2018.

———. "Hands Up at Home: Militarized Masculinity and Police Officers Who Commit Intimate Partner Abuse." *Brigham Young University Law Review* 2015, no. 5 (2015): 1183–1246.

———. "The Impact of Prosecutorial Misconduct, Overreach, and Misuse of Discretion on Gender Violence Victims." *Dickinson Law Review* 123, no. 3 (Spring 2019): 627–60.

———. "The Punishment of Dixie Shanahan: Is There Justice for Battered Women Who Kill?" *Kansas Law Review* 55, no. 2 (January 2007): 269–319. https://doi.org/10.17161/1808.19991.

———. "Transgender People, Intimate Partner Abuse, and the Legal System." *Harvard Civil Rights-Civil Liberties Law Review* 48, no. 1 (March 2012): 51–104.

———. *A Troubled Marriage: Domestic Violence and the Legal System.* New York: NYU Press, 2012.

———. "When Is a Battered Woman Not a Battered Woman? When She Fights Back." *Yale Journal of Law and Feminism* 20, no. 1 (2008): 75–129.

Goodwin, Michele. *Policing the Womb: Invisible Women and the Criminaliza-tion of Motherhood*. New York: Cambridge University Press, 2020.

Grace, Anita. "'They Just Don't Care': Women Charged with Domestic Violence in Ottowa." *Manitoba Law Journal* 42, no. 3 (2019): 153–88.

Grant, Melissa Gira. "Human Trafficking Courts Are Not a Criminal Justice 'Innovation." *The New Republic*, January 7, 2020. https://newrepublic.com/ar ticle/156135/human-trafficking-courts-not-criminal-justice-innovation.

Greene, Christina. "'She Ain't No Rosa Parks': The Joan Little Rape-Murder Case and Jim Crow Justice in the Post–Civil Rights South." *Journal of African American History* 110, no. 3 (2015): 428–47.

Gruber, Aya. *The Feminist War on Crime: The Unexpected Role of Women's Lib-eration in Mass Incarceration*. Oakland: University of California Press, 2019.

Gruber, Aya, Amy J. Cohen, and Kate Mogulescu. "Penal Welfare and the New Human Trafficking Intervention Courts." *Florida Law Review* 68, no. 5 (September 2016): 1333–1402.

Guida, Christine, Kate Mogulescu, Svati Shah, Ariel Wolf, and Margaret Teich. "Sex Work and the Law: Felony, Fetish, or Free Market?" *Cardozo Journal of Law and Gender* 21, no. 2 (2015): 499–525.

Gunter, Joel. "Why Are Crime Victims Being Jailed?" *BBC News*, May 6, 2017. https://www.bbc.com/news/world-us-canada-39662428.

Haines, Faith. "Usually in the Free World." *Tenacious* 40 (Winter 2018): 26–28.

Haley, Sarah. *No Mercy Here: Gender, Punishment, and the Making of Jim Crow Modernity*. Chapel Hill: University of North Carolina Press, 2016.

Halter, Stephanie. "Factors That Influence Police Conceptualizations of Girls Involved in Prostitution in Six U.S. Cities: Child Sexual Exploitation Victims or Delinquents?" *Child Maltreatment* 15, no. 2 (May 2010): 152–60. https://doi.org/10.1177/1077559509355315.

Hamaji, Kate, Kumar Rao, Marbre Stahly-Butts, Janaé Bonsu, Charlene Carruthers, Roselyn Berry, and Denzel McCampbell. *Freedom to Thrive: Reimagining Safety and Security in Our Communities*. Center for Popular Democracy, Law for Black Lives and Black Youth Project, 2017.

Hamberger, L. Kevin, and Theresa Potente. "Counseling Heterosexual Women Arrested for Domestic Violence: Implication for Theory and Practice." *Violence and Victims* 9, no. 2 (1994): 125–37. DOI: 10.1891/0886-6708.9.2.125.

Hamilton, Melissa. "The Sexist Algorithm." *Behavioral Science and Law* 37, no. 2 (2019):145–57.

Harding, David J. "Do Prisons Make Us Safer?" *Scientific American*, June 21, 2019. https://www.scientificamerican.com/article/do-prisons-make-us-safer/.

Harris, Kwaneta. "Untitled." *Tenacious* 41 (Summer 2018): 28–31.

Hatch, Jenavieve. "District Attorney Defends Jailing Rape Victims Who Won't Testify." *HuffPost*, April 19, 2017. https://www.huffpost.com/entry/district-att

orney-defends-jailing-rape-victims-who-wont-testify_n_58f79e42e4b05b9d6
13f8faa.

Hawes, Elizabeth. "Incarcerated Women Are Punished for Their Trauma with
Solitary Confinement." *Truthout*, December 12, 2020. https://truthout.org/ar
ticles/incarcerated-women-are-punished-for-their-trauma-with-solitary-conf
inement/?eType=EmailBlastContent&eId=8235d76f-ab45-4d61-bebb-bce418
902f84.

Hawes, Janelle, and Jerry Flores. "Does Abuse Lead to Incarceration for Girls?
Usually Yes." *Juvenile Justice Information Exchange*, October 4, 2019. https://
jjie.org/2019/09/10/does-abuse-lead-to-incarceration-for-girls-usually-yes/.

Heffron, Laurie Cook, Josie V. Serrata, and Gabriela Hurtado. *Latina Immigrant
Women and Children's Well-Being and Access to Services after Detention.* Saint
Paul, MN: Casa de Esperanza National Latin@ Network for Health Families
and Communities, 2018.

Heintz, Paul. "Guarded Secrets: Claims of Sexual Misconduct, Drug Use Plague a
Vermont Prison for Women." *Seven Days,* December 4, 2019. https://www.se
vendaysvt.com/vermont/guarded-secrets-claims-of-sexual-misconduct-drug
-use-plague-vermonts-womens-prison/Content?oid=29082891.

Heipt, Wendy S. "Girl's Court: A Gender Responsive Juvenile Court Alternative."
Seattle Journal for Social Justice 13, no. 13 (Spring 2015): 803–56.

Hempel, Carrie. "Battered and Convicted—-One State's Efforts to Provide Effective Relief." *Criminal Justice* 25, no. 4 (Winter 2011): 24–33.

Herman, Judith Lewis. "Justice from the Victim's Perspective." *Violence Against
Women* 11, no. 5 (May 2005): 571–602. https://doi.org/10.1177/107780120527
4450.

Hicks, Tyler. "Women in Dallas County Jail Say They Endured Nearly Two Weeks
without Clean Clothes." *Dallas Observer*, January 4, 2021. https://www.dallas
observer.com/news/female-inmates-in-dallas-county-jail-say-they-were-deni
ed-clean-clothes-and-care-11974827.

Hill, Jess. *See What You Made Me Do: Power, Control and Domestic Abuse.*
Carlton, Australia: Schwartz Publishing Pty Ltd., 2019.

Hirschel, David, Philip D. McCormack, and Eve Buzawa. "A 10-Year Study of the
Impact of Intimate Partner Violence Primary Aggressor Laws on Single and
Dual Arrest." *Journal of Interpersonal Violence* 36, no. 3–4 (February 2021):
1356–90. Https://doi.org/10.1177/0886260517739290.

Holt, John, and Lisa McCormick. "Hope for Hope: Kansas Sex Trafficking Victim
Put Behind Bars for Sex Trafficking." *FOX4*, February 24, 2020. https://fox4kc
.com/news/hope-for-hope-kansas-sex-trafficking-victim-put-behind-bars-for
-sex-trafficking/.

Horvatits, Chris. "DA Unhappy That Convicted Murderer Will Walk Out of
Prison after Judge's Order." *WIVB.com*, September 9, 2020. https://www.wivb

.com/news/local-news/da-unhappy-that-convicted-murderer-will-walk-out-of-prison-after-judges-order/.

Hoskins, Zachary. *Beyond Punishment? A Normative Account of the Collateral Legal Consequences of Conviction.* New York: Oxford University Press, 2019.

Howard, Marc Morjé. *Unusually Cruel: Prisons, Punishment, and the Real American Exceptionalism.* New York: Oxford University Press, 2017.

Hua, Julietta. "Telling Stories of Trafficking: The Politics of Legibility." *Meridians: Feminism, Race, Transnationalism* 12, no. 1 (2014): 201–7.

Humphreys, Janice, Elissa S. Epel, Bruce A. Cooper, Jue Lin, Elizabeth H. Blackburn, and Kathryn A. Lee. "Telomere Shortening in Formerly Abused and Never Abused Women." *Biological Research for Nursing* 14, no. 2 (2011): 115–23. https://doi.org/10.1177/1099800411398479.

Hunt, Jerome, and Aisha Moodie-Mills. *The Unfair Criminalization of Gay and Transgender Youth.* Washington, DC: Center for American Progress, 2012. https://cdn.americanprogress.org/wp-content/uploads/issues/2012/06/pdf/juvenile_justice.pdf?_ga=2.213829076.1702118502.1624046510-2103384136.1624046510.

INCITE! Women of Color Against Violence and Critical Resistance. "Statement on Gender Violence and the Prison Industrial Complex," 2001. https://incite-national.org/incite-critical-resistance-statement/ (accessed May 26, 2022).

"Inez Garcia Acquitted of 'Rape-Related' Killing." *Washington Post,* March 5, 1977. https://www.washingtonpost.com/archive/politics/1977/03/05/inez-garcia-acquitted-of-rape-related-killing/68f62287-8f48-4859-999c-f443f8105f09/.

Iskander, Natasha N. "On Detention and Skill: Reflections on Immigrant Incarceration, Bodying Practices, and the Definition of Skill." *American Behavioral Scientist* 63, no. 9 (2019): 1370–88. https://doi.org/10.1177/0002764219835257.

Jacobs, Beth, and Stephanie Richard. "Impact of Criminal Arrest and Detention on Survivors of Human Trafficking." National Survivor Network, 2016. https://nationalsurvivornetwork.org/wp-content/uploads/2017/12/VacateSurveyFinal.pdf.

Jacobs, Michelle S. "Requiring Battered Women Die: Murder Liability for Mothers under Failure to Protect Statutes." *Journal of Criminal Law and Criminology* 88, no. 2 (1998): 579–660.

Jacobsen, Carol. *For Dear Life: Women's Decriminalization and Human Rights in Focus.* Ann Arbor: University of Michigan Press, 2019.

Jacobsen, Carol, and Lora Bex Lempert. "Institutional Disparities: Considerations of Gender in the Commutation Process for Incarcerated Women." *Signs: Journal of Women in Culture and Society* 39, no. 1 (2013): 265–89. https://doi.org/10.1086/670772.

Jacobsen, Carol, Kammy Mizga, and Lynn D'Orio. "Battered Women, Homicide

Convictions, and Sentencing: The Case for Clemency." *Hastings Womens Law Journal* 18, no. 1 (Winter 2007): 31–66.

Jacquet, Catherine O. *The Injustices of Rape: How Activists Responded to Sexual Violence, 1950–1980.* Chapel Hill: University of North Carolina Press, 2019.

James, Andrea. "Ending Incarceration of Women and Girls." *Yale Law Journal Forum* 128 (2019): 772–90.

James, Joy. *Resisting State Violence: Radicalism, Gender, and Race in U.S. Culture.* Minneapolis: University of Minnesota Press, 1996.

James, Sandy E., Jody L. Herman, Susan Rankin, Mara Keisling, Lisa Mottet, and Ma'ayan Anafi. *The Report of the 2015 U.S. Transgender Survey.* Washington, DC: National Center for Transgender Equality, 2016.

Jeltsen, Melissa. "Bresha Meadows Thought You'd Understand." *HuffPost,* October 17, 2019. https://www.huffpost.com/entry/bresha-meadows-thought -youd-understand_n_5da48081e4b087efdbb23973.

———. "The Tortured Life and Tragic Crime of the Only Woman on Death Row." *HuffPost,* November 10, 2020. https://www.huffpost.com/entry/lisa-montgom ery-death-penalty-trump-administration_n_5fa586a3c5b623bfac4f101d.

Jenness, Valerie, Cheryl L. Maxson, Kristy N. Matsuda, and Jennifer Macy Sumner. "Violence in California Correctional Facilities: An Empirical Examination of Sexual Assault." University of California Irvine Center for Evidence-Based Corrections, 2007. https://www.researchgate.net/publication/2678177 59_Violence_in_California_Correctional_Facilities_An_Empirical_Examina tion_of_Sexual_Assault.

Jennings, Angel. "L.A. Sees Parks as a Weapon against Sex Offenders." *Los Angeles Times,* February 23, 2013. https://www.latimes.com/local/la-xpm-20 13-feb-28-la-me-parks-sex-offenders-20130301-story.html.

Johnson, Ida M. "Economic Impediments to Women's Success on Parole." *The Prison Journal* 94, no. 3 (2014): 365–87. https://doi.org/10.1177/00328855145 37760.

Jones, Alexi. "Visualizing the Unequal Treatment of LGBTQ People in the Criminal Justice System." *Prison Policy Initiative,* March 2, 2021. https://www.pris onpolicy.org/blog/2021/03/02/lgbtq/.

Jones, Ann. *Women Who Kill.* New York: Feminist Press, 1996.

Joshi, Holly. Email to author, August 18, 2020.

Juvenile Law Center. "Juvenile Sex Offender Registry (SORNA)." *Juvenile Law Center,* n.d. https://jlc.org/issues/juvenile-sex-offender-registry-sorna.

Kaba, Mariame. *We Do This 'Til We Free Us: Abolitionist Organizing and Transforming Justice.* Chicago: Haymarket Books, 2021.

———. "Yes, We Mean Literally Abolish the Police." *New York Times,* June 12, 2020. https://www.nytimes.com/2020/06/12/opinion/Sunday/floyd-abolish -defund-police.html.

Kaeble, Danielle. *Probation and Parole in the United States*. Washington, DC: US Department of Justice, 2018.

Kajstura, Aleks. "Women's Mass Incarceration: The Whole Pie 2019." *Prison Policy Initiative*, October 29, 2019. https://www.prisonpolicy.org/reports/pie 2019women.html.

Kamis, Tamara, and Emma Rose. "Domestic Violence Survivors Justice Act Gets a Slow Start." *New York Focus*, May 7, 2021. https://www.nysfocus.com/2021 /05/07/domestic-violence-survivors-justice-act-gets-a-slow-start/.

Kang-Brown, Jacob, and Olive Lu. "America's Growing Gender Jail Gap." *New York Review of Books*, May 7, 2019. https://www.nybooks.com/daily/2019/05 /07/americas-growing-gender-jail-gap/.

Kelley, Robin D. G. "Permanent War: How the US Security State Criminalizes and Profits off Its Victims." *Bookforum*, July 21, 2020. https://www.bookfor um.com/politics/how-the-us-security-state-criminalizes-and-profits-off-its-vi ctims-24107.

Kempdaoo, Kamala. "The Modern-Day White (Wo)Man's Burden: Trends in Anti-Trafficking and Anti-Slavery Campaigns." *Journal of Human Trafficking* 1, no. 1 (2015): 8–20.

Kempf-Leonard, Kimberly, and Lisa L. Sample. "Disparity Based on Sex: Is Gender-Specific Treatment Warranted?" *Justice Quarterly* 17, no. 1 (2000): 89–128. https://doi.org/10.1080/07418820000094491.

Kiefer, Michael. "The State of Arizona v. Jodi Arias . . . and Juan Martinez." *Arizona Mirror*, March 27, 2020. https://www.azmirror.com/2020/03/27/the -state-of-arizona-v-jodi-arias-and-juan-martinez/.

Kim, Mimi, "The Carceral Creep: Gender-based Violence, Race, and the Expansion of the Punitive State 1973–1983." *Social Problems* 36, no. 1 (2020): 45–71.

Kiner, Derek. "How the Marissa Alexander Plea Deal Really Went Down." *Folio Weekly Magazine*, December 3, 2014. https://bit.ly/2mhyn8g.

King County Coalition Against Domestic Violence. *Victim-Defendants: An Emerging Challenge in Responding to Domestic Violence in Seattle and the King County Region*. Seattle: King County Coalition Against Domestic Violence, 2003.

Kraft-Stolar, Tamar, Elizabeth Brundige, Sital Kalantry, and Jocelyn Getgen Kestenbaum. *From Protection to Punishment: Post-Conviction Barriers to Justice for Domestic Violence Survivor-Defendants in New York State*. Ithaca, NY: Avon Global Center for Women and Justice and Dorothea S. Clarke Program in Feminist Jurisprudence, 2011. https://scholarship.law.cornell.edu /avon_clarke/2.

Kriel, Lomi, "ICE Deported a Woman Who Accused Guards of Sexual Assault While the Feds Were Still Investigating the Incident." *ProPublica*, September 15, 2020. https://www.propublica.org/article/ice-has-deported-a-woman-who -said-guards-sexually-assaulted-her-while-the-investigation-is-ongoing.

———. "ICE Guards 'Systematically' Sexually Assault Detainees in an El Paso Detention Center, Lawyers Say." *ProPublica*, August 14, 2020. https://www.pr opublica.org/article/ice-guards-systematically-sexually-assault-detainees-in -an-el-paso-detention-center-lawyers-say.

Kruttschnitt, Candace, and Rosemary Gartner. "Women's Imprisonment." *Crime and Justice* 30 (2003): 1–82.

Kruzan, Sara. "Congress Needs to Pass Sara's Law So the Next Sara Kruzan Is Met with Empathy, Fairness." *The Hill*, April 16, 2019. https://thehill.com/blo gs/congress-blog/politics/439011-congress-needs-to-pass-saras-law-so-the-ne xt-sara-kruzan-is-met.

Kubiak, Sheryl Pimlott, Hannah Brenner, Deborah Bybee, Rebecca Campbell, and Gina Fedock. "Reporting Sexual Victimization during Incarceration: Using Ecological Theory as a Framework to Inform and Guide Future Research." *Trauma Violence Abuse* 12, no. 1 (2018): 94–106.

Kubiak, Sheryl P., Stephanie S. Conington, and Carmen Hillier. "Trauma-Informed Corrections." In *Social Work in Juvenile and Criminal Justice Systems*, 4th ed., edited by David W. Springer and Albert R. Roberts, 92–105. Springfield, IL: Charles C. Thomas, 2017.

Kushner, Rachel. "Is Prison Necessary? Ruth Wilson Gilmore Might Change Your Mind." *New York Times Magazine*, April 17, 2019. https://www.nytimes .com/2019/04/17/magazine/prison-abolition-ruth-wilson-gilmore.html#:~:te xt=%E2%80%9Cwhat%20this%20policy%20tells%20me,toward%20people %20who%20hurt%20people.

Lageson, Sarah Esther. "The Purgatory of Digital Punishment." *Slate*, June 24, 2020. https://slate.com/technology/2020/06/criminal-justice-records-online -digital-punishment.html.

Larance, Lisa Young. "Current Controversies: Programs for Women Who Have Used Force in Intimate Relationships." In *Sourcebook on Violence Against Women*, *Third Edition* edited by Claire M. Renzetti, Jeffrey L. Edleson, and Raquel Kennedy Bergen, 320–24. Thousand Oaks, CA: Sage Publications, 2018.

Larance, Lisa Young, and Ashley Rousson. "Facilitating Change: A Process of Renewal for Women Who Have Used Force in Their Intimate Heterosexual Relationships." *Violence Against Women* 22, no. 7 (June 2016): 876–91. https://doi.org/10.1177/1077801215610890.

Larance, Lisa Young, and Susan L. Miller. "In Her Own Words: Women Describe Their Use of Force Resulting in Court-Ordered Intervention." *Violence Against Women* 23, no. 12 (2016): 1536–59. https://doi.org/10.1177/107780121 6662340.

Law, Victoria. "The Abuse Excuse: Dismissing Domestic Violence and Its Effects in the Criminal Court System." *Rewire*, March 8, 2017. https://rewirenewsgro

up.com/article/2017/03/08/abuse-excuse-dismissing-domestic-violence-effec
ts-criminal-court-system/.

———. "After Six Months on Rikers, a Nurse Stands Accused of Murder in a Case
She Says Was Self-Defense." *The Gothamist*, September 9, 2020. https://goth
amist.com/news/after-six-months-rikers-nurse-stands-accused-murder-case
-she-says-was-self-defense.

———. "Immigrants Who Defend Themselves from Sexual Violence Face Prison,
Deportation." *Truthout*, June 10, 2020. https://truthout.org/articles/immigra
nts-who-defend-themselves-from-sexual-violence-face-prison-deportation/.

———. "Maddesyn George Killed Her Alleged Rapist. Prosecutors Blocked Her
Self-Defense Claims." *The Intercept*, October 8, 2021. https://theintercept.com
/2021/10/08/maddesyn-george-self-defense-rape/.

———. "New Report Looks at Strategies to Cut Incarceration of Illinois Women
by Half." *Truthout*, April 29, 2021. https://truthout.org/articles/new-report-lo
oks-at-strategies-to-cut-incarceration-of-illinois-women-by-half/.

———. "A New York Law Could Reduce Sentences for Domestic Violence Survivors. Why Are Judges Reluctant to Apply It?" *The Appeal*, February 24, 2020.
https://theappeal.org/a-new-york-law-could-reduce-sentences-for-domestic
-violence-survivors-why-are-judges-reluctant-to-apply-it/.

———. "New York Lawmakers Fear Court May Render Domestic Violence
Survivor Law 'Meaningless.'" *The Appeal*, September 3, 2020. https://theappe
al.org/new-york-lawmakers-fear-court-may-render-domestic-violence-surviv
or-law-meaningless/.

———. "Punished for Survival: Domestic Violence, Criminalization and the Case
of Naomi Freeman." *Truthout*, December 30, 2015. https://truthout.org/artic
les/punished-for-survival-domestic-violence-criminalization-and-the-case-of
-naomi-freeman/.

———. *Resistance behind Bars: The Struggles of Incarcerated Women*. Oakland:
PM Press, 2009.

Lawston, Jodie M., and Erica R. Meiners. "Ending Our Expertise: Feminists,
Scholarship, and Prison Abolition." *Feminist Formations* 26, no. 2 (2014):
1–25. https://doi.org/10.1353/ff.2014.0012.

Le, Lily. "Gender-Specific Treatment for Female Young Offenders." *Eureka* 3, no.
1 (2012): 26–34. https://doi.org/10.29173/eureka16990.

Lee, Alexander. "Prickly Coalitions: Moving Prison Abolitionism Forward." In
*Abolition Now! Ten Years of Strategy and Struggle against the Prison Indus-
trial Complex*, edited by The CR10 Publications Collective, 109–12. Oakland:
AK Press, 2008.

Lee, Trymaine. "Convicted of Murder as a Teenager and Paroled at 41." *New York
Times*, June 4, 2010. https://www.nytimes.com/2010/06/06/nyregion/06paro
le.html.

Lempert, Lora Bex. *Women Doing Life: Gender, Punishment, and the Struggle for Identity*. New York: New York University Press, 2016.

Leonard, Elizabeth Dermody. *Convicted Survivors: The Imprisonment of Battered Women Who Kill*. Albany: State University of New York Press, 2002.

Levine, Judith, and Erica R. Meiners. *The Feminist and the Sex Offender: Confronting Sexual Harm, Ending State Violence*. London: Verso, 2020.

Levin, Sam. "'Governor, Let Me See My Kids before I Die': Pressure Mounts to Release Elderly Women from Prisons." *The Guardian*, June 3, 2020. https://www.theguardian.com/us-news/2020/jun/03/california-prisons-elderly-women-clemency-coronavirus.

———. "'Traumatized Every Day': Prison Sexual Abuse Survivor Jailed Again—As a Witness." *The Guardian*, September 19, 2016. https://www.theguardian.com/us-news/2016/sep/19/oregon-prison-abuse-victim-brandy-buckmaster-incarcerated.

Levine, Judith, and Erica R. Meiners. *The Feminist and the Sex Offender: Confronting Sexual Harm, Ending State Violence*. London: Verso, 2020.

Linden, Leigh, and Jonah Rockoff. *There Goes the Neighborhood? Estimates of the Impact of Crime Risk on Property Values from Megan's Laws*. Cambridge, MA: National Bureau of Economic Research, 2006. https://doi.org/10.3386/w12253.

Linnane, Rory. "Maricella's Last Breath: She Died Alone in a Cell at 16. Officials Said They Were Devastated. They Didn't Say They Did Anything Wrong." *Milwaukee Journal Sentinel*, October 23, 2020. https://www.jsonline.com/in-depth/news/2020/10/23/warnings-preceded-maricella-chairez-suicide-racine-juvenile-jail-trafficking-maricella-last-breath/3652861001/?Utm_campaign=snd-autopilot.

Logan, TK, and Rob (Roberta) Valente. *Who Will Help Me? Domestic Violence Survivors Speak Out about Law Enforcement Responses*. Washington, DC: National Domestic Violence Hotline, 2015.

Logan, Wayne A. "Challenging the Punitiveness of 'New-Generation' SORN Laws." *New Criminal Law Review* 21, no. 3 (Summer 2018): 426–57.

Lomax, Walter, and Sonia Kumar. *Still Blocking the Exit*. Baltimore: ACLU of Maryland, 2015.

Londberg, Max. "Mom Thrown in Jail Twice While Seeking Civil Order from Same County Magistrate. He Resigned." *Cincinnati (Ohio) Enquirer*, September 15, 2018. https://www.cincinnati.com/story/news/crime/crime-and-courts/2018/09/15/magistrate-who-resigned-sentenced-same-woman-jail-before/1307436002/.

Louis, Errol. "Remember What Parole Is For: People Who Commit Terrible Crimes Can Rehabilitate Themselves." *New York Daily News*, April 4, 2019. https://www.nydailynews.com/opinion/ny-oped-remember-what-parole-is-for-20190404-3dfgxgacbjdjjnnv2nhhe5ufz4-story.html.

Love, Margaret, and David Schlussel. *Pathways to Reintegration: Criminal Record Reforms in 2019*. Washington, DC: Collateral Consequences Resource Center, 2020.

Lowe, Peggy. "Prison Board Says Kansas Governor Should Not Pardon Sex-Trafficked Teen." *KCUR*, November 20, 2019. https://www.kcur.org/news/20 19-11-20/prison-board-says-kansas-governor-should-not-pardon-sex-traffick ed-teen.

Lussenhop, Jessica. "After Years in Prison, Angel Stewart and Other Victims of Violence Ask for Mercy." *Riverfront Times*, March 11, 2015. https://www.riverf ronttimes.com/newsblog/2015/03/11/after-years-in-prison-angel-stewart-and -other-victims-of-violence-ask-for-mercy.

Lydia, Vanessa Patino, and Caroline Glesmann. *Addressing Barriers to Using Respite Beds for Girls Charged with Domestic Violence*. Minneapolis: National Council on Crime & Delinquency, 2019.

Lyon, Andrea D., Emily Hughes, and Juanita Thomas. "The People v. Juanita Thomas." *Women & Criminal Justice* 13, no. 1 (2002): 27–63. https://doi.org /10.1300/j012v13n01_02.

Lyons, Byrhonda. "Victims behind Bars: Trafficking Survivors Still Struggle Despite State Laws." *Cal Matters*, January 27, 2021. https://calmatters.org/jus tice/2021/01/sex-trafficking-victims-prison-california/.

Machado, Carmen Maria. *In the Dream House*. Minneapolis, MN: Graywolf Press, 2019.

Maguigan, Holly. "Battered Women and Self-Defense: Myths and Misconceptions in Current Reform Proposals." *University of Pennsylvania Law Review* 140, no. 2 (December 1991): 379–486.

Mahoney, Martha R. "Misunderstanding Judy Norman: Theory as Cause and Consequence." *Connecticut Law Review* 51, no. 3 (2019): 671–767.

Maldonado, Charles. "Prosecutor Tried to Jail Victim of Alleged Domestic Violence after She Didn't Obey Fake Subpoena." *The Lens*, June 14, 2017. https:// thelensnola.org/2017/06/14/new-orleans-prosecutor-used-fake-subpoena-to -seek-arrest-warrant-for-victim-of-alleged-domestic-violence/.

Mallick, Alexandra, and Kate Chatfield. "California Accomplices to a Felony Shouldn't Be Sentenced Like the One Who Committed the Murder." *Juvenile Justice Information Exchange*, August 8, 2018. https://jjie.org/2018/08/08 /accomplices-to-a-felony-shouldnt-be-sentenced-like-the-murderer-in-califo rnia/.

Marimow, Ann E. "Prisoners Need This Exam to Have a Chance at Freedom. But the Wait in Maryland for a Doctor's Appointment Is Excruciatingly Long." *Washington Post*, April 11, 2019. https://www.washingtonpost.com/local/legal -issues/prisoners-need-this-exam-to-have-a-chance-at-freedom-but-the-wait -in-maryland-for-a-doctors-appointment-is-excruciatingly-long/2019/04/10 /322482b0-562b-11e9-8ef3-fbd41a2ce4d5_story.html.

Marsh, Erin, Brittany Anthony, Jessica Emerson, and Kate Mogulescu. "State Report Cards Grading Criminal Record Relief Laws for Survivors of Human Trafficking." Polaris, American Bar Association, Brooklyn Law School, and University of Baltimore Law School, 2019.

McCarter, Tracy (@mccarter_tracy). "At Riker's I had to submit to FULL BODY strip search w/ cavity search just to get on a COMPUTER to see my family BEFORE & AFTER each televisit. Jails & Prisons replicates violence & control of abusive relationships. This must STOP!! #FreeSurvivors #FreeThemAll #DenimDayNYC." Twitter, April 28, 2021, https://twitter.com/mccarter_tracy/status/1387455948332146695.

McClellan, Cara. *Our Girls, Our Future: Investing in Opportunity and Reducing Reliance on the Criminal Justice System in Baltimore*. New York: NAACP Legal Defense Fund and Education Fund, Inc., 2018. https://tminstituteldf.org/wp-content/uploads/2019/04/Baltimore_Girls_Report_FINAL_6_26_18.pdf.

McCorkel, Jill A. *Breaking Women: Gender, Race and the New Politics of Imprisonment*. New York: New York University Press, 2013.

McDermott, Deborah. "States Working to Toughen Laws against Sex Trafficking: Legislation Aims to Target 'Pimps' with Harsher Penalties." *Seacoast Online*, April 13, 2014. https://www.seacoastonline.com/article/20140413/NEWS/404130344.

McLaurin, Melton A. *Celia, a Slave: A True Story*. New York: Avon Books, 1999.

McLeod, Allegra M. "Envisioning Abolition Democracy." *Harvard Law Review* 132, no. 6 (April 2019): 1613–49.

———. "Prison Abolition and Grounded Justice." *UCLA Law Review* 62, no. 5 (June 2015): 1156–239.

———. "Regulating Sexual Harm: Strangers, Intimates, and Social Institutional Reform." *California Law Review* 102, no. 6 (December 2014): 1553–622.

McMahon, Marilyn. "Homicide, Self-Defence and the (Inchoate) Criminology of Battered Women." *Criminal Law Journal* 37, no. 2 (2013): 79–98.

McMenemy, Jeff. "Fired Dover Cop Seeks Access to Guns While on Bail." *Foster's Daily Democrat*, December 11, 2020. https://www.fosters.com/story/news/crime/2020/12/11/fired-dover-cop-rj-letendre-seeks-access-guns-while-bail/3896909001/.

———. "Police Affidavit Details Letendre Domestic Violence Incident." *Foster's Daily Democrat*, July 21, 2020. https://www.fosters.com/story/news/2020/07/17/wife-files-abuse-complaint-against-dover-officer/113770060/.

———. "Wife Files Abuse Complaint against Dover Officer." *Foster's Daily Democrat*, July 16, 2020. https://www.fosters.com/story/news/2020/07/17/wife-files-abuse-complaint-against-dover-officer/113770060/.

McCray, Rebecca. "Jailing the Victim: Is It Ever Appropriate to Put Someone behind Bars to Compel Her to Testify against Her Abuser?" *Slate*, July 12, 2017. https://slate.com/news-and-politics/2017/07/jailing-the-victim.html.

Meiners, Erica R. "Awful Acts and the Trouble with Normal." In *Captive Genders: Trans Embodiment and the Prison Industrial Complex*, edited by Eric A. Stanley and Nat Smith, 133–42. Chico, CA: AK Press, 2016.

Melamed, Samantha. "Pa. Board of Pardons Recommends Clemency for 8 Lifers, Including 3 Women." *Philadelphia Inquirer*, September 4, 2020. https://www .inquirer.com/news/pennsylvania-board-pardons-commutation-fetterman-sh apiro-reid-wyatt-evans-horton-harris-mojica-stover-20200904.html.

———. "A Philly Woman Killed the Boyfriend Who'd Threatened to Put Her 'In the Grave.' A Jury Found Her Not Guilty." *Philadelphia Inquirer*, December 19, 2019. https://www.inquirer.com/news/philadelphia-letoya-ramseure-cast le-doctrine-women-incarceration-20191219.html.

Melendrez, Alexandra, and Young Women's Freedom Center. *Centering the Lives of San Francisco System-Involved Women and TGNC People: A Participatory and Decolonizing Model*. San Francisco: Freedom Research Institute, 2019.

Melton, Heather C., and Joanne Belknap. "He Hits, She Hits: Assessing Gender Differences and Similarities in Officially Reported Intimate Partner Violence." *Criminal Justice and Behavior* 30, no. 3 (2003): 328–48.

Méndez, Maria. "Gov. Abbott Establishes Clemency Application for Survivors of Domestic Violence and Sex Trafficking." *Dallas Morning News*, February 20, 2020. https://www.dallasnews.com/news/politics/2020/02/20/gov-abbott-est ablishes-clemency-application-for-survivors-of-domestic-violence-and-sex-tr afficking/.

Menjivar, Cecilia, and Shannon Drysdale Walsh. "Gender-based Violence in Central American and Women Asylum Seekers in the United States." *Transla- tional Criminology* (Winter 2019): 12–14. https://cebcp.org/wp-content/uplo ads/2020/04/TC16x-Winter2019.pdf.

Menzel, Margie. "Sex Trafficking Bill Gets OK: Detention Questions Remain." *CBS Miami*, April 10, 2014. https://miami.cbslocal.com/2014/04/08/sex-traffi cking-bill-gets-ok-detention-questions-remain/amp/.

Meyer, Ilan H., Andrew R. Flores, Lara Stemple, Adam P. Romero, Bianca D. M. Wilson, and Jody L. Herman. "Incarceration Rates and Traits of Sexual Minorities in the United States: National Inmate Survey, 2011–2012." *Ameri- can Journal of Public Health* 107, no. 2 (2017): 267–73. https://doi.org/10.21 05/ajph.2016.303576.

Michaels, Samantha. "Courts Are Jailing Victims of Sexual Assault: Yes, You Read That Right." *Mother Jones*, October 31, 2016. https://www.motherjones .com/politics/2016/10/why-are-women-thrown-jail-after-theyre-raped-or-as saulted/.

Miles, Doug. "The System's Response When Victims Use Force: One County's Solution." *Violence Against Women Newsletter* 5, no. 3 (Summer 2007): 1–6.

Miller, Caitlin. "Punishing the Broken and Invisible: How We Have Failed Female Youth Who Are Waived to the Criminal Justice System." *Womens Rights Law Report* 37, no. 1 (2015): 27–59.

Miller, Jody. *Getting Played: African American Girls, Urban Inequality, and Gendered Violence.* New York: New York University Press, 2008.

Miller, Kathryn, Marbre Stahly-Butts, Mecole Jordan-McBride, Kate Levine, Benjamin Tucker, and Kumar Rao. "Changing the Way We See Modern Policing: Abolition or Reform." *Cardozo Journal of Equal Rights and Social Justice* 27, no. 2 (Spring 2021): 435–72.

Miller, Reuben Jonathan. *Halfway Home: Race, Punishment, and the Afterlife of Mass Incarceration.* New York: Little, Brown and Company, 2021.

Miller, Susan L. *Victims as Offenders: The Paradox of Women's Violence in Relations.* New Brunswick, NJ: Rutgers University Press, 2005.

Miller, Susan L., and Michelle L. Meloy. "Women's Use of Force: Voices of Women Arrested for Domestic Violence." *Violence Against Women* 12, no. 1 (2006): 89–115. https://doi.org/10.1177/1077801205277356.

Miller, Susan L., and Patricia Becker. "Are We Comparing Apples and Oranges? Exploring Trauma Experienced by Victims of Interpersonal Violence and Abuse and by Court-Involved Women Who Have Used Force in Relationships." *Journal of Interpersonal Violence* 36, no. 13–14 (July 2021): NP6951–80. https://doi.org/10.1177/0886260518823289.

Miller, T. Christian, and Ken Armstrong. "An Unbelievable Story of Rape." *ProPublica and The Marshall Project*, December 16, 2015. https://www.propublica.org/article/false-rape-accusations-an-unbelievable-story.

Moe, Angela M. "Blurring the Boundaries': Women's Criminality in the Context of Abuse." *Women's Studies Quarterly* no. 3/4 (2004): 116–38. http://www.jstor.org/stable/40004583.

Mogulescu, Kate, and Leigh Goodmark. "Surveillance and Entanglement: How Mandatory Sex Offender Registration Impacts Criminalised Survivors of Human Trafficking." *Anti-Trafficking Review*, no. 14 (2020): 125–30. https://doi.org/10.14197/atr.2012201410.

Molidor, Christian, Richard M. Tolman, and Jennifer Kober. "Gender and Contextual Factors in Adolescent Dating Violence." *Prevention Researcher* 7, no. 1 (February 2000): 1–4.

Moore, Corrine. "8 Women Rescued and Arrested in Central Ohio Human Trafficking Single-Day Sting." *WANE 15*, January 28, 2021. https://www.wane.com/news/national-world/8-women-rescued-and-arrested-in-central-ohio-human-trafficking-single-day-sting/.

Moore, Lori D., and Irene Padavic. "Racial and Ethnic Disparities in Girls' Sentencing in the Juvenile Justice System." *Feminist Criminology* 5, no. 3 (July 2010): 263–85. https://doi.org/10.1177/1557085110380583.

Morabito, Nate. "Advocates Horrified after Domestic Violence Victims Jailed in

Washington County, TN." *WJHL.com*, September 11, 2016. https://bit.ly/2sz eptp.

——. "DOJ Helping after Washington County Domestic Violence Victims Jailed." *WJHL*, October 17, 2016. https://www.wjhl.com/news/doj-helping-aft er-washington-county-domestic-violence-victims-jailed/.

Moreno, Ivan. "Sex Offender Sues Hospital That Won't Let Him Visit Son, 9." *Monterey Herald*, March 9, 2018. https://www.montereyherald.com/2018/03 /09/sex-offender-sues-hospital-that-wont-let-him-visit-son-9/.

Morris, Monique W. *Pushout: The Criminalization of Black Girls in Schools.* New York: New Press, 2016.

Muftić, Lisa R., Jeffrey A. Bouffard, and Leana Allen Bouffard. "An Exploratory Study of Women Arrested for Intimate Partner Violence: Violent Women or Violent Resistance?" *Journal of Interpersonal Violence* 22, no. 6 (June 2007): 753–74. Https://doi.org/10.1177/0886260507300756.

Murphy, Colleen. "The Solitary Confinement of Girls in the United States: International Law and the Eighth Amendment." *Tulane Law Review* 92, no. 3 (February 2018): 697–718.

Musto, Jennifer. *Control and Protect: Collaboration, Carceral Protection, and Domestic Sex Trafficking in the United States.* Oakland, CA: University of California Press, 2016.

Nancarrow, Heather. *Unintended Consequences of Domestic Violence Law: Gendered Aspirations and Racialised Realities.* Basel, Switzerland: Springer International Publishing, 2019.

Nanda, Jyoti. "Blind Discretion: Girls of Color and Delinquency in the Juvenile Justice System." *UCLA Law Review* 59, no. 6 (2012): 1502–39.

National Association of Criminal Defense Lawyers and New York State Association of Criminal Defense Lawyers. *The New York State Trial Penalty: The Constitutional Right to Trial under Attack.* New York, 2021. https://www.nac dl.org/getattachment/1d691419-3dda-4058-bea0-bf7c88d654ee/new_york_sta te_trial_penalty_report_final_03262021.pdf.

National Center for Transgender Equality. *LGBTQ People behind Bars: A Guide to Understanding the Issues Facing Transgender Prisoners and Their Legal Rights.* National Center for Transgender Equality, October 2018. https://trans equality.org/transpeoplebehindbars.

National Council on Crime and Delinquency, and Delores Barr Weaver Policy Center. *Girls in Secure Juvenile Detention in Florida.* Jacksonville, FL: Delores Barr Weaver Policy Center, 2019. https://www.seethegirl.org/wp-cont ent/uploads/2019/09/Girls-in-Secure-Juvenile-Detention-in-FL.pdf.

National Institute of Justice. "Overview of Human Trafficking and NIJ's Role." National Institute of Justice, February 25, 2019. https://nij.ojp.gov/topics/arti cles/overview-human-trafficking-and-nijs-role.

National Institute of Justice and National Institute of Mental Health. *The*

Validity and Use of Evidence Concerning Battering and Its Effects in Criminal Trials: Report Responding to Section 40507 of the Violence Against Women Act. Washington, DC: National Institute of Justice, 1996.

National Survivor Network. "National Survivor Network Members Survey: Impact of Criminal Arrest and Detention on Survivors of Human Trafficking." National Survivor Network, 2016. https://nationalsurvivornetwork.org/wp-co ntent/uploads/2017/12/vacatesurveyfinal.pdf.

Nellis, Ashley. *In the Extreme: Women Serving Life without Parole and Death Sentences in the United States.* Washington, DC: Sentencing Project, 2021.

———. *The Lives of Juvenile Lifers: Findings from a National Survey.* Washington, DC: Sentencing Project, 2012.

———. *No End in Sight: America's Enduring Reliance on Life Imprisonment.* Washington, DC: Sentencing Project, 2021.

Nelson, Blake. "Dozens Suspended at N.J. Prison after Officers Are Accused of Beating Women Inmates." *NJ.com*, January 25, 2021. https://www.nj.com/ne ws/2021/01/dozens-suspended-at-nj-prison-after-officers-are-accused-of-beat ing-women-inmates.html.

———. "Inmate at Troubled N.J. Women's Prison Injured Again after Accusing Officers of Brutal Attack." *NJ.com*, February 24, 2021. https://www.nj.com/ne ws/2021/02/inmate-at-troubled-nj-womens-prison-injured-again-after-accus ing-officers-of-brutal-attack.html.

Nelson, Daniel A., and Natalie Patillo, dir. *And So I Stayed.* 2021.

nemec, blake. "No One Enters Like Them: Health, Gender Variance, and the PIC." In *Captive Genders: Trans Embodiment and the Prison Industrial Complex*, edited by Eric A. Stanley and Nat Smith, 243–61. Chico, CA: AK Press, 2016.

Newman, Andy. "Barred from Her Own Home: How a Tool for Fighting Domestic Abuse Fails." *New York Times*, June 17, 2021. https://www.nytimes.com/20 21/06/17/nyregion/order-of-protection-domestic-violence-abuse.html.

No To Violence. "Predominant Aggressor Identification and Victim Misidentification." No To Violence, 2019. https://ntv.org.au/wp-content/uploads/2020 /06/20191121-NTV-Discussion-Paper-Predominant-Aggressor-FINAL.pdf.

Nobles, Matt R., Jill S. Levenson, and Tasha J. Youstin. "Effectiveness of Residence Restrictions in Preventing Sex Offense Recidivism." *Crime and Delinquency* 58, no. 4 (2012): 491–513.

Nourse, Victoria F. "Self-Defense and Subjectivity." *University of Chicago Law School* 68, no. 4 (2001): 1235–308.

Nozicka, Luke. "Therapist Sexually Abused Women at Missouri Prison for Years." *Kansas City Star*, November 29, 2019. https://www.kansascity.com/news/loc al/crime/article237844334.html.

O'Hagan, Maureen. "In Baltimore, a Victim Becomes a Criminal." *Washington Post*, March 30, 2001. https://www.washingtonpost.com/archive/politics/2001

/03/30/in-baltimore-a-victim-becomes-a-criminal/69e9f6f5-ef03-41dd-9338
-aa3d771ffoc0/.

O'Leary, Christina Hunter. "Addressing the Epidemic of Sexual Assault in California's Immigration Detention Centers." *CSW Policy Brief* 25, 2019. https://es
cholarship.org/uc/item/3t0126k9.

O'Neill, Michael Edmund. "Understanding Federal Prosecutorial Declinations:
An Empirical Analysis of Predictive Factors." *American Criminal Law Review*
41, no. 4 (Fall 2004): 1439–98.

O'Toole, Molly. "19 Women Allege Medical Abuse in Georgia Immigration Detention." *L.A. Times*, October 22, 2020. https://www.latimes.com/politics/story
/2020-10-22/women-allege-medical-abuse-georgia-immigration-detention.

Ocen, Priscilla A. "Awakening to a Mass-Supervision Crisis." *The Atlantic*,
December 30, 2019. https://www.theatlantic.com/politics/archive/2019/12/pa
role-mass-supervision-crisis/604108/?utm_source=twitter&utm_medium=so
cial&utm_campaign=share.

———. "(E)racing Childhood: Examining the Racialized Construction of Childhood and Innocence in the Treatment of Sexually Exploited Minors." *UCLA
Law Review* 62, no. 6 (2015): 1586–641.

Office of the Child Advocate. *From Trauma to Tragedy: Connecticut Girls in
Adult Prison*. Hartford, CT: Office of the Child Advocate, 2008.

Officer, Kelly, Siobhan McAlister, and Katherine Tallan. "Updated Measure
11 Indictments, Convictions, and Sentencing Trends: 2013–2018." Oregon
Criminal Justice Commission, Salem, 2021.

Ohta, Rie, and Clara Long. "How Should Health Professionals and Policy Makers
Respond to Substandard Care of Detained Immigrants." *AMA Journal of
Ethics* 21, no. 1 (2019): E113–18.

Oliver, Ned. "Five Years Later, Virginia Prison Still Not Meeting Terms of Court-
Ordered Settlement over Shoddy Medical Care." *Virginia Mercury*, July 12,
2021. https://www.virginiamercury.com/2021/07/12/five-years-later-virginia
-prison-still-not-meeting-terms-of-court-ordered-settlement-over-shoddy-me
dical-care/.

Opsal, Tara. "'It's Their World, So You've Just Got to Get Through': Women's
Experiences of Parole Governance." *Feminist Criminology* 10, no. 2 (April
2015): 188–207.

Oregon Justice Resource Center. *Herstory Oregon Survey: Intimate Partner Violence and Trauma*. Portland: Oregon Justice Resource Center, 2019. https://st
atic1.squarespace.com/static/524b5617e4b0b106ced5f067/t/5c76c251ee6eb02
22ffd8ba7/1551286870890/HSS+IPV+and+Trauma+Report+FINAL.pdf.

"Oregon Prison Guard Freed on Sex Charge, Victim Detained as Material Witness." *Prison Legal News*, November 7, 2017. https://www.prisonlegalnews.org
/news/2017/nov/7/oregon-prison-guard-freed-sex-charge-victim-detained-ma
terial-witness/.

Osthoff, Sue, and Holly Maguigan. "Explaining without Pathologizing: Testimony on Battering and Its Effects." In *Current Controversies on Family Violence*, edited by Donileen R. Loseke, Richard J. Gelles, and Mary M. Cavanaugh, 225–40. Thousand Oaks, CA: Sage Publications, 2005.

Oudekerk, Barbara A., and N. Dickson Repucci. "Romantic Relationships Matter for Girls' Criminal Trajectories: Recommendations for Juvenile Justice." *Court Review* 46, no. 1–2 (2009–10): 52–57.

Ovalle, David. "She Was Raped by Florida Prison Officers. After Her Drug Death, Supporters Want Justice." *Miami Herald*, August 24, 2021. https://www.mia miherald.com/news/local/community/miami-dade/article253507329.html.

Owen, Barbara. "Women and Imprisonment in the United States: The Gendered Consequences of the U.S. Imprisonment Binge." In *Harsh Punishment: International Experiences of Women's Imprisonment*, edited by Sandy Cook and Susanne Davies, 81–98. Boston: Northeastern University Press, 1999.

Owen, Barbara, James Wells, and Joycelyn M. Pollock. *In Search of Safety: Confronting Inequality in Women's Imprisonment.* Oakland: University of California Press, 2017.

Paiella, Gabriella. "How Would Prison Abolition Actually Work." *GQ*, June 11, 2020. https://www.gq.com/story/what-is-prison-abolition.

Patterson, Evelyn J. "The Dose-Response of Time Served in Prison on Mortality: New York State, 1989–2003." *American Journal of Public Health* 103, no. 3 (2013): 523–28. https://doi.org/10.2105/ajph.2012.301148.

Patterson, Kiahnna, and Adrienne Mayfield. "Break the Cycle: Woman Who Shot Abusive Husband Urges Domestic Violence Survivors to Get Help Early." *WAVY.com*, November 11, 2020. https://www.wavy.com/domestic-violence-aw areness/break-the-cycle-woman-who-shot-abusive-husband-urges-domestic -violence-survivors-to-get-help-early/.

Paul, Deanna. "Murder Case Exposes Bail System's Flaws, Advocates for Abuse Victims Say." *Wall Street Journal*, September 24, 2020. https://www.wsj.com /articles/murder-case-exposes-bail-systems-flaws-advocates-for-abuse-victi ms-say-11600951548.

Pelzer, Jeremy. "Ohio Parole Board Is Secretive and 'Frighteningly Unfair,' Former Member Shirley Smith Says." *Cleveland.com*, January 23, 2019. https://www.cleveland.com/politics/2019/01/ohio-parole-board-is-secretive -and-frighteningly-unfair-former-member-shirley-smith-says.html.

Petersilia, Joan. *When Prisoners Come Home: Parole and Prisoner Reentry.* Oxford: Oxford University Press, 2009.

Peterson, Alyssa. "The Criminalization of Children Forced into Prostitution." *Think Progress*, August 27, 2014. https://archive.thinkprogress.org/the-crimin alization-of-children-forced-into-prostitution-d24632f27627/.

Phillips, Geneva. "What Happens in Prison Stays in Prison: The Willful Medical Neglect and Deaths of the Incarcerated." *Tenacious* 43 (Winter 2020): 30–38.

Phipps, Alison. *Me, Not You: The Trouble with Mainstream Feminism*. Manchester, UK: Manchester University Press, 2021.

Pilkington, Ed. "'There Was a Lot of Shame': Meet the Sex Offender 'Who Is Not a Sex Offender.'" *The Guardian*, October 1, 2018. https://www.theguardian.com/us-news/2018/oct/01/there-was-a-lot-of-shame-meet-the-sex-offender-who-is-not-a-sex-offender.

Pishko, Jessica. "Expert: Crime Registries Turn People into Pariahs with 'Very Little to Lose.'" *The Appeal*, July 20, 2018. https://theappeal.org/expert-crime-registries-turn-people-into-pariahs-with-very-little-to lose/.

———. "Serving Life for Surviving Abuse." *The Atlantic*, January 26, 2015. https://www.theatlantic.com/national/archive/2015/01/serving-life-for-surviving-ab use/384826/.

Potter, Hillary. *Battle Cries: Black Women and Intimate Partner Abuse*. New York: New York University Press, 2008.

Poulin, Anne Bowen. "Female Delinquents: Defining Their Place in the Justice System." *Wisconsin Law Review* 1996, no. 3 (1996): 541–76.

Powers, Kirsten. "Angela Corey's Overzealous Prosecution of Marissa Alexander." *Daily Beast*, July 19, 2013. https://bit.ly/2rpbnk6.

"Prosecution Sums Up in Lucas Trial." *San Francisco Chronicle*, April 4, 1957.

Rajan, Mekha, and Kathy A. McCloskey. "Victims of Intimate Partner Violence: Arrest Rates across Recent Studies." In *Backs against the Wall: Battered Women's Resistance Strategies*, edited by Kathy A. McCloskey and Marilyn H. Sitaker, 24–48. Abingdon: Routledge, 2009.

Ramsey, Carolyn. Forthcoming. *Houses of Pain: Domestic Violence and Criminal Justice, 1880–1994*. Cambridge, UK: Cambridge University Press.

Ramsey, Carolyn B. "The Stereotyped Offender: Domestic Violence and the Failure of Intervention." *Penn State Law Review* 120, no. 2 (Fall 2015): 337–420.

Randall, Mike. "Nicole Addimando's Sentence Reduced under Domestic Violence Survivors Justice Act." *Poughkeepsie Journal*, July 14, 2021. https://www.poughkeepsiejournal.com/story/news/local/2021/07/14/murderer-nicole-addiman do-sentence-reduced-domestic-violence-act/7967311002/.

Rankin, Bill. "Court Strikes Down Lifetime Electronic Monitoring of Sex Offenders." *Atlanta Journal Constitution*, March 4, 2019, https://www.ajc.com/news/local/court-strikes-down-lifetime-electronic-monitoring-sex-offenders/FiuH bWK5NfopOTcgqD8IMO/.

Rantala, Ramona R. *Sexual Victimization Reported by Adult Correctional Authorities*. Washington, DC: US Department of Justice, 2018.

Reamer, Frederic G. *On the Parole Board: Reflections on Crime, Punishment, Redemption, and Justice*. New York: Columbia University Press, 2017.

Rhine, Edward E., Joan Petersilia, and Kevin R. Reitz. "Improving Parole Release in America." *Federal Sentencing Reporter* 28, no. 2 (December 2015): 96–104.

Rhor, Monica. "Pushed Out and Punished: One Woman's Story Shows How

Systems Are Failing Black Girls." *USA Today,* May 15, 2019. https://www.usat oday.com/in-depth/news/nation/2019/05/13/racism-black-girls-school-discip line-juvenile-court-system-child-abuse-incarceration/3434742002/.

Richie, Beth E. "Abolition Feminism: The Heart and Soul of Transformative Justice." Webinar, October 22, 2020. https://nnedv.zoom.us/rec/play/lR6hyv5 qq-2YsxLpdzYqGWtIPb98n9b8mDLIvqVhbK6ss31hfZFjHODnuRBTK6JhU XdfbApVcMdhVVjt.Qq5SOPKQtpP603a7.

———. *Arrested Justice: Black Women, Violence, and America's Prison Nation.* New York: New York Univ. Press, 2012.

———. *Compelled to Crime.* New York: Routledge, 1996.

———. "Keynote: Reimagining the Movement to End Gender Violence: Anti-Racism, Prison Abolition, Women of Color Feminisms, and Other Radical Visions of Justice." *University of Miami Race and Social Justice Law Review* 5, no. 2 (Summer 2015): 257–74.

———. "NBWJI Book Club: Arrested Justice." Webinar, December 17, 2020. https://www.nbwji.org/post/nbwji-book-club-announcement-arrested-jus tice.

Ritchie, Andrea J. *Invisible No More: Police Violence against Black Women and Women of Color.* Boston: Beacon Press, 2017.

Roberts, Anna. "Arrests as Guilt." *Alabama Law Review* 70, no. 4 (2019): 987–1030.

Robinson-Oost, Amy. "Evaluation as the Proper Function of the Parole Board: An Analysis of New York State's Proposed Safe Parole Act." *CUNY Law Review* 6, no. 1 (Winter 2012): 129–200.

Romain, Danielle M., and Tina L. Freiburger. "Chivalry Revisited: Gender, Race/Ethnicity, and Offense Type on Domestic Violence Charge Reduction." *Feminist Criminology* 11, no. 2 (April 2016): 191–222.

Rooney, Andy. "Celeste Declares Open Season on Ohio Men." *Columbus Dis-patch*, December 28, 1990, 11A.

Ross, Luana. *Inventing the Savage: The Social Construction of Native American Criminality.* Austin: University of Texas Press, 1998.

Rowe, Ashley. "Judge Has Mercy on Buffalo Woman for Man's Murder, Grants Freedom under New Law." *WKBW.com*, September 9, 2020. https://www.wk bw.com/news/local-news/judge-has-mercy-on-buffalo-woman-for-mans-mur der-grants-freedom-under-new-law.

Ruhland, Ebony L., Edward E. Rhine, Jason P. Robey, and Kelly Lyn Mitchell. *The Continuing Leverage of Releasing Authorities: Finding a National Survey.* Minneapolis, MN: Robina Institute of Criminal Law and Criminal Justice, 2016.

Russo, Ann. *Feminist Accountability: Disrupting Violence and Transforming Power.* New York: New York University Press, 2019.

Saar, Malika Saada, Rebecca Epstein, Lindsay Rosenthal, and Yasmin Vafa. *The

Sexual Abuse to Prison Pipeline: The Girls' Story. Washington, DC: Human Rights Project for Girls, Georgetown Law Center on Poverty and Inequality and Ms. Foundation for Women, 2015.

Samuels, Liz, and David Stein. "Perspectives on Critical Resistance." In *Abolition Now! Ten Years of Strategy and Struggle against the Prison Industrial Complex*, edited by The CR10 Publications Collective, 1–14. Oakland, CA: AK Press, 2008.

Sanders, Sam. "Florida Woman in 'Stand Your Ground' Case Accepts Plea Deal." National Public Radio, November 25, 2014. https://n.pr/2hexdxf.

Sangoi, Lisa Kanti, and Lorie Smith Goshin. "Women and Girls' Experiences before, during, and after Incarceration: A Narrative of Gender-based Violence, and an Analysis of the Criminal Justice Laws and Policies That Perpetuate This Narrative." *UCLA Women's Law Journal* 20, no. 2 (2014): 137–68. https://doi.org/10.5070/l3202021355.

Sawyer, Wendy. "The Gender Divide: Tracking Women's State Prison Growth." *Prison Policy Initiative*, January 9, 2018. https://www.prisonpolicy.org/reports/women_overtime.html.

Sawyer, Wendy, and Peter Wagner. "Mass Incarceration: The Whole Pie 2020." *Prison Policy Initiative*, March 24, 2020. https://www.prisonpolicy.org/factsheets/pie2020_allimages.pdf.

Scarduzio, Jennifer A., Kellie E. Carlyle, Kate Lockwood Harris, and Matthew W. Savage. "'Maybe She Was Provoked': Exploring Gender Stereotypes about Male and Female Perpetrators of Intimate Partner Violence." *Violence Against Women* 23, no. 1 (January 2017): 89–113. https://doi.org/10.1177/1077801216636240.

Scelfo, Julie. "Bad Girls Go Wild." *Newsweek*, June 12, 2005. https://www.newsweek.com/bad-girls-go-wild-119637.

Schaffner, Laurie. "Female Juvenile Delinquency: Sexual Solutions, Gender Bias, and Juvenile Justice." *Hastings Women's Law Journal* 9, no. 1 (1998): 1–26.

Schechter, Susan. *Women and Male Violence: The Visions and Struggles of the Battered Women's Movement.* Cambridge, MA: South End Press, 1982.

Schenwar, Maya, and Victoria Law. *Prison by Any Other Name: The Harmful Consequences of Popular Reforms.* New York: The New Press, 2021.

Schneider, Rachel Zimmer. *Battered Women Doing Time: Injustice in the Criminal Justice System.* Boulder, CO: FirstForum Press, 2014.

Schreyer, Natalie. "A Prisoner of War Story: The Life and Captivity of Lisa Montgomery—the First Woman to Be Executed by the Federal Government in 68 Years." *Ms. Magazine*, January 11, 2021. https://msmagazine.com/2021/01/11/lisa-montgomery-only-woman-on-federal-death-row-death-penalty-execution/.

Schwartz, Jennifer, Darrell J. Steffensmeier, and Ben Feldmeyer, "Assessing Trends in Women's Violence via Data Triangulation: Arrests, Convictions,

Incarcerations, and Victim Reports." *Social Problems* 56, no. 3 (2009): 494–525. https://doi.org/10.1525/sp.2009.56.3.494.

Schwartzapfel, Beth. "Want to Shrink the Prison Population? Look at Parole." *The Marshall Project*, February 11, 2019. https://www.themarshallproject.org /2019/02/11/want-to-shrink-the-prison-population-look-at-parole.

Seattle Police Department (@seattlepd). "In our experience, victims are forced into prostitution through violence, deception and other factors not of their choosing. Diversion options can be limited, and we may need to arrest them to disrupt the cycle of violence and abuse. (2 of 3) cc @ ericacbarnett @ kromandavid. For people trafficked into prostitution, jail can be a safer place than out on the street. That said, our primary enforcement focus will ALWAYS be those who profit from and support this form of human trafficking. (3 of 3) cc @ericacbarnett @kromandavid." Twitter, October 2, 2019, 9:05 p.m. https://twitter.com/seattlepd/status/1179563139118952448.

Segrave, Marie, and Bree Carlton. "Women, Trauma, Criminalisation and Imprisonment." *Current Issues in Criminal Justice* 22, no. 2 (November 2010): 287–306.

Segrave, Marie, Dean Wilson, and Kate Fitz-Gibbon. "Policing Intimate Partner Violence in Victoria (Australia): Examining Police Attitudes and the Potential of Specialization." *Australian and New Zealand Journal of Criminology* 51, no. 1 (2018): 99–116.

Seigel, Micol. *Violence Work: State Power and the Limits of Police*. Durham, NC: Duke University Press, 2018.

The Sentencing Project. *Incarcerated Women and Girls*. Washington, DC: Sentencing Project, 2020. https://www.sentencingproject.org/publications/in carcerated-women-and-girls/.

———. *Women and Girls Serving Life Sentences*. Washington, DC: Sentencing Project, 2019.

Sered, Susan Starr, and Maureen Norton Hawk. "Beyond Recidivism and Desistance." *Feminist Criminology* 16, no. 2 (2020): 165–90.

Sered, Susan S., and Maureen Norton-Hawk. *Can't Catch a Break: Gender, Jail, Drugs and the Limits of Personal Responsibility*. Oakland: University of California Press, 2014.

Shakur, Assata. "Women in Prison: How It Is with Us." *The Black Scholar* (April 1978). https://www.historyisaweapon.com/defcon1/shakurwip.html.

Shammas, Victor L. "The Perils of Parole Hearings: California Lifers, Performative Disadvantage, and the Ideology of Insight." *PoLAR: Political and Legal Anthropology Review* 42, no. 1 (2019): 142–60. https://doi.org/10.1111/plar .12275.

Shamus, Kristen Jordan. "5 Michigan Women Lifers Want Clemency. Will Gov. Rick Snyder Grant It?" *Detroit Free Press*, December 19, 2018. https://www.fr

eep.com/story/news/2018/12/19/michigan-women-prison-clemency-governor
-rick-snyder/2219515002/.

Shapiro, Joseph, Jessica Pupovac, and Kari Lydersen. "In Prison, Discipline
Comes Down Hardest on Women." National Public Radio, October 15, 2018.
https://www.npr.org/2018/10/15/647874342/in-prison-discipline-comes-do
wn-hardest-on-women.

Sharp, Susan F. *Mean Lives, Mean Law: Oklahoma's Women Prisoners*. New
Brunswick, NJ: Rutgers University Press, 2014.

Shear, Pinky. "A Prison Guard Raped Me and Threatened My Life. Now I Fight
for Others' Lives." *Truthout*, August 3, 2021. https://truthout.org/articles/a-pr
ison-guard-raped-me-and-threatened-my-life-now-i-fight-for-others-lives/.

Sheehy, Elizabeth. "Battered Women and Mandatory Minimum Sentences."
Osgoode Hall Law Journal 39, no. 2 and 3 (Summer/Fall 2001): 529–54.

Sheehy, Elizabeth, Julie Stubbs, and Julia Tolmie. "Battered Women Charged
with Homicide in Australia, Canada and New Zealand: How Do They Fare?"
Australian & New Zealand Journal of Criminology 45, no. 3 (December
2012): 383–99. https://doi.org/10.1177/0004865812456855.

———. "Defences to Homicide for Battered Women: A Comparative Analysis of
Laws in Australia, Canada and New Zealand." *Sydney Law Review* 34, no. 3
(September 2012): 467–92.

Sherman, Francine T. "Justice for Girls: Are We Making Progress?" *Criminal
Justice* 28, no. 2 (July 26, 2013): 9–17.

———. *Unintended Consequences: Addressing the Impact of Domestic Violence
and Mandatory and Pro-Arrest Policies and Practices on Girls and Young
Women*. Portland, OR: National Crittenden Foundation, 2016.

Sherman, Francine T., and Annie Balck. *Gender Injustice: System-Level Juvenile Reforms for Girls*. Portland, OR: National Crittenton Foundation and
National Women's Law Center, 2015.

Shugerman, Emily. "A Kansas Law School Student Reported a Rape. Then Police
Arrested Her." *The Daily Beast*, November 11, 2019. https://www.thedailybea
st.com/kansas-prosecutors-drop-false-report-charges-against-rape-accuser
-she-says-the-nightmare-is-not-over.

Simkins, Sandra B., Amy E. Hirsh, Erin McNamara, and Marjorie B. Moss. "The
School to Prison Pipeline for Girls: The Role of Physical and Sexual Abuse.'"
Children's Legal Rights Journal 24, no. 4 (Fall 2004): 56–57.

Simkins, Sandra, and Sarah Katz. "Criminalizing Abused Girls." *Violence Against
Women* 8, no. 12 (December 2002): 1474–99. https://doi.org/10.1177/1077801
02237966.

Simon, Jonathan. *Governing through Crime: How the War on Crime Transformed American Democracy and Created a Culture of Fear*. New York: Oxford
University Press, 2009.

Sinon, Brianna M. "Failing Girls: A Cure Worse Than the Disease—Charging,

Trying and Sentencing Female Juvenile Offenders as Adults." *Howard Scroll: The Social Justice Law Review* 7 (2004): 32–90.

Sivin, Alana. "Oregon's Fight to End Mandatory Minimum Sentences." *The Appeal Live*, March 17, 2021. https://www.facebook.com/1692312484375663 /videos/149426516968909.

Slater, Dashka. "Can You Talk Your Way Out of a Life Sentence?" *New York Times Magazine*, January 1, 2020. https://www.nytimes.com/2020/01/01/magazine /prison-parole-california.html.

Sledge, Matt. "One of Louisiana's Oldest Incarcerated Women Is Free; Prosecutors Say She Was Wrongly Convicted." *Nola.com*, May 17, 2021. https://www -nola-com.cdn.ampproject.org/c/s/www.nola.com/news/courts/article_02129 3b2-b66b-11eb-8a4c-3f6115400cbc.amp.html.

———. "Two More Settlements Reached in Fake Subpoena Lawsuit as DA Leon Cannizzaro's Term Draws to Close." *NOLA.com*, January 2, 2021. https://www .nola.com/news/courts/article_391c3486-4b94-11eb-844f-3bad6d43ce8d.html.

Slipke, Darla. "Mother Imprisoned under Failure to Protect Laws Reflects on First Months of Freedom." *The Oklahoman*, February 3, 2020. https://www.ok lahoman.com/article/5653956/mother-imprisoned-under-failure-to-protect -laws-reflects-on-first-months-of-freedom.

Small, Julie. "#MeToo Behind Bars: Records Shed Light on Sexual Abuse inside State Women's Prisons." *KQED*, November 14, 2019. https://www.kqed.org/ne ws/11786495/metoo-behind-bars-new-records-shed-light-on-sexual-abuse-in side-state-womens-prisons.

Smith, Jordan. "Landmark California Law Bars Prosecutors from Pursuing Murder Charges against People Who Didn't Commit Murder." *The Intercept*, November 23, 2018. https://theintercept.com/2018/11/23/california-felony -murder-rule/.

Snyder, Rachel Louise. "When Can a Woman Who Kills Her Abuser Claim Self-Defense?" *The New Yorker*, December 20, 2019. https://www.newyorker.com /news/dispatch/when-can-a-woman-who-kills-her-abuser-claim-self-defense.

Solutions Not Punishment Collaborative. *"The Most Dangerous Thing Out Here Is the Police": Trans Voices on Police Abuse and Profiling in Atlanta*. East Pont, GA: Solutions Not Punishment Collaborative, 2016.

Spade, Dean. "The Only Way to End Racialized Gender Violence in Prisons Is to End Prisons: A Response to Russell Robinson's 'Masculinity as Prison.'" *California Law Review Circuit* 3 (2012): 182–93.

Sprang, Ginny, Jennifer Cole, Christine Leistner, and Sarah Ascienzo. "The Impact of Safe Harbor Legislation on Court Proceedings Involving Sex Trafficked Youth: A Qualitative Investigation of Judicial Perspectives." *Family Court Review* 58, no. 3 (July 2020): 816–31. https://doi.org/10.1111/fcre.12519.

Stahl, Aviva. "The Shocking, Painful Trauma of Being a Trans Prisoner in Solitary Confinement." *Vice*, January 22, 2016. https://www.vice.com/en/article/qkgq

97/the-shocking-painful-trauma-of-being-a-trans-prisoner-in-solitary-confin
ement.

Steadman, Otillia. "More Than 1,000 Open Prostitution Cases in Brooklyn Are
Going to Be Wiped from the Files." *BuzzFeed News*, January 28, 2021. https://
www.buzzfeednews.com/article/otilliasteadman/prostitution-loitering-cases
-brooklyn.

Stillman, Sarah. "America's Other Family-Separation Crisis." *The New Yorker*,
October 29, 2018. https://www.newyorker.com/magazine/2018/11/05/americ
as-other-family-separation-crisis.

———. "Why Are Prosecutors Putting Innocent Witnesses in Jail?" *The New
Yorker*, October 17, 2017. https://www.newyorker.com/news/news-desk/why
-are-prosecutors-putting-innocent-witnesses-in-jail.

Stoddard, Martha. "Report: Multiple Leadership, System Failures Led to Crisis
at Nebraska Youth Treatment Center." *Omaha World-Herald*, January 5, 2021.
https://omaha.com/news/state-and-regional/report-multiple-leadership-syst
em-failures-led-to-crisis-at-nebraska-youth-treatment-center/article_2d4412
00-4fae-11eb-91db-43fbffc656a2.html#tracking-source=home-top-story-1.

Stone, Rebecca, Susan Sered, Amanda Wilhoit, and Cherry Russell. *Women,
Incarceration, and Violent Crime: A Briefing in Response to Plans for Build-
ing a New Women's Prison in Massachusetts*. Boston, MA: Women and
Incarceration Project at Suffolk University, 2021.

Straus, Murray. "Thirty Years of Denying the Evidence on Gender Symmetry in
Partner Violence: Implications for Prevention and Treatment." *Partner Abuse*
1 (2010): 332–62. DOI: 10.1891/1946-6560.1.3.332.

Strom, Kevin J., Tara D. Warner, Lisa Tichavsky, and Margaret A. Zahn. "Policing
Juveniles: Domestic Violence Arrest Policies, Gender, and Police Response to
Child–Parent Violence." *Crime & Delinquency* 60, no. 3 (April 2014): 427–50.
https://doi.org/10.1177/0011128710376293.

Subramanian, Ram, and Alison Shames. *Sentencing and Prison Practices in
Germany and the Netherlands: Implications for the United States*. New York:
Vera Institute of Justice, 2013.

Sufrin, Carolyn, Lauren Beal, Jennifer Clarke, Rachel Jones, and William D.
Mosher. "Pregnancy Outcomes in U.S. Prisons." *American Journal of Public
Health* 109, no. 5 (May 2019): 799–805. https://doi.org/10.2105/AJPH.2019
.305006.

Sullivan, Irene H. "Raised by the Courts-Umatilla." *Juvenile and Family Court
Journal* 61, no. 3 (2010): 36–40. https://doi.org/10.1111/j.1755-6988.2010.010
45.x.

Survived & Punished. "Action Toolkit to Free Assia." https://docs.google.com/doc
ument/d/1uSC2aCbAmEu3Wog07FGAg_1UooleEJN6cdYg1QVatXo/edit.

Survived & Punished (@survivepunish). "It's breathtaking to connect with
powerful survivors behind bars and to see them released and doing incred-

ible anti-violence advocacy in the 'free world.' Releases are acts of survivor solidarity. Releases are having survivors' backs. #EmergencyReleaseNow #ExposeYourDA." Twitter, August 20, 2020, 5:00 p.m. https://twitter.com/sur vivepunish/status/1296552720468283393.

Survived & Punished New York. *No Good Prosecutors Now or Ever: How the Manhattan District Attorney Hoards Money, Perpetuates Abuse of Survivors, and Gags Their Advocates.* New York: Survived & Punished New York, 2021.

———. *Preserving Punishment Power: A Grassroots Abolitionist Assessment of New York Reforms.* New York: Survived & Punished New York, n.d.

———. "Vision & Purpose." *Free: Survivors* 1 (2019): 1–29.

Swavola, Elizabeth, Kristine Riley, and Ram Subramanian. *Overlooked: Women and Jails in an Era of Reform.* New York: Vera Institute of Justice, 2016.

Syedullah, Jasmine. "The Hearts We Beat: Black Feminist Freedom in the Hold of Slavery." Webinar, February 10, 2021. https://www.youtube.com/watch?v=r h9XfeKva8c.

Tarrant, Stella, Julia Tolmie, and George Giudice. *Transforming Legal Understandings of Intimate Partner Violence.* Victoria, Australia: Australia's National Research Organisation for Women's Safety Limited, 2019.

Taylor-Thompson, Kim. "Girl Talk—Examining Racial and Gender Lines in Juvenile Justice." *Nevada Law Journal* 6, no. 3 (Spring 2006): 1137–64.

Tereshchuk, David, and Laura Fong. "U.S. Jail Populations Drop but Not for Women." *PBS News Hour Weekend,* June 30, 2019. https://www.pbs.org/news hour/show/u-s-jail-populations-drop-but-not-for-women.

Thornton, William. "Alabama Woman Who Killed Alleged Rapist Back in Jail for Going to Trunk-or-Treat." *AL.com,* November 4, 2021. https://www.al.com/ne ws/2021/11/alabama-woman-who-killed-alleged-rapist-back-in-jail-for-going -to-trunk-or-treat.html.

Thuma, Emily. *All Our Trials: Prisons, Policing, and the Feminist Fight to End Violence.* Urbana: University of Illinois Press, 2019.

———. "Joan Little." In *No Selves to Defend: A Legacy of Criminalizing Women of Color for Self-Defense,* edited by Mariame Kaba, 20–22.Tolmie, Julia, Rachel Smith, Jacqueline Short, Denise Wilson, and Julie Sach, "Social Entrapment: A Realistic Understanding of the Criminal Offending of Primary Victims of Intimate Partner Violence." *New Zealand Law Review* no. 2 (March 2018): 181–217.

Torres, Angel C., and Naima Paz. *Denied Help! How Youth in the Sex Trade and Street Economy Are Turned Away from Systems Meant to Help Us and What We Are Doing to Fight Back.* Chicago: Young Women's Empowerment Project, 2012.

Tully, Tracey. "31 Guards Suspended at a Women's Prison Plagued by Sexual Violence." *New York Times,* January 28, 2021. https://www.nytimes.com/2021 /01/28/nyregion/edna-mahan-correctional-facility-abuse.html.

United States Commission on Civil Rights. *Women in Prison: Seeking Justice Behind Bars*. Washington, DC: US Commission on Civil Rights, 2020.

United States Department of Justice. *Investigation of the Edna Mahan Correctional Facility for Women (Union Township, New Jersey)*. Washington, DC: US Department of Justice, 2020.

———. *Investigation of the Julia Tutwiler Prison for Women and Notice of Expanded Investigation*. Washington, DC: US Department of Justice, 2014.

———. *Investigation of the Lowell Correctional Institution—Florida Department of Corrections (Ocala, Florida)*. Washington, DC: US Department of Justice, 2020.

———. *Report and Recommendations Concerning the Use of Restrictive Housing*. Washington, DC: US Department of Justice, 2016.

———. *Review of the Federal Bureau of Prisons' Management of Its Female Inmate Population*. Washington, DC: US Department of Justice Office of the Inspector General, 2018. https://oig.justice.gov/reports/2018/e1805.pdf.

Van Cleve, Nicole Gonzalez. *Crook County: Racism and Injustice in America's Largest Criminal Court*. Palo Alto, CA: Stanford University Press, 2017.

van der Leun, Justine. "Confinement and Contagion." *New York Review of Books*, October 8, 2020. https://www.nybooks.com/articles/2020/10/08/confinement-and-contagion/.

———. "Death of a Survivor." *New Republic*, May 3, 2020. https://newrepublic.com/maz/article/157589/death-survivor.

———. "The Evidence against Her." *Medium*, May 27, 2020, https://gen.medium.com/nikki-had-proof-shed-been-abused-but-was-it-enough-for-self-defense-bd9f196396eb.

———. "'I Hope Our Daughters Will Not Be Punished.'" *Dissent*, June 29, 2020. https://www.dissentmagazine.org/online_articles/i-hope-our-daughters-will-not-be-punished.

———. "'No Choice but to Do It.'" *The Appeal*, December 17, 2020. https://theappeal.org/criminalized-survivors-survey/.

Vanderford, Anna (Joe). "Minnesota Malice." *Tenacious* 44 (n.d.): 56–60.

Vansickle, Abbie, and Weihua Li. "Police Hurt Thousands of Teens Every Year. A Striking Number Are Black Girls." *The Marshall Project*, November 2, 2021. https://www.themarshallproject.org/2021/11/02/police-hurt-thousands-of-teens-every-year-a-striking-number-are-black-girls?utm_medium=email&utm_campaign=newsletter&utm_source=opening-statement&utm_term=newsletter-20211102-2658.

Vasquez, Tina. "Exclusive: Georgia Doctor Who Forcibly Sterilized Detained Women Has Been Identified." *Prism*, September 15, 2020. https://prismreports.org/2020/09/15/exclusive-georgia-doctor-who-forcibly-sterilized-detained-women-has-been-identified/.

Vergano, Dan. "The Criminal Justice System Is Bad for Your Health, Warns New

York City's Health Department." *BuzzFeed News*, August 5, 2019. https://www
.buzzfeednews.com/article/danvergano/new-york-health-risk-criminal-jus
tice.

Walker, Lenore E. *The Battered Woman Syndrome*. New York: Springer Publishing Company, 2017.

Wallace, Lewis. "Inez Garcia." In *No Selves to Defend: A Legacy of Criminalizing
Women of Color for Self-Defense*, edited by Mariame Kaba, 10–12.

———. "Lena Baker." In *No Selves to Defend: A Legacy of Criminalizing Women of
Color for Self-Defense*, edited by Mariame Kaba, 8–9.

Walklate, Sandra, and Kate Fitz-Gibbon. "Why Criminalise Coercive Control?
The Complicity of the Criminal Law in Punishing Women through Furthering
the Power of the State." *International Journal for Crime, Justice and Social
Democracy* 10, no. 4 (2021): 1–12.

Walters, Joanna. "An 11-Year-Old Reported Being Raped Twice, Wound Up with
a Conviction." *Washington Post*, March 12, 2015. https://www.washingtonpo
st.com/lifestyle/magazine/a-seven-year-search-for-justice/2015/03/12/b1cccb
30-abe9-11e4-abe8-e1ef6oca26de_story.html.

Wang, Esther. "Cyntoia Brown, Bresha Meadows, and How the 'Criminal Legal
System Disappears Survivors.'" *Jezebel*, December 28, 2018. https://www.new
sbreak.com/news/1209144831970/cyntoia-brown-bresha-meadows-and-how
-the-criminal-legal-system-disappears-survivors.

WarBonnett, Darcy K., Deborah Bounds, Karen R. Paese, lois landis, and shannon r. houser. "Women in Prison Tell It Like It Is." *Our Sisters in Prison: What
Are They Doing There?* 31, no. 2 (2001): 9–12.

Watson, Liz, and Peter Edelman. "Improving the Juvenile Justice System for
Girls: Lessons from the States." *Georgetown Journal on Poverty Law and
Policy* 20, no. 2 (Winter 2013): 215–68.

Weber, Andrew, and Jerry Quijano. "Activists Call on Travis County to Say No to
New Women's Jail." *Kut 90.5*, June 7, 2021. https://www.kut.org/crime-justice
/2021-06-07/activists-call-on-travis-county-to-say-no-to-new-womens-jail?fb
clid=IwAR1Xro9usyXxWVo6sAqUKvmSvl4mQVEjkuk4gbEJP9pOpIw545H
Bx7u-dTo.

Weisberg, Robert, Debbie A. Mukamal, and Jordan D. Segall. *Life in Limbo: An
Examination of Parole Release for Prisoners Serving Life Sentences with the
Possibility of Parole in California*. Stanford, CA: Stanford Criminal Justice
Center, 2011.

Weiss, Debra Cassens. "Children Paid for Sex Acts Were Aggressors, Judge Says
While Sentencing 67-Year-Old Man." *ABA Journal*, February 4, 2019. https://
www.abajournal.com/news/article/young-teens-paid-for-sex-acts-were-aggre
ssors-judge-says-while-sentencing-67-year-old-man.

Weissman, Deborah M. "Gender Violence, the Carceral State, and the Politics of Solidarity." *University of California Davis Law Review* 55, no. 2 (2021): 801–73.

West, Carolyn M, "'Sorry, We Have to Take You In': Black Battered Women Arrested for Intimate Partner Violence." In *Backs against the Wall: Battered Women's Resistance Strategies,* edited by Kathy A. McCloskey and Marilyn H. Sitaker, 87–112. New York: Routledge, 2009.

Western, Bruce. *Homeward: Life in the Year after Prison.* New York: Russell Sage Foundation, 2018.

Weston, Rebecca, Linda L. Marshall, and Ann L. Coker. "Women's Motives for Violent and Nonviolent Behaviors in Conflicts." *Journal of Interpersonal Violence* 22, no. 8 (2007): 1043–65.

West-Smith, Mary, Mark R. Pogrebin, and Eric D. Poole. "Denial of Parole: An Inmate Perspective." *Federal Probation* 64, no. 2 (December 2000): 3–10.

White, Gary. "Path to Healing: Programs Give Sex-Trafficking Victims a Chance at Recovery." *The Ledger,* October 12, 2014. https://www.theledger.com/story /news/2014/10/13/path-to-healing-programs-give-sex-trafficking-victims-a-c hance-at-recovery/26996935007.

Whitehorn, Laura. Introduction to *Resistance behind Bars: The Struggles of Incarcerated Women,* by Victoria Law, i–xv. Oakland, CA: PM Press, 2009.

Whittier, Nancy. *Frenemies: Feminists, Conservatives, and Sexual Violence.* New York: Oxford University Press, 2018.

Wicentowski, Danny. "Angel Stewart Won Parole in Missouri. She Still Has a Second Life Sentence in Iowa." *Riverfront Times,* August 27, 2018. https:// www.riverfronttimes.com/newsblog/2018/08/27/angel-stewart-won-parole-in -missouri-she-still-has-a-second-life-sentence-in-iowa.

Williams, Clarence. "Where Sugar and Spice Meet Bricks and Bats." *Washington Post,* December 8, 2004. https://www.washingtonpost.com/archive/local/20 04/12/28/where-sugar-and-spice-meet-bricks-and-bats/a83ad0a8-fd37-42e5 -9cec-e6eb0798da41/.

Witherspoon, Paula Rae. "My Story." In *Captive Genders: Trans Embodiment and the Prison Industrial Complex,* edited by Eric A. Stanley and Nat Smith, 235–40. Oakland, CA: AK Press, 2015.

Wolf, Angela, Barbara E. Bloom, and Barry A. Krisberg. "The Incarceration of Women in California." *University of San Francisco Law Review* 43, no. 1 (Summer 2008): 139–70.

Woolington, Rebecca. "Ex-Prison Guard Guilty in Sexual Misconduct Case; Accuser Freed after 50 Days in Jail." *The Oregonian,* October 7, 2016. https:// www.oregonlive.com/hillsboro/2016/10/ex-prison_guard_guilty_of_sexu .html.

Wu, Henry, and Alexandra Yelderman. *Prosecution at Any Cost? The Impact of Material Witness Warrants in Federal Human Trafficking Cases.* Washington, DC: Human Trafficking Legal Center, 2020.

Yaroshefsky, Ellen. "State of Washington v. Sherrie Lynn Allery: Victor Despite Conviction." In *Trial Stories*, edited by Michael E. Tigar and Angela J. Davis, 13–46. New York: Foundation Press, 2008.

Yepsen, David. "Let Shanahan Case Run Course." *Des Moines Register*, May 16, 2004, p. 3.

Zaitzow, Barbara H. "Pastel Fascism: Reflections of Social Control Techniques Used with Women in Prison." *Women's Studies Quarterly* 32, no. 3/4 (Fall-Winter 2004): 33–48.

Zuckerman, David, and Brooke Cucinella. "Read These Stories before Voting to Make Pardons More Difficult." *Morning Call*, November 2, 1997. https://www.mcall.com/news/mc-xpm-1997-11-02-3174641-story.html.

Index

Abbott, Greg, 162
abolition, xi, 18, 24, 184–88, 195
abolition feminism, x–xi, 23, 170–71, 184,
    186–94
accomplice liability, 77, 79
ACES. *See* adverse childhood experiences
Adam Walsh Act. *See* Sex Offender Registra-
    tion and Notification Act
Adams, LaTasha, 69
Adams v. Hanson, 69
Aday, Ronald, 108
Addimando, Nikki, 102–4, 146, 190
Adkins, LeeAnn, 129–30, 134–35
adverse childhood experiences, 26
AjeeDaPoet, 118
Aldrich, Keiana, 28, 34, 144
Alexander, Marissa, 1, 19–20, 75, 86, 190
Alford plea, 28
Allen, Johnny, 33–34
Allery, Sherrie, 59
Alligood, Clarence, 4
Alvarado, Michael, 77
Ammons, Linda, 157
Amos, Kevin, 89
Anderson, Devon, 68, 70
Angiolillo, Daniel, 99
anti-rape movement, 4–5

anti-trafficking laws, 8, 21
anti-trafficking movement, 80
anti-violence movement, 18, 20, 186, 188–90,
    194
Arias, Jodi, 90
arrest, 2, 22, 46–57; consequences of, 46,
    56–57, 91; credibility and, 51–54; experi-
    ence of, 54–57; of girls, 25–26, 30–32,
    42–43; justifications for, 47–54; of lesbi-
    ans and bisexual women, 46–47; as res-
    cue, 47, 49, 53; stereotypes and, 43, 51, 53;
    of transgender people, 47, 50, 52, 55–56;
    of victims of gender-based violence, 33,
    46–48, 50; of women of color, 46–47,
    50–51
Atkins, Maryanne, 39–40
Aviram, Hadar, 152

Bachman, Michael, 14
bail, 7, 22, 27, 56, 67–68, 70–74, 188, 190–91
Bailey, Rudeara, 78–79, 105, 181
Baker, Lena, 3
Baker, Robert Jr., 164
Baker County Detention Center (FL), 127
Balzer, Brian, 68
Barker, Stacy, 117
Barnett, Ashley, 17, 100–1

Founded in 1893,
UNIVERSITY OF CALIFORNIA PRESS
publishes bold, progressive books and journals
on topics in the arts, humanities, social sciences,
and natural sciences—with a focus on social
justice issues—that inspire thought and action
among readers worldwide.

The UC PRESS FOUNDATION
raises funds to uphold the press's vital role
as an independent, nonprofit publisher, and
receives philanthropic support from a wide
range of individuals and institutions—and from
committed readers like you. To learn more, visit
ucpress.edu/supportus.